ALLEN PHOTOGRAPHIC GUIDES

ALL ABOUT LAMINITIS

CONTENTS

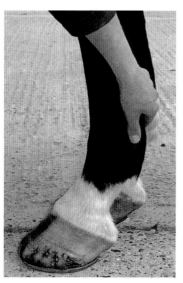

WHAT IS LAMINITIS?

Laminitis is a common disease which affects a horse's or pony's whole body and shows itself as painful feet. A pony with laminitis will lean back to try and take the weight off its painful feet.

WHAT HAPPENS IN THE FOOT

The easy way to understand this is to remember that horses and ponies balance all the weight of each leg on the equivalent of our middle finger. The hoof wall is like our finger nail but it wraps right around the foot and is strengthened by the hard sole underneath. Together the hoof and sole act as a fairly rigid box to protect the bones inside. The **laminae** line this box and are visible (see arrow on photograph below) when the hoof is removed from the foot. Laminae are delicate structures which interweave like a sophisticated 3-D zip fastener binding together the hoof and bone.

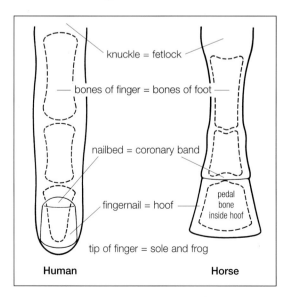

knuckle = fetlock

bones of finger = bones of foot

nailbed = coronary band

fingernail = hoof

pedal bone inside hoof

tip of finger = sole and frog

Human   **Horse**

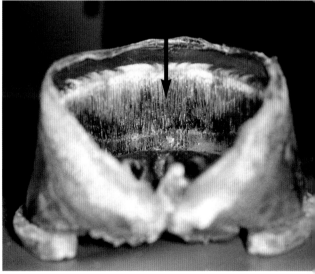

These laminae have a tightly pleated appearance (see arrow on photograph of a slice cut from a horse's foot). If all the laminae within one foot were spread out they would cover a tennis court, which shows how closely knitted they really are.

The inner surface of the wall of the hoof is attached to the outer covering of the **pedal bone** (i.e. the main bone of the foot) by a sliding joint similar to that found between the human finger nail and its nail bed. The **sensitive laminae** wrap around the pedal bone and contain many nerves and blood vessels. The **insensitive** or **horny laminae** are on the inner surface of the hoof wall. As the hoof grows towards the ground, the insensitive laminae slide slowly over the sensitive laminae. The horn of the insensitive laminae is usually unpigmented and can be seen on the bearing surface of a freshly trimmed foot as the **white line**. In a laminitic foot this may be wider than normal (see arrow on photograph).

The laminae are essential to the support of the animal's weight; several hundred kilograms are transmitted from the limb, via the pedal bone, to the wall of the hoof through the laminae.

VET'S VIEW

The laminae form a vital bond between the hoof and the pedal bone supporting the weight of the horse.

WHAT HAPPENS WHEN LAMINITIS DEVELOPS?

When laminitis develops, these delicate laminae were thought to become inflamed, i.e. hot, swollen and painful. The suffix 'itis' means inflammation, so laminitis means inflammation of the laminae. In fact the disease is not simply due to inflammation, but this name has stuck.

The bond between the laminae is loosened in laminitis by pressure of fluid leaking from the damaged sensitive laminae. This is extremely painful for the horse or pony involved. There is no room for the laminae to swell within the rigid box of the hoof and heat, pain and lameness result. In severe cases, this fluid and blood may build

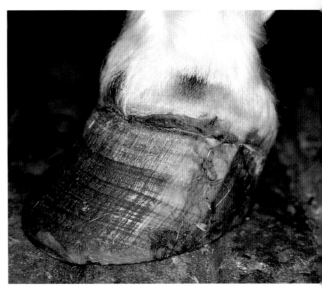

up enough pressure to burst out at the coronary band at the top of the hoof.

ROTATION OF THE PEDAL BONE

Once laminitis starts, urgent treatment is needed to remove the cause and reduce the damage to the feet. Without this, the laminae will start to die because the swelling raises pressure and reduces their blood supply. As this happens, the pedal bone will shift because the laminar bond is no longer there to hold it in place. The combined forces of the weight of the pony from above, plus the tendons pulling from the heels and the extra pressure inside the hoof will all act together to cause the pedal bone to rotate or to sink within the hoof. The diagram shows a section through a normal foot (left) and a foot damaged by laminitis (right).

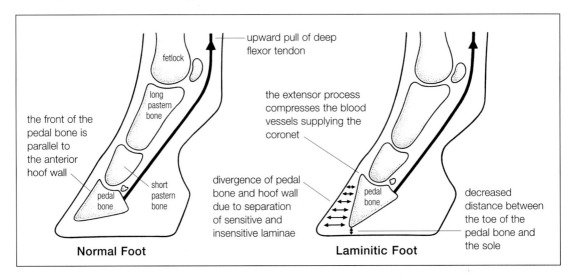

upward pull of deep flexor tendon

fetlock

long pastern bone

the front of the pedal bone is parallel to the anterior hoof wall

pedal bone

short pastern bone

Normal Foot

the extensor process compresses the blood vessels supplying the coronet

divergence of pedal bone and hoof wall due to separation of sensitive and insensitive laminae

pedal bone

decreased distance between the toe of the pedal bone and the sole

Laminitic Foot

The photograph shows the rotated pedal bone nearly through the sole of the foot and the damaged laminae can be seen as an area of bleeding.

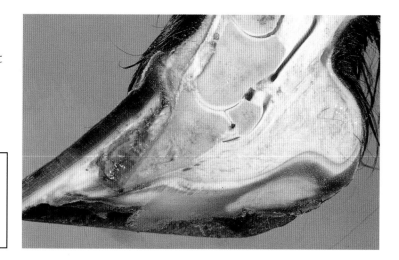

TYPES OF LAMINITIS

Subacute laminitis is the mildest form of the condition where some signs are present, but they are not as severe as in the acute cases. Such cases will usually clear up without permanent damage to the feet, but if care is not taken it can happen again and gradually become worse.

Acute laminitis is the early stage of the condition when the horse or pony is uncomfortable and showing lameness but major changes have not yet happened within the foot. It is an *emergency* and proper treatment needs to be started at once to prevent serious damage.

Chronic laminitis occurs when the pedal bone has rotated or sunk or if the condition has been going on for more than 48 hours.

Founder is an American term used to describe the more severe case of laminitis in which the laminae are tearing and the pedal bone is unstable and dropping.

Sinkers are the most severe laminitis cases, where the laminar bond has been destroyed right around the foot, so that the whole pedal bone is loose within the foot. The pedal bone will drop and it can literally sink through the sole of the foot. With a sinker, a gap at the coronary band can be felt. This is a bad sign.

In the very worst cases, (such as in the one below), the entire hoof wall and sole can separate from the foot.

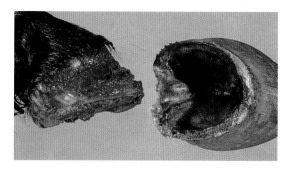

THE SIGNS TO LOOK OUT FOR

A horse or pony with laminitis is said to look like a cat on a hot tin roof. Their feet hurt and they simply do not know which one to stand on. Look out for one or more of these signs, which should act as a warning of laminitis:

- Lameness in one or more limbs. It is most common in the front feet, occasionally present in the hind limbs and rarely present in one leg only.

- A reluctance to move, or a stiff pottery gait always suggests laminitis. In mild cases it is most obvious when they turn and they may lean awkwardly like this pony (see right). If worse, they move reluctantly, rocking their feet from heel to toe as they try to reduce the pain.

- A horse or pony which lies down a lot. This may be all that you notice at first. They are lying down for a reason: to get the weight off their sore feet.

- Standing uncomfortably. Many laminitic cases will stand with their front legs stretched forward to throw their weight on to their heels away from their painful toes. They will also have their back legs well forward underneath them. Often they will shift their weight from one foot to another.

- A reluctance to lift their feet up. If the feet are sore they will not want to put more weight on the other legs. So be aware of this when picking out the feet or when the feet are trimmed and reshod by the farrier.

- Looking unwell and uncomfortable. The pain from the feet will cause an increase in the pulse and respiratory rate.

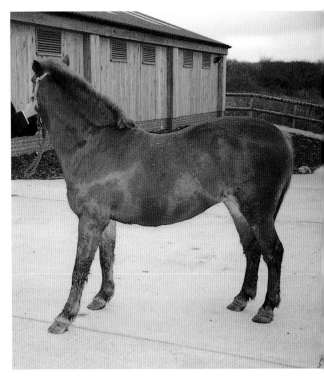

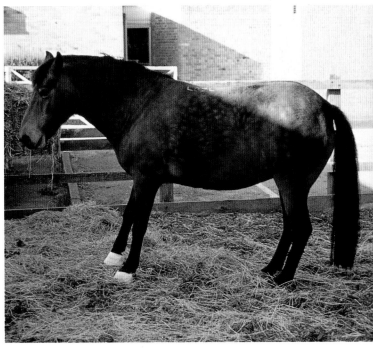

WHAT TO LOOK FOR IN THE FEET

- **Heat** in the feet may be noticeable, especially around the coronary band. Never depend on this as a sign of laminitis because it is possible to have severe laminitis without obviously warm feet. The feet may be warm for other reasons as well as laminitis.

- If laminitis is present, a stronger than normal **digital pulse** may be felt where the artery runs over the fetlock (see right). This happens because of the change in blood flow to the foot and will be more obvious on the affected feet. Compare the different feet. If there is an abscess or some other foot problem developing, that too may cause a more pronounced pulse to be present. If you find a pounding digital pulse in more than one foot the most likely cause is laminitis. You rarely see foot abscesses in more than one foot at once unless it is associated with laminitis. The photo shows a foot being treated for a laminitis-associated abscess.

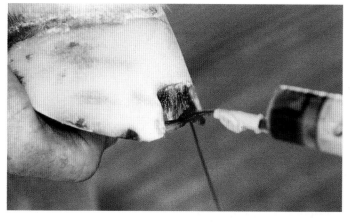

- Examination by your vet or farrier will demonstrate increased **sensitivity to pressure** with hoof testers especially in the area of the sole between the point of the frog and the toe. This is the delicate area beneath the tip of the pedal bone where there will be pain from pressure as it rotates. With serious cases, even gentle pressure in this area with your thumbs will cause discomfort.

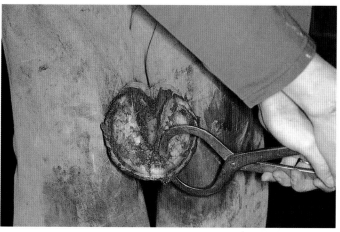

SIGNS OF CHRONIC LAMINITIS

The worst chronic cases are obvious because you will see the signs already described in a horse or pony that is crippled. The difficulty is detecting the mild chronic cases, in particular how do you know if an animal that you are considering for purchase has a laminitis problem.

Signs of chronic laminitis include:

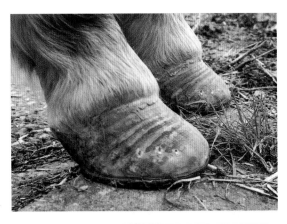

- **Intermittent lameness** especially on stony ground. Typically this is the pony which is said to 'feel his feet'.

- Often footsore or lame after having the feet trimmed or reshod.

- **Abnormal hoof growth** seen as diverging rings around the hoof wall (see top right), which are wider at the heel than at the toe. This will be associated with an abnormally shaped foot; characteristically long toes with overgrown heels (see arrow showing damaged laminae).

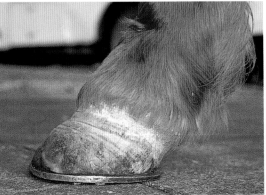

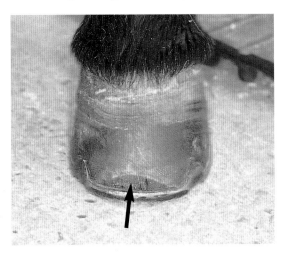

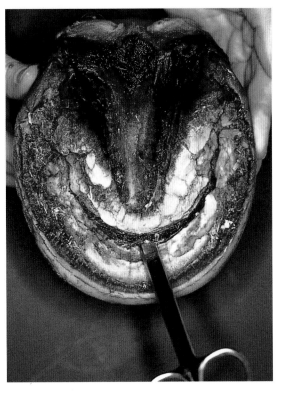

- The sole of the foot may drop because of the shift of the pedal bone, making the sole flatter. In the worst cases it will bulge out and actually be convex. The pedal bone may even drop through the sole (see right).

- **Pus in the foot** is common because of the abnormally weak horn growth and the increased chance of infection developing in the diseased tissue of the foot.

- A **wider than normal white line** at the ground surface. Frequently you can see red or pink areas of blood staining (from the diseased laminae) particularly when the farrier trims the feet (see right). This is a weakness and again increases the chances of infection.

- **Seedy toe** is the name for infection and damage in the area at the front of the foot, and commonly follows laminitis.

- Ponies which have previously had laminitis frequently have thick cresty necks where fat deposits have accumulated and these may persist even when they lose weight elsewhere.

If you are in any doubt you should seek your vet's advice.

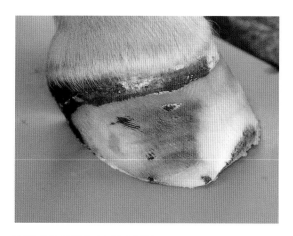

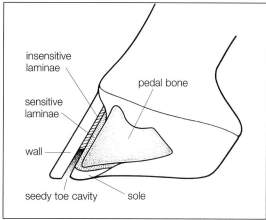

insensitive laminae

pedal bone

sensitive laminae

wall

seedy toe cavity   sole

IS IT LAMINITIS?
THE DIFFERENTIAL DIAGNOSIS

Any of the signs described can suggest that your horse or pony is suffering from laminitis. If you are in any doubt, ask your vet immediately. Remember that treating laminitis as an emergency in the early stages increases the chances of a full recovery.

Often your farrier will warn you that there are suspicious changes in the feet. Many people confuse the signs they see with something else. Sometimes the horse that cannot move because of laminitis is thought to have a bad back or to have azoturia, which is when they 'tie up' with muscle cramps. Occasionally a laminitic animal, which is lying down a lot because of its painful feet, can be incorrectly considered to have colic.

DIAGNOSIS

Usually the clinical signs will make it obvious for your vet to tell whether a horse or pony has laminitis. It can, however, be confusing particularly in the early stages, or if only one foot is affected. In these cases it is important to eliminate other causes of lameness.

Vets use a grading system for laminitis called the Obel grading system based on findings established over 50 years ago. Sadly laminitis has not changed since then. It is a classification from grade one to four, where four describes the worst cases when an animal spends most of its time lying down and has to be forced to move. This classification is based on the degree of lameness, and is a good way for vets to compare different cases. It helps with treatment and gives a guide to the severity of the case. The higher the Obel grade of lameness, the greater the likelihood of permanent damage to the laminae. Unfortunately many people are not aware that laminitis is present until the disease has reached grade three, which is when the horse moves reluctantly and objects to picking up a foot because of the pain in the other feet. By this stage, significant laminar degeneration may have already happened, reducing the chances of a full recovery.

WHAT CAUSES LAMINITIS?

To understand the treatment of laminitis you need to know about the causes of the condition. Everyone thinks of the little fat pony – the 'stomach on legs' – which overeats whilst out on lush spring grass. These are the commonest laminitis cases that we see, simply because British native ponies have evolved to live on poor mountain and moorland grazing. When they are faced with rich, well-fertilised paddocks instead of the odd sprig of heather and gorse they can rapidly develop problems.

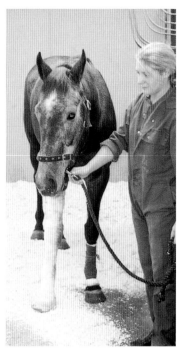

Other conditions that cause laminitis include:

- **'Bingeing'**, i.e. overfeeding of any sort, especially grain if an animal gets into a feedstore, excess grazing of well-fertilised pasture or a sudden change to a high energy diet.

- **Overfat** animals, show horses for example, kept in excessively good condition.

- **Illness**, particularly digestive disorders, possibly after severe colic or diarrhoea, and other conditions such as liver disease.

- Mares that have recently foaled and **retain their afterbirth** (placenta), will develop infections and consequently laminitis (see above left).

- **Severe lameness** in one leg from other causes resulting in excessive weight bearing in the remaining limbs and, possibly, subsequent laminitis (see above).

- **Irregular or incorrect trimming** of the feet and bad shoeing. Feet which are untrimmed are more prone to laminitis (below left). Untreated and untrimmed laminitic feet will produce this Turkish slipper appearance (below right) if neglected.

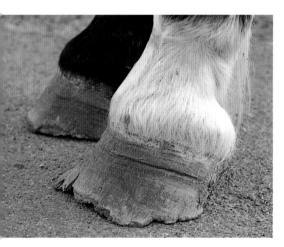

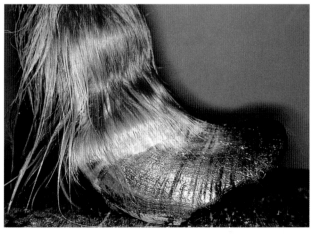

- **Trauma** to the feet due to excessive concussion from too much work on the hard ground causing laminar tearing.

- **Drug treatment** side-effects can result in laminitis. The risk is highest with steroid therapy.

- **Hormonal problems**, in particular those associated with pituitary gland overactivity in old ponies can result in laminitis. This can be due to a tumour and may be associated with Cushing's disease. A typical feature of this is a curly long-haired coat (see right) which may be present even in summer. It is usually seen in old ponies and typically they may drink excessive amounts of water. Laminitis can also occasionally occur with thyroid gland disease.

- **Stress** of any sort, travelling long distances for instance, especially if the animal is overweight to start with. Again, think of some unfortunate over-weight and over-travelled show horses!

Laminitis in horses and ponies is a little like headaches in people. They can occur for a multitude of reasons but, whatever the cause, the end result is similar. People have 'brain ache' and horses and ponies have aching feet. Donkeys can develop laminitis too, especially if they are over-weight.

THE TECHNICAL DETAILS. WHY DOES LAMINITIS DEVELOP?

To compare laminitis with the human brain again: it is well known that if the brain is starved of oxygen for a very few minutes because of an interruption to the blood supply – if, say, the heart stops beating during a heart attack – then, tragically, brain damage can occur. It is similar with laminitis.

The healthy hoof has an extremely good blood supply to the laminae through a mass of tiny blood vessels. When this blood supply is disrupted the laminae suffer. If the blood supply is blocked for long enough then the laminae are damaged, become swollen, degenerate and die. This damage can be seen when the laminitic foot is trimmed (see right). As this happens, fluid leaks within the area of damage which, with the swelling, causes severe pain. This is because the hoof is an enclosed box which cannot expand. When fluid leaks within it, the internal pressure builds up and it is this that makes the pain so severe. This pain makes the whole situation worse by increasing the shock, stress and illness.

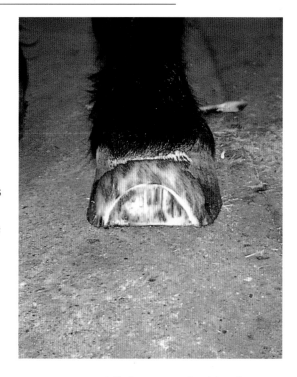

Why is the blood supply to the laminae damaged in the first place? Vast amounts of veterinary research have been done to try to establish why laminitis occurs; there are plenty of theories, but there is no simple explanation.

It is thought that somehow the circulatory system is affected producing a rise in the blood pressure. This is detectable by the increased digital pulse. This causes blood to be shunted away from the laminar region by a combination of the tiny blood vessels shutting down, blood clots forming and blocking blood flow, plus swelling around these critical blood vessels causing compression. All this stops the blood going to these vital structures. The rise in blood pressure is thought to be caused by either metabolic, toxic or vascular factors which are triggered by any of the predisposing causes. Current thought favours the vascular theory, which means there is direct disruption to the circulation. Certainly new research on a small number of cases has shown that using compounds to reduce blood pressure experimentally can help. Continuing research is bound to produce new theories.

VET'S VIEW

Changes can occur very quickly; experiments have shown that they can start to happen within two to three hours, and pedal bone rotation can follow within a couple of days so treatment needs to be started as soon as possible.

TREATMENT

Laminitis therapy is based on:
1. The need to control pain.
2. Restoring the blood circulation in the feet to normal.
3. Stabilising the pedal bone and preventing it sinking or rotating, if possible. Once the pedal bone shifts, many cases will never recover and others take over a year to return their feet to near normal.

There are many different treatments used and it is difficult to know which form of therapy has the greatest effect on any one case.

The first, and most important, thing for you and your vet to do is to attempt to **control the cause** of the laminitis. For instance, horses and ponies that develop acute laminitis on lush pastures should be removed from the grass that is effectively 'poisoning' them. A horse which has binged on grain will require large amounts of liquid paraffin by stomach tube to neutralise any toxins in the gut, and speed removal from the gut.

Often, the underlying cause is not clear and a careful clinical examination and blood tests may be required to investigate this.

Control of pain is vital in stopping the vicious circle of more pain, further increases in blood pressure and worsening of the laminitis.

Your vet may prescribe non-steroidal anti-inflammatory drugs such as:

- **phenylbutazone** commonly called 'bute';
- **flunixin meglumine** (trade name Finadyne);
- **meclofenamic acid** (trade name Arquel);

These powerful drugs reduce pain and control inflammation, and are very commonly used in the treatment of laminitis. Powders given in a feed will act less rapidly than injections. You also need to provide a feed to put it in, which is not ideal if you are trying to reduce the rations of a fat pony! A course of treatment may need to be started off with an intravenous injection of a suitable painkiller.

It must be remembered that such drugs can disguise the signs by masking pain. It is important to establish the cause as well. Overlooking the cause can be compared to taking aspirin if your own feet hurt because your shoes are uncomfortable, when what needs to be done is to change your shoes!

Pain may also be controlled by using a local anaesthetic in the form of a nerve block to stop the pain in the foot. The disadvantage of this is that if a seriously affected laminitic case can no longer feel its feet, it may move more than it should and damage the laminae further. It has been known for the whole hoof to fall off in this way. The only time I would ever consider doing it is if I had no choice but to move a laminitis case, for instance, to take x-rays and provide treatment.

Control of high blood pressure and improving blood flow to the laminae is also important.

- Your vet may prescribe drugs such as **acetylpromazine** (often called ACP) to do this. This is also a mild tranquilliser and can help to calm a distressed horse. Other drugs sometimes used include **isoxuprine**, a vasodilator (i.e. a drug to open up blood vessels), which is designed to help the blood flow through the foot, although how effective it actually is in laminitis is uncertain, and **heparin**, which has been used to reduce blood clotting; some studies have shown it helps. New drugs (such as glyceryl trinitrate paste) to reduce blood presssure are being researched.

- Tubbing the feet in warm water with added Epsom salts particularly at the start of treatment can help improve the circulation. Warm water hosing – or bags of warm water around the feet (see right) – is good, if practical, but is unlikely to alter the outcome of the case in the long term; short term, it may help ease the pain.

- Traditionally cold water hosing was done because it provided temporary relief by reducing the heat in the feet, but long term it does not help as it reduces the blood flow to the feet. In the same way, ice packs and standing a horse in cold water makes them feel better but for a short while only. It is useful if you have to move them or if they are seriously distressed.

Foot care in acute laminitis is directed at preventing the pedal bone from rotating or sinking:

- The horse should not be moved more than is essential because movement may cause more laminar damage. The old idea of forcing a laminitis case to walk is *wrong*. If you think about it, it is bound to make them feel worse.

- Allow them box rest until they can walk around the stable comfortably without pain or lameness. It is best if a laminitic is kept stabled. By choice, use a very deep (about 30 cm) newspaper or shavings (clean whitewood ideally) bed so that they can lie down and take the weight off their sore feet. A deep bed

must also be soft, dry and clean as if they do lie down a lot they may develop the horse equivalent of bed or pressure sores (see above). The Americans often use a sand stall designed so the patient can stand on deep sand which helps provide good uniform support for the feet. If you use straw, watch that they do not eat it.

- Frog supports may be used. These are either made from bandages or are commercially available devices, such as Lily pads (see below). Whichever type of

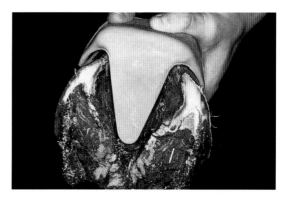

support is used, it must be positioned 1 cm behind the trimmed point of the frog. These may help to reduce pressure on the sole and provide extra support. A deep, soft standing area will give extra comfort and can be used as well as supporting the feet (see right). Foot supports are a temporary help but in some cases can increase discomfort, in which case radiographs are needed to check the pedal bone position.

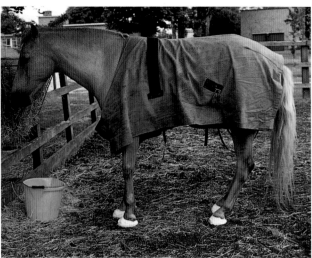

- Radical trimming of the feet should be avoided in acute laminitis. It is best to see how the laminitis progresses before deciding to do anything drastic to the feet. Taking the shoes off often increases the degree of lameness but may be necessary to search for infection in the foot. If the shoe has to come off, then it is often worth trimming an overlong toe, but otherwise wait.

Feeding is important, particularly in the typical fat pony laminitis cases.

> ### VET'S VIEW
> The rule is: reduce the quantity and quality of feed.

- Feed hay not concentrates and do not allow grazing. The amount of hay depends on its quality, but feed the minimum of the poorer quality hay; as a rough idea, give a fat Shetland less than one kilo of hay twice a day and a tiny amount of a high fibre feed.

- Never starve the patient completely as this can cause other problems, particularly fat metabolism mix-ups. Feeding is critical if you have an in-foal mare with

laminitis: ask your vet for advice on how to feed her.

- If a pony is suddenly stabled after being at grass, they may become constipated, so feed small bran mashes with added Epsom salts and check to make sure they are passing droppings.

- Any feed should be divided up and given little and often, three or four times a day. There are special high fibre feeds which are useful for laminitics. The aim is to feed a high fibre diet, which is low in carbohydrates.

    It helps to keep the laminitic on a non-edible bed such as shavings or peat so they cannot eat it. If you scatter their hay in the bedding it takes them more time to eat their reduced ration and helps avoid boredom.

- A good supplement to help hoof quality is also advisable: ask your vet to recommend one. There is a large range on the market and you should use one which contains methionine, biotin and zinc to improve the hoof wall. It is also advisable that it should be low in sodium, which is one of the components of salt.

It is not a good idea to give laminitic cases any extra salt although potassium chloride (30 g daily) may help instead.

There are many other laminitis feed supplements available, ask your vet if any are worth using for your case.

TREATMENT OF CHRONIC LAMINITIS

If the laminitis becomes chronic, everything suggested so far will still apply but there will be serious changes in the foot which will require drastic treatment to correct. Such cases used to be considered hopeless. These days it may be possible to get very sick horses or ponies sound again with careful and complicated treatment. If it is going to be effective it will require a lot of effort and attention from you as the owner, and an equine veterinary surgeon and a knowledgeable farrier who have plenty of experience in dealing with such cases. Everyone will need to work together as a team, and understand what is needed. The aim is to use corrective trimming and shoeing to improve the hoof and gradually return the pedal bone to its normal position (see diagram below).

Radiographs (x-ray pictures) should be taken in any laminitis case that continues to get worse, or is failing to respond to treatment. Your vet may well attach metal markers to the foot to show up the front of the hoof and also underneath the point of the frog on the radiograph. These provide a useful means of seeing how bad the case is and what chance it has of recovering. It is important to prevent suffering in hopeless cases, and radiographs can be used to help decide if treatment is worthwhile.

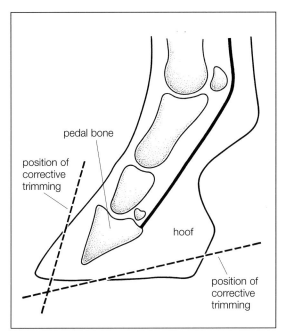

pedal bone

position of corrective trimming

hoof

position of corrective trimming

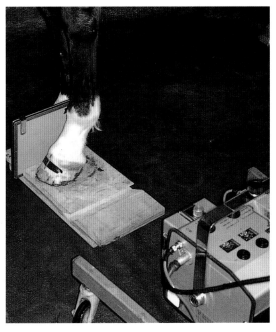

This radiograph shows the metal markers and serious changes in the form of pedal bone rotation and sinking (illustrated by arrows 1) and a gas shadow in front of the pedal bone (illustrated by arrow 2). To obtain good quality pictures you may need to transport the laminitic to a veterinary clinic, if your vet feels it is safe for the patient to travel.

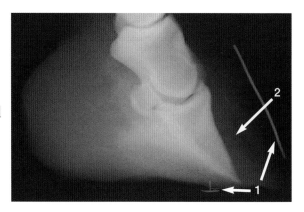

X-ray pictures provide a very helpful guide for your farrier by allowing him to see exactly where the pedal bone is within the foot. This allows the foot to be improved and reshaped by:

- Removing the underrun sole and opening and draining any abscesses.

- Shortening the toes.

- Cutting and trimming back the heel; care needs to be taken not to take off too much heel because it can cause more discomfort by affecting the pull from the tendons at the back of the foot. Often there is much discussion about how much to lower the heels; this has to be judged from the radiographs and the results of trimming. Recently, in America, they have been using a shoe with heel wedges to lift the heel, which has helped in some cases.

- Rasping back the front of the hoof wall to bring it parallel with the pedal bone.

It often helps to take radiographs as the feet are being trimmed, to check progress. Ideally the vet and farrier can do this together at the veterinary clinic so that they can take more x-ray pictures as required. It will be necessary to repeat the trimming every four to six weeks because

the hoof grows rapidly in laminitis cases, particularly at the heel. More radiographs may then be required.

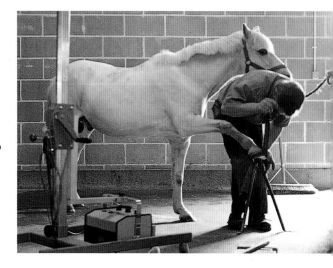

SHOEING FOR LAMINITIS CASES

There are many different techniques used, but it is crucial that the foot is properly reshaped first. Most laminitics do better when shod, simply because the shoe will help to protect the tender foot. Hammering on the shoe, however, may be painful. This can be helped by:

1. Shoeing the worst foot first, so they can then weight-bear more comfortably once that first shoe is fitted.
2. Using glue-on shoes, such as these glue-on bar shoes. (see opposite above)

3. Using local anaesthetic nerve blocks to stop the pain in the foot. This must be done very carefully by your vet and farrier because, without feeling in the foot, it can be more difficult to fit a shoe, which may make the laminitis worse. This is *not* ideal and is not recommended.

The type of shoe used will depend on how bad the laminitis case is but, whichever shoe is used, the aim is to:

1. protect the painful area of the sole and hoof wall from ground contact;
2. prevent further tissue destruction or rotation of the pedal bone;
3. provide support for the foot;
4. help healing of the foot.

The ideal shoe does not exist and what works well for one case is not always as good for another. The final choice will depend on the expertise and experience of your farrier. Follow the advice of your veterinary surgeon and farrier and 'keep it simple'! Do not expect complicated treatment when it is not necessary.

- Mild cases of laminitis often respond very well to a wide-webbed seated-out shoe. It is seated out on the inside to relieve pressure on the sole and help reduce bruising. Quarter clips instead of a toe clip can also help with this sort of shoe because this reduces the pressure on the toe.

- More support is provided by using a bar shoe (such as the straight bar shoe, below left). Sometimes this is combined with a pad as well. The bar increases the load-bearing surface, whilst pads are said to protect the sole from bruising. Any pad which covers the whole of the sole, will prevent you seeing what is going on there. It is possible to trim the pad to leave just that directly under the shoe where, in theory, it helps by increasing the elevation of the foot from the ground. There are also special pads designed with built-in frog supports such as Theraflex shoe inserts. Pads may not work as well in practice as in theory, but bar shoes on their own can make a laminitic much more comfortable. Egg bar shoes are sometimes used successfully to provide extra heel support (below right).

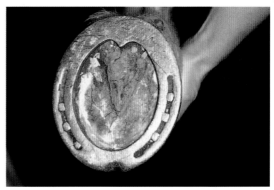

- Open-toed shoes, which are really a normal shoe fitted back to front, have been tried. These lift the sole from the ground and so appear to produce an improvement at first. The problem is that they do not provide support for the pedal bone, which will frequently continue to rotate or drop. Such shoes can aggravate the situation although, initially, they seem to produce an improvement.

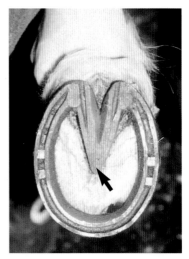

- Heart bar shoes have become trendy recently, although they have been in use for well over one hundred years. Their aim is to provide support for the pedal bone and help stabilise it. Some say it helps push the pedal bone back into place, but I cannot believe that any shoe could do this with the whole weight of a horse above it. Many modifications of the heart bar have been devised such as flexible heart bars, but the principle is the same for all of them. The positioning of the tip of the bar is critical; it should not extend too far towards the toe because it may damage the already compromised blood vessels. Anything touching the sole may hinder the blood supply in that area. As a rule of thumb, a margin of frog should be visible around the edge of the bar of the shoe (see arrow on top photograph). Your vet and farrier will require radiographs to do this properly. It is a skilled job to fit heart bar shoes correctly. With a well-fitted heart bar shoe, the horse will be more comfortable as soon as it is applied. A local anaesthetic nerve block should never be used for this procedure because, without sensation in the foot, it is impossible to tell if the horse is comfortable on this special shoe.

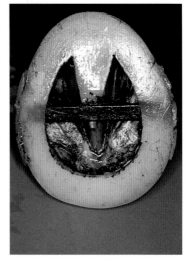

- A good combination of plastic and steel, glue-on, adjustable heart bar shoes have been developed by Robert Eustace. These are very good when the feet are too sore to accept a nailed-on shoe (centre photograph).

SURGICAL TREATMENTS FOR LAMINITIS

1. **Dorsal hoof wall resection** is used in some advanced cases of laminitis. It involves removing the front of the hoof wall usually using a small power drill. It is done for the following reasons:
   - to relieve the pressure due to the accumulation of fluid within the non-expandable box of the foot;

- to help improve the damaged blood supply by releasing pressure on some blood vessels;
- to encourage regrowth of the new horn at the correct angle parallel to the pedal bone.

When, or if, to do it is a decision for your vet and farrier. They may consider a hoof wall resection if radiographs show gas and fluid within the foot or if the hoof wall is no longer attached because of laminar separation. It is a controversial technique, which can work very well, but can also cause more complications. It will mean a lot of effort from you, your vet and farrier. It will be costly because it has to be combined with radiographs, special shoeing and careful cleaning and dressing of the feet. Once the front of the hoof is removed it has to be treated like an open wound. It will take between six and twelve months for fresh hoof to grow down over the area. During this time there is a risk of infection developing. It must be kept clean either by dressing with bandages, or as it improves by using antiseptic spray, which is the blue colour shown in the top photograph.

2. **Dorsal hoof wall drilling**. Instead of removing large areas of the front of the hoof, holes are drilled through the front of the hoof using radiographs for guidance. This is a compromise which allows fluids to drain, yet is not as radical as removing the whole affected area. It is not always very effective as the holes may not be sufficient to allow drainage and it is difficult to be sure the correct spot is drilled to produce good drainage. The lower photograph shows one hole drilled and the area for hoof wall resection marked.

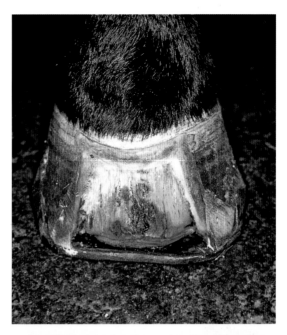

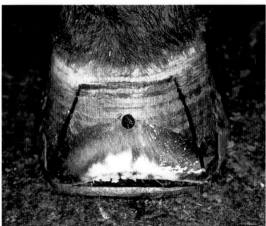

3. **Cutting the deep flexor tendon or the associated check ligament** has been used as a treatment. It appears to relieve the pain but rarely alters the ultimate outcome.

All the surgical procedures for laminitis are salvage procedures and should not be undertaken lightly. Regrettably they are not always successful, but then they are only ever carried out on the very worst cases. It is far better if the situation is never allowed to deteriorate to that stage.

PROGNOSIS

It has to be said that one of the most frustrating aspects of looking after a laminitis case is the difficulty in predicting which way it is going to go. The prognosis in any laminitis case is guarded. Mild cases will often get better quickly with rapid treatment and the right management. The problem is that many will recur unless very strict preventative measures are carried out.

More severe cases will respond well to foot trimming and careful shoeing, but can take many months to recover. The very worst cases are unlikely to be able to return to work. If they are unlikely to ever go sound, there comes a point when everyone must think seriously about whether it is right to prolong a laminitic's miserable life in a starvation paddock with permanently sore feet. To make this decision you will need the help and advice of your vet and farrier, who should have had experience with such cases before.

Factors important in determining the prognosis include:

- MOST IMPORTANT: the **degree of pain** and suffering;

- **how long** the laminitis has been going on;

- the **number of feet** affected;

- the **degree of lameness**;

- the **severity of changes on x-ray** pictures;

- the degree of **infection** in the foot;

- the **response to treatment** so far;

- the **ability** of everyone concerned to manage the case;

- any **other disease** also involved.

PREVENTION

Good management can reduce the chance of your horse or pony developing laminitis. It helps to use a weight tape regularly to monitor their dimensions. Your horse or pony is too fat if you cannot feel its ribs.

It is important to:

- Restrict grazing, particularly on lush, well-fertilised fields. Restricted grazing is most essential when the spring grass comes through and in the autumn when there is a late flush of growth. I always see lots of laminitis in October!

- If you have a high laminitis risk candidate, which means almost any pony, limit their grazing to a couple of hours a day. Use a starvation paddock (as illustrated), or bring them in, or use a muzzle if they will tolerate it. Remember that any animal left in a starvation paddock without exercise may well become bored and bad-tempered.

- Monitor condition with a weight band or at least by measuring their girth regularly.

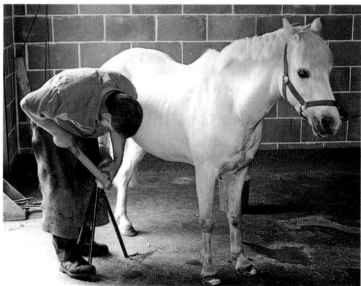

- Keep the feet trimmed and shod regularly to avoid mechanical strains on the foot.

- Laminitis can be caused by fast work on hard surfaces. Too much trotting on the road will tear the laminae and result in laminitis. People always forget this, so be careful on the hard ground.

- Lock your feed room to prevent anyone, four- or two-footed, entering uninvited!

- Obtain prompt treatment for any illness, particularly colic or any foaling problems in a mare. Remember laminitis can follow on from numerous things in the same way that headaches do in humans.

VET'S VIEW

The bottom line is look after your horse or pony properly.

ACKNOWLEDGEMENTS

I would like to thank everyone who has helped and advised me, in particular all my colleagues at the Bell Equine Veterinary Clinic and everyone who allowed me to photograph their horses and ponies. I am also indebted to Mr. P. D. Clegg, Mrs. A. B. Clegg. Mrs. S. F. Devereux, Prof. S. Love, Mr. J. O'Keeffe, Dr. C. M. Riggs, Mr. P. H. P. Savage, Mr. T. M. Stern and Mr. K. J. Willard for their contributions. Most of all, I am very grateful to my husband Adam for all his support.

My thanks are also due to *Horse and Hound* for their help and for allowing me to use the heading VET'S VIEW in this book.

British Library Cataloguing-in-Publication Data.
A catalogue record for this book is available from the
British Library

ISBN 0.85131.660.3

© J. A. Allen & Co. Ltd., 1996

Published in Great Britain in 1996 by
J. A. Allen & Company Limited,
1 Lower Grosvenor Place, Buckingham Palace Road,
London, SW1W OEL

Design and Typesetting by Paul Saunders
Cover photograph by Bob Langrish
Printed in Hong Kong by Midas Printing Ltd.

Joan Stanley-Baker is a graduate of Bennington College in Vermont, and earned her D.Phil in Chinese Art History at the University of Oxford. She has been studying various aspects of Asian art since 1964 and spent four years studying the arts of Japan *in situ*. She was inaugural curator of Asian art at the Art Gallery of Greater Victoria, B.C., Canada, and has taught Chinese and Japanese art history at the University of Melbourne, National Taiwan and National Ts[illegible] Universities, and was founding professor of art history and art [illegible] Tainan National College of the Arts, Taiwan. Her books [illegible] study [illegible] Japanese reception and transformation of Chinese [illegible]ing, *The Transmission of Chinese Idealist Painting to* [illegible] *the Early Phase* which examines the transformation [illegible] in trans-cultural adaptation (1992), and the highly [illegible] of the nature and function of forgeries in Chinese pa[illegible]*ers Repainted: Wu Zhen (1280–1354) Prime O*[illegible]*tions* (1995).

World of Art

This famous series provides the widest available range of illustrated books on art in all its aspects. If you would like to receive a complete list of titles in print please write to:

THAMES & HUDSON
181A High Holborn
London WC1V 7QX

In the United States please write to:

THAMES & HUDSON INC.
500 Fifth Avenue
New York, New York 10110

Printed in Singapore

Enichi-bō Jōnin
Myōe Shonin meditating
(detail). See III. 67

Joan Stanley-Baker

Japanese Art

167 illustrations, 48 in colour

THAMES & HUDSON

© 1984 and 2000 Thames & Hudson Ltd, London

First published in the United Kingdom in 1984
by Thames & Hudson Ltd, 181A High Holborn,
London WC1V 7QX

Revised and expanded edition 2000

ISBN 0-500-20326-1

Printed and bound in Singapore by C.S. Graphics

Contents

Author's note

For clarity regarding their source, the names of monks, monasteries, artists and artworks originating in China are given in their Chinese form, while those of Japanese origin are given in Japanese. The Chinese suffix meaning temple, *-si*, appears as *-ji* in Japanese, and its Japanese equivalent is *-tera* or *-dera*: hence such names as Tōdaiji, Hōryūji, Wakakusadera.

Chinese words for painting, *hui* and *hua*, become *e* and *ga* in Japanese. They occur frequently as suffixes in words referring to styles or techniques, and are hyphenated only in the *-e* form to avoid ambiguity in reading: *onna-e, tsukuri-e*, etc. Special terms are capitalized only when preceded by proper names (eg *Kara-e*, Chinese-style painting; *Nihonga, Yamato-e*, Japanese-style painting); proper names functioning as verbs, however (eg japanization), are not capitalized, following such precedents as romanization or pasteurization.

Chapter 1:   Introduction

This book addresses itself to those who come to Japanese art for the first time, and introduces some of the more significant artistic innovations made on Japanese soil. The aim has not been to be comprehensive; certain major aspects of art and their traditions are not covered, major traditions which can best be seen in a fuller social context, such as Nō and Kabuki theatre, dance (some deriving from ancient Polynesian origins), and the tremendous achievements of swordsmiths and makers of miniatures. Those aspects which have been selected are intended to demonstrate the breadth and resilience of Japan's artistic spirit, which has withstood successive cultural inundations from the continent and emerged highly selective, adaptable, and always fully able to rediscover its own artistic roots.

Another purpose of the book is to identify those aspects of the Japanese spirit which were developed in art forms. Artists, especially up to the Muromachi period, were often working with, and transforming, basically incompatible foreign ideas. This seems to me a greater challenge than the unhindered development of indigenous artistic traditions. To have continually taken and transformed diverse influences (whether from Korea, China, the South Seas, Europe or America) is a unique achievement. Japanese culture in general may be likened to an oyster, opening itself up to repeated onslaughts from the ocean and transforming grains of continental grit into pearls. These transformations obviously reflect Japanese preferences; but, more importantly, they indicate a particular kind of perception: it is possible to identify the patterns of adaptation which appear when Japanese art ingests new stimuli. Because they reflect cultural or ethnic traits, these patterns remain constant despite differences in source, in genre, or in time.

At the same time, the swing of the Japanese psychological pendulum seems wider than that of other peoples, and this is reflected in opposing tendencies in the arts. One tendency is to mirror the external world as it is perceived (direct imitation). A mirror of public manifestations (in institutions, diplomacy, in architecture or the arts) is held up to the world, so to speak, and keeps outsiders from penetrating the essential delicacy and emotional vulnerability of Japanese sensibility. Seeing in Japan a mirror-likeness of himself, the outsider loses interest and ceases to threaten.

The second tendency is introspective and insular, and fosters a creative urge to unparalleled delicacy and poetic imagery. Innate potentials, fully realized, gave birth to art forms and expressions unique to Japan. One is even tempted to propose that the subtlety, poignancy and sense of vulnerability in Japanese culture in general are protected from external disturbance and survive precisely by means of the public manifestations, the 'mirror' that Japan chooses to show to the world.

Examples of the first, mirror-image tendency, are the Asuka-Nara periods (when whole communities of continental artisans were imported), the late Kamakura and Muromachi periods (when Japanese artists were commissioned to work in Chinese styles), the Meiji period (when vast numbers of foreign experts, this time from Europe and North America, were imported to found schools of art, and when Japanese students were sent abroad in hundreds), and finally post-second-world-war Japan, whose art tries to be indistinguishable from its Western models, in spite of the cultural and social differences between Tokyo or Osaka and New York, Cologne or Paris. It is, however, the more introspective tendencies which best reveal Japanese uniqueness and ingenuity; the range includes the arts of Jōmon man, those of the Heian, Momoyama and early Edo periods.

It could be argued that in the absence of indigenous traditions and without artistic importations from abroad, throughout Japanese history, there would have been no ideas to work on, and little Japanese art. There are nevertheless distinct ways in which the Japanese have reacted to foreign stimuli. These are, on the one hand, a spontaneous identification with and rapid absorption of those new ideas which struck a responsive chord in the Japanese artist, and on the other, when required by self-conscious patrons, the mastery of styles and processes which might at first seem unbridgeably alien or mysterious. Given that most artistic processes and styles were imported, it may be that the phases of introspection, when native traditions flourished, were times when artists enjoyed greater freedom in their selection and handling of styles, while the more assertive, outward-directed phases were times when the patrons' choices were conditioned by the prestige they sought to gain from mirroring some external style.

Non-Japanese viewers tend to respond more readily to the introspective phases (where the art is more characteristically

'Japanese'); the assertive or public phases inevitably invite comparisons with the original models, when the Japanese version usually appears to fail. (In passing, it is interesting to note that the Emperors and the aristocracy in general have consistently favoured indigenous and introspective tendencies in the arts.) For instance, Japanese examples of calligraphy in the regular Chinese script of *kaishu* or semi-cursive *xingshu* styles, by even the greatest monks who had lived and studied in China during the ninth and tenth centuries, cannot compare at first glance, in nobility, gravity or structural prowess, with corresponding examples by great Chinese masters. On the other hand, it is difficult for the non-Japanese to detect the 'japanization', the tendency towards a more sensuous line reflected in the Japanese hand. In Muromachi ink landscapes which evolved from Chinese 'Ma-Xia' styles, connoisseurs of the Chinese prototypes lament the unhealthy appearance of the trees, the lack of solidity in the rocks and coherence in the pictorial structure, but do not see that in Japanese hands it is not the rocks and trees which represent early fifteenth-century ideals but the expansive, evocative space for which the trees and rocks serve merely as points of departure. In the same way, in the 'post-Impressionist' paintings of Sakamoto Hanjirō (1889–1956), it is not so much that his horses lack muscular structure or that his space lacks definition; what matters is the way in which his brushstrokes, oil-textures and choice of colours all help to convey a mood of autumnal gloom and elegiac *tristesse*.

In the last twelve hundred years or so, when most imported cultural stimuli reached Japan from China, what was the response of the Japanese artist? How did he select and transform his models? These quests offer some of the great fascinations of Japanese art, and the solutions found are an index to its supreme vitality and durability. For no two peoples could be more disparate. The ancestor-worshipping Chinese, for example, developed a sinewy, three-dimensional ideographic script for their monosyllabic language, and constructed a moral philosophy based on a profound respect for man and the brotherhood of all mankind. A great deal of Chinese imports to Japan thus reflect concern with continuation of lineages and permanence. The polysyllabic Japanese, on the other hand, communicates with whimsical deities through songs and dances, and his poetry is permitted the minutest emotive indulgences. With no eye on eternity, he quickens at the sight of unexpected beauty and cherishes its impermanence.

In the Heian period, aristocratic Japanese courtiers personally directed the development of indigenous art-forms and revealed

their natural preference for the motifs (subdued colours, rolling contours, seasonal flowers) natural to the Yamato plains where they lived. Since these were totally unlike the 'monumental' vistas of granite peaks and vast distances characteristic of Chinese landscape-painting, the result was a transformation of Chinese source-material so profound that its Chinese origins became irrelevant. (By contrast with this delicate art, intended for private enjoyment, public images in Heian halls of state, like the outsize murals of Chinese-style worthies ranged in strict vertical parallel, reflect the protective mirror of image-makers seeking parity with the outside world.)

In view of their relationship, it is worth discussing in general the differences between Chinese and Japanese art. Chinese forms tend to be self-contained and relaxed, while Japanese forms are affected by the overall composition of a picture, and emotional tension charges both motifs and the space around and between them. The inward-directed motifs of Chinese paintings tend to stress solidity and depth (an effect often achieved by the complex interweaving of brushstrokes), whereas the motifs in Japanese painting, each conceived as part of a larger emotional whole, tend to reach laterally across the picture-plane in a 'layered' technique, and to be drawn together by the treatment of the intervening space. The ease and grandeur of Chinese art generate forms which are malleable: each can be slightly changed in space without disturbing the overall visual harmony. Japanese art, by contrast, is often focussed on nuances of emotion, and works tend to be so charged with tension that altering the position of any part would drastically change the overall effect.

This intense feeling for texture, colour, form and space is intended to satisfy the spectator's need for emotional assurance and calm. Stepping-stones leading to a gate, for example, slow the visitor's pace. In a tea-house interior, a feeling of calm is generated by the asymmetrical balance of the space, the warm hues and 'woolly' surface textures. The Way of Tea in particular highlights this aspect of Japanese sensibility, where environment is structured to induce contemplation and calm, to promote a sense of social equality and brotherhood lacking in the rigid social hierarchies of the real world. Japanese critics express their preference for Korean peasant ware over the cool perfection of Chinese celadons by saying that 'the imperfect Korean bowl waits for me even when I am not at home, whereas the Chinese bowl waits for no one.' This sentiment is an index of the inter-relationship between human beings and objects which permeates Japanese life,

1. Stepping-stones laid in moss: a characteristic garden path.

2. *Bizen* unglazed vase showing straw marks, with asymmetrical ear-loop handles. Momoyama. (See p. 158)

3. *Kōgō*, incense-box, shaped like the comic character Oto Gozei. Earthenware, with overglaze enamels. Edo.

4. *Minka*, farm-house, of the Tsubokawa family. Late 17th century.

and which causes their 'worship of the imperfect' (i.e. the natural). A smooth celadon bowl, like the majestic Chinese landscape, is too perfect, too awesome: to the Japanese eye it seems severe, it 'waits for no one', and does not need human sympathy or audience participation to visualize its innate perfection.

From the first moment we look at Japanese art, we are invited to relate in a personal way to the human qualities of imperfection built into the artwork, to the beauty of rooms with unadorned walls and textured surfaces, to artefacts like unglazed Bizen pottery, where straw wrappings have been fired to leave uneven markings on the body; we are invited to discover the strong emotive qualities of an anonymous water-jar or dish, the wit of an incense-box shaped like an actress, or the deliberate fomality of a dinner-service created for a nobleman. In each case the artist gives himself wholly to the work, and reveals an unparalleled awareness of his medium, to the peculiarities of which he responds in a symbiotic way. There is no boundary between planes, between art and man.

Nothing expresses a people's spirit more than its folk crafts, and Japan's *mingei* have dazzled art-lovers around the world. Here generosity of spirit, love of simplicity, and perception of beauty in all natural things is manifest. The simple Japanese farm-house, for

example, with its rough-hewn wooden beams, unpainted walls and thatched roof, inspired the highly sophisticated, tea-house oriented *sukiya* architecture so influential today. In simple lacquers such as the horned wine-bucket, exactly the same kind of peasant strength and forthrightness are expressed. There is no nervousness here about symmetry or glossy surfaces; indeed, there is an easy magnanimity often lacking in the arts of the ruling classes.

In every facet of life, the Japanese have always devoted themselves to bringing about that sense of peace and harmony, of warmth and comfort, which they feel to be an essential part of beauty. In a Japanese meal, for example, quantities which would seem alarmingly frugal to a Chinese gourmet are attractively arranged in a variety of vessels, and are served in slow and graceful sequence on lacquered trays. Quantity is not a concern. Instead, Japanese consciousness works through an aesthetic appreciation of the entire physical and psychological context of the meal. This includes sharply tuned sensory perceptions, but above all it satisfies the diner's senses. The timing of the dishes, and their appearance in bowls of varied shape, decoration and materials, are beautifully harmonized. The hungry Chinese would perhaps be astonished to realize that the feeling of satisfaction arises not from gorging oneself, but from savouring the carefully timed harmony of the food and its service (even down to the meticulously dressed attendant's gait and movements). Appreciation of such subtleties is essential to the enjoyment of Japanese culture in general, and of its arts in particular.

In the same way, the key to understanding the relationship of the Japanese artist or craftsman to his work lies in one word: union. Whether it be the chopstick-rest one finds in a fish restaurant, or a signed painting, one sees a particularly developed symbiosis bonding the artist or craftsman and the product. Painters of old caught exactly this quality of creative absorption in their depictions of carpenters, tatami floor-mat and bamboo-blind makers and mounters of paintings. In literature, the perfection of *renga* or linked verse is believed to come only through repeated group practice among the poets. More than in any other culture, Japanese poets incorporate each other's essence; potters incorporate the essence of the potting process (including finger-prints and kiln accidents); woodworkers or print-makers incorporate woodgrain and chisel marks as an integral and essential part of the finished work.

The artist and his materials, clay, wood or ink-brush and paper, together create the work. This factor is of paramount importance.

5

5. Horned *sake* cask. Black lacquer. H. 57 cm. 19th century.

Considerations basic to other cultures, such as personal uniqueness, the obliteration of all traces of the creative process (such as
rough edges, fingerprints or chisel marks), as well as preconceived
margins or the distinction of planes, are often of no importance. A
six-sided Japanese box may be decorated in one continuous design
which surrounds the form and unifies the planes. The common –
and curious – practice in other cultures of decorating ceramic vessels in arbitrary registers is joyfully absent from Japanese ceramics, where decoration and form are aspects of a single whole.

When patrons demanded imported qualities unpalatable to
Japanese taste (such as unequivocal statement, regularity, repetition, hard or shiny surfaces, equilateral symmetry, monumentality, rigid spaces in roads or rooms – in short, any qualities which
stress self-sufficiency with the least hint of predictability), the
artist's response was usually to adjust and transform in accor-
dance with his own feeling and personal taste. Philosophy, interest
in building up in depth (whether in architectural space or dense
brushstrokes on a painting surface), concepts of permanence and
immutability are to a large extent alien. But these qualities are
often precisely those which generated the Chinese forms which
later entered Japan, and it is with this basic incompatibility in mind
that we must watch Japan's genius unfold, untiringly transforming the continental model to suit its own expression. The poet
Shinkei (1406–75) describes the way to artistic maturity thus (the
italics are mine):

> Unless a verse is by one whose very being has been transfixed
> by the truth of the *impermanence* and *change* of this world,
> so that he is never forgetful of it in any circumstance,
> it cannot truly hold *deep feeling*.

Chapter 2: Prehistoric Period (11th mil. BCE–6th c. CE)

Japanese archaeology is the oldest and most systematic in East Asia. At its official centenary in 1977, one hundred thousand sites had been documented, yielding a fascinating array of artefacts ranging from Paleolithic tool-kits to Mesolithic and Neolithic ceramics. Many of these are so distinct in style from those of Japan's immediate continental neighbours as to suggest possible migrations from as far west as the Mediterranean

Its geographical situation, at the eastern extreme of the Asian continental land mass, may have made prehistoric Japan the terminal point for numerous cultural migrations by peoples from Europe, Central Asia and the Altaic Mountain range, and Siberia. Seafaring peoples from South China, Southeast Asia and the Polynesian isles have also left their cultural imprint on Japanese architecture, dance and vowel structure.

From earliest times, the blend of differing cultural styles is evident. The ceramic strata unearthed by archaeology reveal legacies from cultures widely differing in social structure, religious ceremonies and cuisine.

Archaeologists divide the Japanese Paleolithic Age into two periods, Early (50,000–30,000 BCE) and Late (30,000–11,000 BCE). The division comes with technological evolution from crude and simple scrapers and cutting tools to more sophisticated blades, knives and small tools for engraving, drilling, scraping and piercing.

Jōmon culture (11,000–300 BCE)
Japanese archaeologists date the following, or Mesolithic, period (characterized by a hunting, fishing and gathering way of life) from 11,000–300 BCE. It is also called by the blanket name Jōmon ('cord-impressed'), after the distinctive surface decoration of its pottery. However, the very first pottery of all (11,000–*c.* 7500) is startlingly different from what followed, and more closely resembles the work of Neolithic societies elsewhere in the world. These early vessels were quickly and easily made, by kneading and punching in the hand, and utilized the natural qualities of clay.

They had smooth sides and generous interiors, enabling easy storage and retrieval, as befits utilitarian vessels used for food; they were sparingly decorated. Some scholars term this ware 'incipient-' or 'proto-' Jōmon, suggesting a continuity and internal development between it and Jōmon wares. But the new ware, 'Archaic' or 'Earliest' Jōmon, suggests markedly different attitudes to ceramic form and also to everyday eating and living. It seems doubtful that both styles could have come from a single developing culture; It would be more appropriate therefore to call this earliest phase pre-Jōmon.

Archaic or Earliest Jōmon ware first appeared around 7500 BCE. Examples have been found along the whole main archipelago from Hokkaidō to Okinawa, and on outlying islands such as Tsūshima, Sado, Oki and the Izu isles. It is highly textured, incised or cord-impressed, and has the qualities of low-relief sculpture. It is usually built up from piled-up clay coils, hand-joined inside and outside, and the outer surface is entirely covered with texture decoration, painstakingly applied. The typical pot is conical in form with a sharply pointed bottom, a flaring, often quatrifoil rim and a constricted interior. This form is far more difficult and time-consuming to make than are pots with open interiors such as the pre-Jōmon ware. Even more time-consuming is the application of the cord marks (by rolling a cord-covered stick smartly along the still damp, fragile surface of the clay cone), even if the pot were upturned with the point on top. For ordinary household storage or cooking, such elaborate effort far exceeds necessity and one must ask: what was the real function of these early vessels which were un-pot-like, hard to make, unlidded and impractical?

Middle Jōmon sees even more extraordinary developments. The base is flattened, the rim rises majestically to a height equalling the vessel body, and the lip is often topped with rippling scallops. The entire surface is alive with curvilinear, high-raised decoration with writhing coils forming spirals, S-shapes and meanders; the soaring, flame-like loops are charged with an intensity suggesting an outreach toward the supernatural. There is still a marked absence of 'tableware': bowls, dishes, cups, ewers or amphorae. Vessels of the period are mostly elaborate urns or jars, and were probably used for making ritual offerings.

In the Late Jōmon period (2500 BCE onwards) another dramatic change reflects the arrival of a ceramic-rooted culture which emphasized the natural properties and forms of clay. There is a hint of Central Asian styles, with double-rhyton-shaped vessels, pouring vessels with open and closed spouts and short, squat,

6

6. *Umataka* fired clay urn in basketwork form. H. 32 cm. Middle Jōmon.

7. Clay figurine showing crown-shaped hair and 'insect' eyes. H. 36 cm. Terminal Jōmon.

lidded pots with cylindrical spouts attached. Bowls and round-bottomed vessels reappear, as well as amphorae with narrowed necks and serving-bowls with handles. These indicate a major shift in culinary habits, which includes the discovery of fermentation. (The new typological development, however, retains the raised surface designs characteristic of Jōmon ware.)

From 1000–300 BCE (Terminal Jōmon), stemmed ware began to appear: shallow serving-bowls and amphorae with long narrow necks. These suggest acquaintance with wheel-thrown ware, though they themselves remain hand-built. Once again, the exact function of some vessels is hard to determine. A stemmed dish with an openwork dome, reminiscent of metalwork, for example, could have been used as an oil lamp or a hand-warmer.

It would seem that Jōmon culture did not develop entirely in isolation during its ten thousand year span, and that significant changes in Jōmon man's habits were periodically introduced. Aside from its spectacular pottery, Jōmon culture produced decorated blades of ivory, horn and bone, bracelets and earrings.

For his spiritual needs, Jōmon man carved figurines from stone and moulded them in clay. At about the same time that Middle Jōmon pottery urns were developing elaborate features, these figurines also underwent a dramatic transformation.

Previous figurines had minimal facial features (such as a pinched nose and punctures for eyes); mid-Jōmon figurines have raised-line eyebrows and rather startling eyes: large perforations, round or almond shaped. By Late Jōmon (2500–1000 BCE) they assume a mask-like quality and in some areas become highly ornate with shamanistic features surmounted by all kinds of decorative paraphernalia. At the end of the period, in Terminal Jōmon (1000–300 BCE), extremely sophisticated vessels and figures appear. The hollow body (whether of pot or figurine) is covered with elaborate, raised cord-impressed patterns and the figurines have enormous insect or shell shaped eyes. This kind of cord-impressed pattern, 7 over a plain 'cord-erased' background, is a particularly sophisticated use of 'negative' (ie, undecorated) space. Although their ritual use is still unknown, these late figurines have such enormous, horizontally slitted eyes that some scholars say they are the product of an age of deep superstition and fear; it is, however, difficult to reconcile superstition and fear with the uninhibited decoration also characteristic of these artefacts, which seems far more readily attributable to Jōmon man's exuberance and general delight in 'the dance of life'.

The most significant religious legacy of the Jōmon period is the stone circles and menhirs found in the Tōhoku area in Akita 8 and further north in Hokkaidō, some measuring as much as thirty metres across. Each centres on a square burial-pit in which bones were placed, covered with pebbles. These tombs resemble those found in Siberia from the Bronze Age into the early Iron Age. A peculiarly Japanese feature of each site, however, is the placing of a

8. *Nonakado* stone group in 'sundial' arrangement at the centre of a burial pit. Late Jōmon.

large upright stone in the centre from which other long stones, laid flat, radiate like the spokes of a wheel. This sundial-like arrangement suggests an agrarian society, aware of seasonal changes; but the link – if any – with the following Yayoi culture is not yet clear.

Yayoi culture (c. 300 BCE–c. 300 CE)

Yayoi culture derives its name from the characteristic wheel-thrown pottery first discovered at the Yayoi site near Tokyo. This is entirely different from Jōmon ware. Some scholars believe that the Yayoi (called the Wa or Wo people by Chinese chroniclers) were the first people to settle in Japan whom we might recognize as Japanese today. They arrived from the continent and settled on the southern tip of the Korean peninsula and in northern Kyūshū. They had a highly civilized technology of bronze and iron, wheel-thrown ceramics and wet-rice cultivation. Their sea-borne trade flourished, reaching as far as Lolan, the Han Commandery in Northern Korea. They drove the Jōmon people north and south; though traces of Jōmon styles of pot-decoration remained in northern Japan throughout the Yayoi period, elsewhere (beginning in northern Kyūshū and spreading gradually through Honshū) wheel-thrown Yayoi pottery effectively replaced the earlier Jōmon ware.

Ceramics of the Yayoi period included combed bowls, jars with 9 wide bellies and flaring necks, lidded jars and tall urns. Towards the middle Yayoi period there began to appear goblets, narrow-necked bottles, high-footed wide dishes, ewers and handled cups. All of these indicate a high level of skill with the potter's wheel: it is clear that 'tableware' had now begun to replace largely ritual pots. (The existence of vessels containing traces of grain confirms the agrarian nature of this age.)

The new, wheel-thrown wares have smooth surfaces, and the red or incised decoration tends to be horizontal, combed or zigzag bands across the vessel. This contrasts with the tactile surface and predominantly vertical decoration of Jōmon pottery.

Since metallurgy was introduced to Japan and not indigenously developed, bronze and iron appeared simultaneously around the third century BCE. But the introduced forms were quickly adapted to serve the needs of Yayoi man: bronze war-swords from the continent, for example, became, in the hands of native craftsmen, broader and longer peace-swords for use in burials. One of the most striking importations of all was the *dōtaku* bronze bell, 10 with its characteristic oval shape and protruding flanges. At first

9. Clay pitcher showing horizontal decoration and openwork footrim. H. 22 cm. Mid-Yayoi.

10. *Dōtaku* ritual bronze bell. H. 44.8 cm. Late Yayoi. (Note the similar shape of the Kofun tomb in Ill. 11.)

these bells were small, but they were gradually made larger and larger, and were often adorned in twelve sections to symbolize the twelve-month year. The magical *ryūsui*, or flowing-water designs (C- or S-spirals in bands of parallel raised lines) meander in zig-zags. (These patterns are also found on pottery and tombs; they became part of the later Japanese artistic vocabulary.) Some of the later bells rise splendidly in majesty, with double C-spirals extending beyond the flanges which are now entirely ornamental; they may have been used in ritual, perhaps as symbols of state. *Dōtaku* bells are found in isolated areas, far from settlements and carefully buried. They seem a purely Yayoi phenomenon; certainly they were never made again once the Kofun culture appeared.

While intimate Yayoi contact with Korea is well documented, evidence also suggests some form of direct contact with China. A great number of Chinese bronzes, especially Han mirrors, have been found in Yayoi sites, far more numerous than those found in Korea and those of Korean manufacture. This suggests not only direct contact with China, but also a marked selectivity on the part of the Yayoi when it came to imported artefacts.

Mirrors, *dōtaku*, ceremonial swords, and cashew-nut-shaped jades and agates (*magatama* or Korean fertility jewels) are the principal ritual art objects of the Yayoi period. They are propitiatory objects, and show dependence on the land and the weather. The robust, surface-oriented sculptural forms of the Jōmon hunter give way to more stately, noble vessels more demonstrative of the potter's craft: exterior shape conforms to interior space, and the decoration is simple and understated. Quiet dignity is achieved through purified forms.

Compared to the previous Jōmon or subsequent Kofun cultures, the Yayoi seem to have been particularly civilized, peaceful and refined, using advanced technology to bring about a rise in living standards and to contribute to a religious consciousness which seems more rational and serene than in other periods. It is in the time of the Yayoi that a preference for artistic purity, in both form and decoration, first appears. This purity is the quintessential expression of Shintō (Way of the Gods), the spiritual belief and practice which is thought to have developed about this time. The *kami* or super-consciousness is thought to reside everywhere: in ancient trees, in enormous boulders, in elevated wooden shrines plainly made and without decoration. The love of unadorned materials and pristine freshness, those fundamental attributes of Japanese art, first found expression in the Yayoi period.

The Kofun period (300–600 CE)

The third and last prehistoric period is named after its characteristic tumuli, or *kofun*: huge, mounded tombs, at first round, then keyhole-shaped.

The earlier tombs, found in many areas, from southern Kyūshū to northern Tōhoku, number in the thousands. The earliest of all are concentrated in the Yamato Plains, and continue the traditions of Yayoi culture. It may even be argued that the early Kofun tombs are actually an extension of Yayoi burial practice. But as individual tombs grow in size and cost, we may infer rising despotism and centralized control. The use of cosmic mirrors, for example, is common to both. The grandest tombs of all are close in time and are not found inland, but on the Kawachi Plain in Osaka Prefecture, near the Inland Sea. They are Imperial mausolea, and the finest of them, such as those of the Emperors Ōjin (reigned *c.* 346–95) and Nintoku (reigned *c.* 395–427) are situated by the port, suggesting that these early rulers had come into Japan from the continent, via northern Kyūshū, advancing along the Inland Sea to the Kinai region, where they settled.

The largest mausoleum is that of the Emperor Nintoku. It 11 consists of a rounded, keyhole-shaped mound with trapezoidal elevations in front (thought to have been a ritual altar). If we include the three surrounding moats, the total length of the tomb is 480 metres, and at its highest point the mound rises to 35 metres. The area is 110,950 square metres (about 458 acres); the total volume 1,405,866 cubic metres. The archaeologist Umehara Sueji has calculated that if one person could move about one cubic metre of earth a day, it would have taken a thousand people, working daily, four years to complete the mound.

A characteristic feature of Kofun tombs is pottery figures called *haniwa*. These first appeared (as jars with stands) in the Okayama region facing the Inland Sea; later (in the fourth century) they became cylindrical and were placed 'on guard' around the central area of each tomb; later still they were placed in concentric circles enclosing an earthen platform at whose centre was the pottery house, thought to be the abode of the dead person's soul, and also surrounded by pottery shields and ceremonial sunshades. At the end of the fourth century, *haniwa* became anthropomorphic, hollow figures dressed in minutely detailed costumes. During the sixth century animals (chickens, horses, wild boar, deer, dogs, cats, cattle and fish) were added. These were placed in rows facing outwards, above ground; the sacred central area was reserved for birds, boats and houses, presumably linked symbolically with the transport of the soul to its final resting-place.

The human *haniwa* figures – many with deep-set eyes and 12 abundant curly hair, some with distinctly Caucasian and Central Asian features – give a fascinating glimpse of the society which created them. They include falconers, grooms, farmers, soldiers in armour, priestesses, court ladies, and musicians and dancers posed as if performing for the deceased.

From the fifth century onwards, Kofun artefacts begin to suggest the presence of a new, equestrian and military culture. It shares features with the contemporary Silla culture of Southern Korea, and many types of artefacts appear on both sides of the Tsushima Straits. There are gilt-bronze accoutrements of the mounted archer: crowns adorned with 'branches' from which hang golden leaves and *magatama* jewels, bronze stirrups, openwork pommels and peaked golden helmets; even domestic objects like mirrors and bracelets are often adorned with horsebells. A bronze crown is surmounted by horses in silhouette, and by jingling leaf-discs. Finally there is the Silla/Sueki ware, a thin, highfired, dark pottery in metallic forms with jingling attachments.

Below

11. Aerial view of the thrice-moated 'keyhole' tumulus of Emperor Nintoku. Kofun.

Opposite

12. *Haniwa* figure: farmer carrying plough blade. H. 92 cm. Excavated from a tomb. Late Kofun.

13. Takehara dolmen wall-painting of man leading a horse. Late Kofun.

14. Bronze mirror with *chokkomon* design. 5th century.

(There are stylistic affinities here with Scythian and Central Asian cultures: not only the tree-imagery and the openwork design, but motifs like the gryphon and palmette, imported from even further west. The enormous range of trade as far as the Mediterranean is shown by the presence, in one sixth-century tomb, of a glass bowl made in Persia.)

A striking late Kofun development in Kyūshū was the dolmen type of tomb, whose stone-lined inner chambers had decorated walls and sometimes contained stone sarcophagi decorated with incised or painted designs. (The colours are red hematite, black charcoal, yellow ochre, white china clay and green chlorite.) The earliest of these tombs (those in the centre of present-day Kumamoto) are decorated with red and black diamond patchwork. Later, painted tombs appeared over a wider area; those in the northern area of Fukuoka are decorated with the figures of horses, grooms, birds and boats a well as with the magic spirals and concentric circles found elsewhere. Large drawings of quivers, and double C-coils, are prominent, as are the horses, birds and boats associated with the soul's last journey.

The most striking image which can be associated with the Kofun period is the decorative motif known as the *chokkomon* ('straight-lines-and-arcs'). This consists of a series of broken arcs

drawn over opposed diagonals or crosses, and was apparently
made using compasses and a ruler. The *chokkomon* design is found
in places and on objects associated with burial: incised, for example, on the walls of tombs and sarcophagi, or part of the decoration
of *haniwa* quivers and bronze mirrors. This is one of the first of
those striking conjunctions of straight and curved lines which
became such a prominent feature of later Japanese art.

14

Chapter 3:   Asuka and Nara (552–794)

Shintō shrines

The religious practice of the early Japanese was based on a profound sense of awe for natural manifestations such as sun, water, trees, rocks, sound and silence. Man's response to these phenomena was to purify himself and to identify sacred precincts. Much later this practice was named Shintō (Way of the Gods), to distinguish it from Buddhism which had entered Japan in the sixth century, bringing with it a full panoply of architecture, doctrine and indoor ceremonies. Although later Shintō developed its parallels in architecture, art, clergy and forms of ritual, it is essentially an indigenous religion with neither dogma, scriptures nor form.

It seems safe to say that the earliest sacred precincts were places of particular beauty, demarcated by rudimentary stone boundaries and by simple, pre-architectural monuments (such as rock piles surmounted by stones) indicating the places where sacred presences were first sensed. Monuments of this kind still survive in the precincts of the Ise Jingū. Here worship took its purest form, in total silence with no ritual. (Construction of the earliest Shintō shrines seems related to palace architecture of the Tumulus period, and is characterized by simplicity of both form and material.) In the Ise Jingū precinct, a raised-floor building with a giant thatched gable supported by nine huge pillars is reached by an outside ladder, set at a steep angle. (Reconstructions of another ancient site, Izumo Taisha, in western Japan, facing 15 Korea, suggest a particular sense of mystery and also the intimacy, darkness and warmth associated with the sacred domain of the spirit or *kami*. The worshipper climbs a long flight of steps and, once inside the hall, proceeds beyond the central pillar and turns right to the innermost quadrant before reaching the *sanctum sanctorum*. All this is in marked contrast to the foursquare centrality of Buddhist architecture, where icon images dominated huge open spaces in stone-paved, ground level monastic halls.)

The Ise Jingū, on the eastern coast, is both the ancestral shrine 16 of the imperial family and the national shrine. It has been rebuilt every twenty years since the reign of Emperor Temmu (reigned

15. Izumo Taisha Shintō shrine (rebuilt 1744), showing covered stairway (and main sanctuary with deep thatch).

672–686), sixty times altogether by 1993. The space is dominated by two compounds, the western Naikū and the eastern Gekū, thought to have been first built in the fourth and late fifth centuries respectively. They are dedicated to Amaterasu no Ōmikami (Heaven-illuminating Great Spirit, the daughter of Izanagi no Mikoto), traditional ancestor of the imperial house, and to Toyoukeno Ōkami (Great Spirit of Food Abundance and grandson of Izanagi no Mikoto, provider of the Five Grains). The site is among tall evergreens near the Isuzu River; its cool stillness is broken only by the clatter of cleanwashed pebbles underfoot, and it is said to have been chosen by Amaterasu herself, in an apparition to Princess Yamato early in the first century CE.

Each compound is divided into an eastern and western sector; when one sector is in use, the other is kept empty, white and still,

16. The Ise Jingū shrine. Site dates from the 4th century.

with its ground-covering of pebbles. Each compound is rectilinear, enclosed by four layered wooden fences. The buildings are aligned along the central north-south axis, beginning with thatched and gabled gates set into the southern fences. The main sanctuary (or *shōden*), three bays wide and two bays deep, is poised aloft on a structure of pillars and surrounded by a covered veranda. The approach is by a stairway leading to the central bay. Some elements, such as alignment, the layered enclosure and the metal decorative accents may be later features incorporated from continental architecture, but distinguishing native characteristics remain: the roof with its forked finials pointing skywards at either end, the heavy ridge pole topped by cylindrical, tapered billets laid crosswise along its length, and the main pillars which are embedded directly in the ground, not set in foundations. The general impression is of abstract design, of planes, angles, circles in simple

but dynamic interaction. The natural colours and textures of the wood and pebbles are not sullied; the effect is warm; the atmosphere is one of intimacy and awe.

In spite of the arrival and dominance of Buddhism, Shintō shrines continued to be built in serene woods and beside quiet shores, and were later often incorporated into Buddhist compounds, representing as they did local manifestations of universal Buddhist values. Shintō silence, its simplicity and its direct yet undefined interaction between man and nature or spirits are characteristic Japanese additions to, or modifications of, imported religion, just as the same qualities modify imported art.

Asuka 552–646

The introduction of Buddhism, striking as it did at the core of Japanese spiritual consciousness, exerted a profound and far-reaching effect upon all aspects of Japanese life. The higher presence (or *kami*), of which the Japanese were so intensely aware, and which possessed no specified form or attribute, now appeared in a plethora of human guises. Principles of the faith were expounded in Chinese texts and by the clergy; regiments of monks and nuns performed minutely prescribed religious functions inside vast halls filled with anthropomorphic statues, illumined with candles and befogged with incense. The stillness was broken by chanting to the beat of drums, gongs and bells.

With the coming of Buddhism, Japan was introduced to a concept of systems, routines and regulations. Buddhism channelled silent and spontaneous interaction with spirits into an organized programme of ritual observance, and explained the mysteries of life by the Law of Cause and Effect. The new theology, with its inexorable focus on the after-life, must have both disturbed and inspired followers of Shintō, who suddenly found previously vague sentiments now clearly articulated and vigorously systematized. The Aryan mind of India had been absorbed in metaphysical subtleties for centuries and had learned to analyse phenomena and control consciousness even before the birth of Gautama (567–488 BCE), the historical Buddha. After attaining total enlightenment the Buddha explained that existence is a continuing series of transformations and that salvation from suffering and death lies in detachment from desires.

Buddhism arrived in Japan from Korea after centuries of development on the Continent. The king of Paekche (Kudara) in the south-eastern corner of the Korean peninsula presented a gilt-bronze image of Buddha to Emperor Kimmei of Japan in 552 CE, with the assurance that 'this doctrine can create religious merit and retribution without measure or bounds, and lead one to a full appreciation of the highest wisdom'. The emperor, who had no wish to offend native spirits, was grateful but cautious: he allowed the powerful Soga family to practise the new religion before all others.

In fact, many members of the immigrant community in Japan prior to 552 had been Buddhists. The Korean scholar Wani is recorded to have introduced (Chinese) writing to Japan in 405; other immigrants, in charge of various *be* (hereditary guilds specializing in painting, weaving, saddlery) had settled in the Yamato area during the reign of Emperor Yūryaku (457–79). By the Asuka period, every major building project was using imported Korean specialists, many of whom subsequently settled. (Although immigrant Chinese craftsmen are mentioned, some families for several generations, artistic contact, like religious contact, between Japan and China during the Asuka period was largely by way of Korea. Korean dress was worn at court, as evidenced by the two Paradise embroidery panels (*Tenjūkoku Mandala*) produced by court ladies in 622 for the heavenly repose of Prince Shōtoku: see page 34.)

Prince Shōtoku (573–621) and the rise of Buddhism
The Asuka period is particularly notable for life and activities of Prince Umayado, better known by his Buddhist name Shōtoku (Sagely and Virtuous), an avid scholar and learned statesman whose cultural activities substantially advanced Japanese civilization. In the arts, this period reflects cultural links with the Korean peninsula rather than with China, in particular with the kingdoms of Koguryō to the north and Paekche to the southwest.

Born into a court that for twenty-one years had been receiving Buddhist images from Korea and was now coming to terms with the new faith, Shōtoku grew up in an atmosphere of cultural ferment. The powerful pro-Buddhist Soga clan was resisting pressure from conservative elements (notably from the custodian of Shintō rituals, Nakatomi, and the military chief Mononobe, who together burned down chapels built on Soga instructions, and hurled their Buddhist statutes into the Naniwa canal). Soga no Umako (died 626) placed his niece on the throne as Empress Suiko (reigned 592–628) and ordered Prince Shōtoku, then only nineteen years old, to act as Regent. This turned out to be Soga's greatest deed, and the Suiko reign saw the rise of a literate culture that permeated the social and political life of the aristocracy.

Prince Shōtoku was an ardent Buddhist scholar. At court he lectured and wrote commentaries on the Vimalakirti sūtra, the *shōman-gyō*, and the *Lotus Sutra*. Contact with China was opened in 607 when he dispatched a scholar to Sui China to study Buddhism and ordered the first compilation of the history of Japan (now lost). In 604 he had decreed the famous Seventeen Articles, aiming at social harmony, in an attempt to centralize power and to unify the various clan-chiefs whose rivalries had hitherto dominated Japanese life.

The Prince built his palace at Ikaruga overlooking the Yamato River (which flowed to nearby Naniwa, gateway to Korea). Next to it he built a Buddhist temple, called the Wakakusadera. Soga no Umako built another temple, the Hōkōji, in 596. (Both this and the Wakakusadera were laid out in imitation of contemporary Paekche style, with the southern gate close to the inner gate, and the sūtra repository, belfry and lecture hall to the north, outside

17, 18. The Hōryūji compound, pagoda to west, Golden Hall to east; and detail view of the pagoda. Late 7th century.

the compound.) By 614, over half a century since the presentation of the first Buddhist statue to Japan, there were 46 temples and 1385 ordained monks and nuns.

After Shōtoku's death the Soga clan sought to replace his influence with their own, arrested his son, and killed or forced his family to suicide. They burnt down the Ikaruga Palace in 643, and in 670 burnt the Wakakusadera itself. However, Shōtoku's legacy, the primacy of learning and of moral values, had been so firmly implanted among the aristocracy and the clergy that the ruined temple was soon rebuilt. The new compound, now called the Hōryūji, lay to the northwest of the Wakakusadera site. The layout of the original Wakakusa temple was a rectilinear walled compound whose three basic structures – the *chūmon* or inner gate, the pagoda and the main Golden Hall – were aligned on a south–north axis, facing south involving the worshipper in a northward progression from one holy building to another in a straight line. In

17

this layout the pilgrim's path necessitated a physical encounter with the tower-like pagoda. This structure evolved from the Indian stupa, by way of Northern Wei Chinese cave temples characterized by their central four-sided votive pillars around which pilgrims would have practiced energetic circumambulation. The pagoda like the stupa was the reliquary and as such was the most powerful source of sacred presence (or energy) in any religious compound. Physical interaction with sacred energy had been central to continental practice where walking clockwise around the relic, stupa or central pillar energized and charged the faithful with divine blessings. Such energetics can be traced back from Alexandrine India to Bronze Age Crete and her mountain cave or subterranean pit sanctuaries where central pillars are surrounded with implements for ritual libation. Circumambulation, coil-motion, magnetic fields and divine energy fields had been interrelated in ritual since the dawn of Eurasian civilization. But now the psycho-physical aspect of religion was to lose its primacy to a politicization and secularization of Buddhism, both on the continent and in Japan. 18

The rebuilt Hōryūji compound, for example, now laid its long side on the east-west axis, with the *chūmon* at the southern end, slightly to the west. The pagoda was now to the west, and the Golden Hall to the east; both were equidistant from (that is, they were either side of) the *chūmon* and simultaneously visible to the worshipper as he entered. Instead of progressing into the depths of the compound with an obligatory reverencing of the reliquary or pagoda, the pilgrim now made a lateral turn either way. From this time forward the pagoda lost its function of the primordial central pillar and became increasingly an instrument of decoration, later even appearing, as in the New Yakushiji, Nara, as a guardian-like pair, recalling the secular drum and bell towers of imperial China. This eschewing of linear penetration in favour of lateral movement is one of the basic traits of japanization and is repeatedly met throughout Japanese history.

The Tamamushi Shrine

This portable wooden shrine is the oldest architectural example surviving from the Asuka period. Housed in a temple which escaped burning, it was later moved to the Hōryūji. The bronze filigree bands ornamenting the pedestal and architectural members were once inlaid with the iridescent wings of the *tamamushi* beetle, hence its name. (Although the same type of beetle is found in Korea, the choice of camphor and cypress wood native to Japan is 19

19, 20. The Tamamushi Shrine, with its roof of camphor and cypress wood; and tiger *jātaka*, oil on lacquered cypress, the left panel from the base of the shrine. Mid-7th century.

evidence of Japanese manufacture, some time during the late Asuka period (*c.* 650), when many of the statues for the original Wakakusadera were being produced.) The shrine's hipped and gabled roof is tiled in such a way as to mark a distinct break between the upper and lower portions, whereas the rebuilt Hōryūji temple has roofs tiled in one continuous plane, although the rafters beneath show a separation between the sharply pitched upper section and the more gently curving lower section. This method gives the roof an effect of curvature and lightness which characterizes Asuka architecture.

Asuka painting
Widescale destruction has left very little evidence of Asuka painting, but surviving works in lacquer and in embroidery hint at a

thriving co-existence of styles imported from a variety of sources. On the Tamamushi Shrine, for example, the lacquered wood is painted over with an oil-based paint in four colours. This *mitsuda-e* technique has distant origins in Persia and its appearance here has puzzled those who hold China's silk routes to be the only trading link between the Mediterranean and the Pacific. However, centuries of Scytho-Siberian activities in Korea are confirmed by the equestrian artefacts in metal found in royal tombs in Silla's Kyongjū area, almost identical to those excavated in Japan from the Kofun and the Asuka periods. Sillan golden drinking vessels pre-date those (admittedly more advanced) of mid-Tang China by nearly three centuries, and it is possible that Persian oil-painting techniques were transmitted to Japan before China. It is reasonable to postulate a 'northern route' which linked West to East, bypassing China. The actual style of the Tamamushi oil paintings, however, also transmitted through Korea, distinctly recalls Northern and Western Wei prototypes from the Dunhuang Buddhist caves in China, not forgetting that the Northern Wei were possibly a Tungusic people who hailed from the Central Asian Steppes.

On the left panel of the base of the Tamamushi Shrine is a very early example of that style of narrative painting which achieved unparalleled heights in later Japanese art. It is a *jātaka* (a tale depicting one of the Buddha's previous lives). As Prince Mahāsattva hunts in the mountains with his two brothers, he comes upon a starving tigress and her seven cubs. The brothers flee, but Mahāsattva offers his own flesh for nourishment. This act of compassion ensures advancement to Buddhahood in a future life. The panel tells the story in three sequential scenes: on the cliff the prince doffs his robe; he plunges down the chasm; he is then shown at the bottom, being devoured by the grateful tigress. His body is lithe and graceful; the flowing lines and the tendency toward attenuation are characteristic of mid-century sculpture. These schematized rocks, also to be found in early Korean art, derive from Chinese Six Dynasties painting. In mid-seventh century Japan we clearly see sympathetic and sensitive reception of cultural and technical ideas from earlier Continental Buddhist art. Their swift assimilation confirms the enormous appeal of the new religion.

When Shōtoku Taishi died in 621, a pair of tapestries (*Tenjūkoku* or Paradise Mandala) was designed by immigrant artists from the Continent and handsewn by court ladies. Surviving fragments show figures in contemporary Koguryō

20

21

21. Tenjūkoku Mandala (detail). Embroidered silk. 622.

dress. This indicates that the prince and his court wore Koguryō style robes in real life. The Sui-Tang style robe in which the prince is shown in the famous posthumous painting of which a copy survives, now in the Imperial Collection, is doubtless a fabrication of Nara-period artists in the flush of Chinese fashions and therefore a misleading anachronism. Korean elements permeated the lifestyles of the aristocracy throughout the seventh century. Even an eighth-century burial mound recently excavated at Takamatsu reveals murals of figures in Koguryō dress (now up-dated, reflecting Tang proportions and poses). It would seem that an intimate (familial?) relationship between Japanese aristocracy and Korean royal households was maintained long after contact with Sui and Tang China, and that the transition from Korea-derived to China-derived styles we see in the arts may belie the Korean origins or ethnicity of Japan's royal family and aristocracy.

Asuka sculpture

Shōtoku's principal Buddhist master was Hye-cha, a Koguryō monk whose state-oriented Buddhism (from Northern Wei China) differed from the politically more liberal southern Buddhism of Paekche and Liang China, where monks did not have to reverence the sovereign. However, the influence of Buddhist

22. Guze Kannon (detail). Gilded camphor wood. H. 197 cm. Early 7th century.

diplomats, monks, artisans and painters from both Korean kingdoms had been felt in Japan since the mid-sixth century. It can be assumed that a variety of contrasting styles flourished during the Suiko period; the Hōryūji temple alone reveals several artistic tendencies.

One source is non-Chinese, the Scytho-Siberian equestrian culture already seen in the earlier Kofun period. This appears both in the openwork metal crowns which Shiba Tori (a third-generation Chinese member of the saddlers' guild) used on his Buddhist sculptures (see below). Another is the series of square panels with bull's eye circles and triangles that front the overhead canopies (like the Kofun murals in the stone dolmens of Fukuoka and Kumamoto). These alternating, repeated geometric forms hark back to Northern Wei Buddhist cave decor in Dunhuang.

Yet another source is revealed in the angular, severe and archaistic sculptural style of Shiba Tori's actual sculptures. Tori school works were the offcial style of the Suiko reign; they include the Asuka Great Buddha (cast for the Hōkōji temple in 606 and since extensively restored and poorly remodelled), the Yakushi healing Buddha cast in 607 for the ailing Emperor Yōmei (Shōtoku's father and Suiko's brother), the tall wooden standing statue of Guze Kannon made for Prince Shōtoku before his death in 621, as well as the Shaka Triad cast in 623, and several of the so-called 'Forty-Eight (bronze) Statues of Hōryūji' now in the Tokyo National Museum. These Tori works derive their regal stiffness from sixth-century Koguryō bronze statuettes: they are conceived frontally, in terms of planes and tubes, and have typical facial characteristics: the Buddha's eyes slant upwards, the nose is long, flared at the bottom, and forms a conspicuous triangle in the ovoid, tubular face, and the mouth is set close under the nose, which makes the chin appear somewhat large. The deep trough beneath the nose cuts into the upper lip, forming the Tori hallmark: twin points rising at a prominent angle. The lips, in simple angled planes, are pulled back forming the 'archaic smile'. The dimple beneath the lower lip is deeply etched. The neck is a smaller cylinder beneath that of the head; the shoulders are set four-square. The body is conceived as front-facing, upright blocks; the muscles lack articulation beneath the drapery. These characteristics link the Tori style, by way of Koguryō reinterpretation, to earlier Chinese Wei sources.

Koguryō Buddhist philosophy may account for the stern mien of Tori's main figures, but mention should be made of the gently rounded and tender quality of his peripheral figures (for example

22

23

23. Shaka Triad. Bronze. Middle figure h. 86.3 cm, attendants 91 cm. Hōryūji Golden Hall, 623.

the small seated Buddhas on the mandorla cast in relief), qualities common in the second half of the seventh century, but already evident in Tori's time. The meditating bodhisattva Maitreya in the Kōryūji is carved from a hollowed block of red pine, a tree which grows abundantly in Korea but not in Japan. (Japanese wooden sculptures are made either from camphor or Japanese cypress.) Its style and details are related to the famous gilt-bronze meditating bodhisattva in Seoul's Toksu Palace Museum. The eyebrows arch out and up; the eyes are narrow slits with a straight upper lid and the lower curved; the nose is narrow, and distinctly ridged. The groove beneath it flares as it reaches the lips which (unlike the simple lateral planes of the Tori school) bifurcate to left and right. The chin is less prominent than that in the Tori style, and the face more rounded. The body inclines gently forward, and the bare torso tapers inwards below the breast. An impression of gentleness and absorption is part of the sculptor's intention.

24

An exquisite bodhisattva in the Chūgūji convent in Hōryūji shares the characteristics of the Kōryūji figure and of the Toksu (Seoul) bodhisattva except that the downward-arching eyebrows here add an air of beatific tenderness. (There are several sculptural affinities amongst the three pieces: the spherical modelling of the eyeballs, the articulation and inclination of the torsos, the proportion of arms and legs.) Unfortunately, we know nothing of the carving and dedication of this beautiful statue, but as it is housed in Hōryūji it may have been associated with Prince Shōtoku and Korea.

Recent investigations have established a southern provenance for the Toksu Palace Museum bodhisattva. In 541, King Songmyong of Paekche had sent to the Chinese Liang court for Buddhist texts, craftsmen and painters. The resultant softening of the style in the latter sixth century can be seen not only in the Toksu gilt bronze meditating bodhisattva but also in its Kōryūji and Hōryūji sisters. In 603 Paekche presented a gilt seated meditating bodhisattva to Prince Shōtoku. The Prince charged a nobleman to venerate it, and the nobleman built the Hachioka-dera (Kōryūji) to house it. From separate historical accounts scholars have identified the Kōryūji red pine Maitreya as the 603 gift from Paekche. (Originally this work had been gilt.) The Chūgūji bodhisattva is made of the camphor wood typical of Japanese sculpture. Its remarkable resemblance to the Kōryūji and Toksu works, and the absence of its continuation in Japan, suggest its being the work of a Korean sculptor, perhaps resident in Japan. The presence of the soft contemporary Paekche style in Japan by the first decade of the seventh century may account for the softened contours of peripheral Tori school works even during this most severe and archaistic phase of Japanese Buddhist sculpture.

Another craftsman who, like Tori, was of Chinese descent and who worked in the Koguryō-derived angular style in Hōryūji, was Aya no Yamakuchi no Ōkuchi Atahi. Among other works, he produced the Four Celestial Guardians or Heavenly Kings (*shitennō*) for the Golden Hall, some time before the Taika Reform of 646 (which ended the Soga clan's power and patronage). The Four Kings show an advance in volumetric and three-dimensional sculpture, even though they have the unmistakable archaistic Tori stamp. They are more rounded and the faces are fuller and more expressive. Many of the so-called 'Forty-Eight Buddhist Statues' originally associated with Hōryūji (now in the Tokyo National Museum) are of obvious Korean manufacture, but there are also several examples in the Tori style. In short, although during the

24. Meditating Miroku Bosatsu. Red Pine. Kōryūji, Kyoto. H. 123.5 cm. 603?

25. Meditating bodhisattva (detail). Camphor wood. Chūgūji convent. H. 87.5 cm. Early 7th century.

25

27

pre-Taika period under Soga influence the severe northern Korean style was dominant, it coexisted with styles of southern Korean origin. After the Taika Reformation, however, gentler styles superseded the Tori style. Among the Forty-Eight Statues there are many with child-like proportions: large heads, hands and feet, and small bodies. The faces have highly arched, rounded eyebrows set high above heavy-lidded, narrow-slitted eyes; the noses are shorter than those of the Tori school, and the mouths are set lower, giving smaller, rounded and fleshy chins. This child-like style seems to have influenced many larger figures during the second half of the seventh century, the Hakuhō period, 645–710. For example, in the Kannon figures of Kinryūji and Hōryūji (with hair parted in the middle, high above the brow and temple and looped over long ears), the beatific smile suggests innocence and the inner peace of meditation. The same child-like style appears in the flying wooden apsaras which adorn the canopy over the main figures in the Hōryūji's Golden Hall. Seated on lotus blossoms, and playing musical instruments, they appear to descend from heaven on flying tendrils. Although made during the Hakuhō period, such child-like works probably derive from the Paekche style already gleaned from the tiny gilt-bronze Asuka figurines. True Hakuhō sculpture does not appear until the end of the seventh century, in the Yakushiji Triad.

26

The Hakuhō (White Phoenix) period 645–710
In the 660s, at the same time that Silla was conquering both Paekche and Koguryō, Chinese Tang was entering its most glorious phase. In Japan, as a result of the Taika reform and the removal of the Soga clan from power and patronage, the flood-gates were opened to Chinese influences. Hakuhō sculpture shows these influences in substantial works of imperial grandeur. There is new-found authority and grace; sculpture is rounded and more realistic.

One of the most powerful Hakuhō sculptures is the larger-than-life group of gilt-bronze statues in the Yakushiji. The seated Yakushi (Healing Buddha) is flanked by two bodhisattvas, Nikkō (Sunlight) and Gakkō (Moonlight), for which there are no prototypes in the Hōryūji Treasure Museum or among the Forty-Eight statuettes. They are realistically conceived in the round rather than frontally, and are in *contraposto* stance, weighted on the inner foot, swinging the upper torso outwards. The faces are full, almost spherical and the chins droop toward the necks and thence to the chests, in three fleshy wrinkles. These bodhisattvas, like the Shō

28

26. One of six standing
bodhisattvas (detail). Camphor
wood. Style probably derived
from Paekche. H. 85.7 cm.
Late 7th century.

27. Zōchō Ten (Virudhaka), one
of the Four Guardian Kings from
Hōryūji. Carved wood.
H. 20.7 cm. Before 646.

Kannon housed in the Kondō of the same temple, have upswept hair which culminates in a high topknot and is secured on the forehead with a trifoliate crown. Both the Shō Kannon and the Yakushi, perhaps because they are principal rather than flanking figures, are more conservative in style and have little turning of the torso, as the body weight is centred. These figures show a clear High Tang influence in their rounded lips and faces, and in their expressions of deep absorption. This influence may also be seen in the Hōryūji paradise murals which date from the same period.

Bronze sculpture in Hōryūji was more conservative in idiom and, even toward the end of the century, retained vestiges of the Tori style. Among the most beautiful works here are the Yumetagai (Dream-changing) Kannon and the Amida Triad of Lady Tachibana's Shrine. They have the fuller proportions, characteristic chins and sloping necks of the Yakushiji figures; but the facial modelling is rather restrained, with angular lines along the brows, nose and lips (which rise in twin points and bear the Tori

29
30

28. (*left*) Gakkō, from Yakushi Triad. Gilt bronze. H. 315.3 cm. Hakuhō, 688.

29. (*above*) Yumetagai Kannon. Bronze. H. 85.7 cm. Late Hakuhō.

30. (*right*) Amida Triad, seated on lotus blooms, in Lady Tachibana's Shrine. Gilt bronze. H. 33 cm. 733.

31. Bodhisattva Monjū from
Hōryūji Pagoda. Clay.
H. 50.9 cm. Early Tempyō, 711.

cylindrical dimple beneath). These pieces exude a full, quiet aristocratic confidence, and may be the work of a small group of conservative craftsmen who maintained Tori traditions in the face of
imported Chinese styles and techniques. Korean artisans, for
example, who painted the Hōryūji murals and sculpted the extensive clay panorama of Buddha's nirvana in the Hōryūji Pagoda,
entirely ceded to the onslaught of Chinese Tang realism.

These clay sculptures are built into niches in the four corners
of the pagoda and were completed in 711, one year after the capital
moved to Nara, the start of the Tempyō period. In a scene depicting the conversation between the Buddhist layman and scholar
Yuima (Vim-alakīrti) and the bodhisattva Monjū (Mañjuśrî) the
latter looks as if he could have stepped out of one of the newly-
completed murals in the Kondō (Golden Hall). Wearing flowing
robes and a jewelled necklace, the bodhisattva sits full-faced in

31

regal pose, his wavy, backswept hair in a high topknot. The dress of the lay onlooker is in High Tang style. The concept of these figures is no longer frontal and linear: there is a strong feeling of volume and the beginning of torso articulation and motion.

The Hōryūji murals

The most magnificent examples of late Hakuhō painting are the murals of the rebuilt Hōryūji Golden Hall. The murals are over 3 metres high; the four large central ones measure 2.5 metres across and the eight corner ones 1.8 metres. They are a very rare example of mural painting: this may have been the first time a monastery was so decorated. (The usual wall-decoration in Buddhist halls, before and since, was hangings of painted, woven or embroidered silk.) The Golden Hall was completed some time between 680 and 690, and the murals finished by around 711.

The artisans, of immigrant Chinese and here mostly Korean descent, had been organized into craft guilds responsible for the decoration of palaces and temples. The Taihō-ryō decree of 701 established a Painters' Bureau (*edakumi-no-tsukasa*) under the Ministry of Internal Affairs, and was presided over by three civil offcials. The bureau had four master-painters (*eshi*) and sixty ordinary painters (*edakumi*) living in the metropolitan area, and several groups of private painters living in the provinces (*sato-eshi*) who could be summoned to the capital for large-scale projects. The institution of official painters existed in some form or other for another thousand years, until the Meiji restoration of 1868.

To make the murals, the Kondō wall surface was first covered with a layer of fine white clay. Then the artisan transferred the design from a pouncing pattern using a fine even red or ink line, then added colours including cinnabar, red ochre and red lead for the reds, ochre and litharge for yellow, malachite for green and azurite for blue. The figures have the same sensuous and fleshy presence as Chinese High Tang painting of the period, such as those in the Dunhuang caves dating to 642 and 698 CE, with the bodies slightly twisted and relaxed in *tribhanga* or *contraposto* pose which separates the planes of torso, upper and lower abdomen and places the weight on one leg, with the other slightly lifted in motion. The most famous of the figures is perhaps the Kannon (Avalokiteśvara) in the Amida Paradise on the West Wall. Full, sensuous lips and long, deep-set eyes are vestigial traces of its Indian and Khotan sources and, still more distant in time and space, of ancient Greece. The magnificent presence of the deity is captured with firm technical assurance. The stylistic relationship

34

with the line-drawn bodhisattva on the door panels of the Lady Tachibana Shrine is unmistakable, suggesting variant pouncing patterns from the same source. When the Kondō was completed the effect of the Paradise images, flanked by bodhisattvas, and with apsaras flying overhead in prayerful attitudes, must have been resplendent and inspiring. And when the Shaka Triad for the original temple was moved in, it must have seemed odd, being much too small for the enlarged hall and by now looking rather antiquated in style.

Buddhism and centralized power

When Prince Shōtoku embraced Chinese statecraft and Buddhism, he had envisioned the first, based on Confucian ethics, as underpinning the whole administrative and penal system; Buddhism remained for him a private personal faith. Church and state did not converge, as in Europe, until over a century later, in the person of Emperor Shōmu (reigned 724–749). In 741 Shōmu launched a massive building programme of Buddhist monasteries and temples throughout the land, ostensibly for the protection of the nation, but also as a compelling monument to his imperial authority. (This in fact ran counter to the basic tenet of Buddhism, which aims at the salvation of the individual soul, sees no class distinctions and is universally benevolent.) The new monasteries were created and served by labour conscriptions which recruited untold numbers of the nation's population, including slave groups, to the service of the government. Buddhist monks were no longer free to preach the sūtras as they saw fit, nor were monks and nuns permitted to hold religious observances on unauthorized premises. The entire chuch had come under the protection, and the control, of the throne.

Tempyō religious art: the Tōdaiji 752

In his zeal Emperor Shōmu removed a small mountain in Nara to make way for the largest Buddhist monastery in the land, the Tōdaiji or Eastern Great Temple. In 743 he vowed to cast a massive image of the Rushana Buddha (Universal Light, Vairocana); the project was properly begun in 745. All the copper in the land was commandeered for the colossal statue which towered over 14 metres high; Japanese bronze ran out and bronze-casting thereafter ceased for centuries. The Great Buddha symbolized the dominance of Buddhism and its spread among the populace. It was no longer a private faith for the leisured but had become the most powerful spiritual force all over the land.

The Tōdaiji project exacted a huge toll in money and labour. An estimated ten per cent of the populace, down to the poorest beggars, contributed in some way or another; there were 50,000 carpenters and over 370,000 metal smiths. The casting was begun in Shōmu's palace grounds in Shigaraki; but after numerous failures the site was changed to Nara in 745 and the work was completed after four more years. The largest wooden structure in the world was built around it; its front of eleven bays was some 73 metres across and tied into a cloister of 154 bays. Its proportions and roof pitch may have roughly resembled that of the Shōsōin repository which is one of three storehouses among the numerous structures in the original compound. Twin pagodas, now emblems of imperial power rather than the source of sacred energy, rose three times the height of the Hōryūji Pagoda, soaring 100 metres into the air. With its numerous gates, halls and sub-temples, the Tōdaiji compound is the largest in Japan and dominated the new capital of Heijō (Nara). In a spectacular ceremony, attended by every member of court and the clergy, the monastery and Great Buddha of Nara were dedicated in 752. But in the half century that

32. Head of Fukūkenjaku Kannon in the Sangatsudō. Gilded dry lacquer. H. 360.3 cm. 746.

33. Rushana Buddha, in Tōshōdaiji. Gilded dry lacquer. H. 4m. 759.

followed, its power overshadowed the government and the Court was forced to seek yet another site for its capital.

The Great Buddha of Nara we see today has been reworked several times and the Buddha Hall is a much reduced and squared-off version of its once magnificent proportions. For a glimpse of the original Great Buddha, in all the splendour of gold-leaf gilt, we must resort to two sculptures, and to an early painted illustration. Both statues were made in dry lacquer, no more copper being available. The contemporaneous Fukūkenjaku Kannon of 746 is the main statue in Tōdaiji's Hokkedo (Lotus Hall) sub-temple, commonly called the Sangatsudō (Third Month Hall). It stands nearly 4 metres tall, and is probably the work of the sculptors responsible for the Great Buddha, headed by Kuni-naka Muraji Kimimaro. It is an eight-armed bodhisattva whose third left hand holds a rope to symbolize the salvation of souls. As the bodhisattva towers over a high wooden pedestal, its majestic, serene face is usually missed by viewers. The cheeks and chin are full but not heavy; the long, slanted eyes are modelled with curved upper lids which give them a gentle, loving expression beneath arched and bevelled brows. A large vertical third eye is partially open in the forehead and a black pearl decorates the spot between the brows. The mouth is modulated and full, with upper and lower lips in symmetrical M and W shapes which echo the curves of the rest of the face. The elaborate silver crown is encrusted with thousands of precious stones, pearl, agate and crystals, and is swathed with chains holding beads carved in the ancient *magatama* shape. A twenty-centimetre silver Amida Buddha stands in the middle, hands spread in the *mūdra* of bestowing peace of mind. Although the Kannon clearly reflects Tang features, the Amida's face shows vestigial traces of the Koguryō mien, in the eyes and two sharp points rising in the centre of the upper lip.

The other statue which may give us a glimpse of the Great Buddha is in the Golden Hall (Kondō) of Tōshōdaiji, west of Nara. It is a seated Vairocana or Rushana Buddha, 4 metres high, and was made of gilded dry lacquer in 759. An elaborate aureole originally had one thousand seated Buddhas in thirty-two clusters, most of which are still in place. The Rushana Buddha's face is more heavy-set than that of the Sangatsudō Kannon and the neck-folds are modelled around a dropped chin. The eyes look down from under thick, curved lids, and slant to the nose in an expression more severe than compassionate, more lordly than tender. The original Great Buddha of Tōdaiji designed as Emperor Shōmu's symbol of state may well have combined the qualities of these two

32

33

34. Kannon from the Amida Paradise on the Hōryūji murals. 711. (Damaged by fire in 1949.)

works, a severe but benevolent colossus which radiated protective light over the land. From a twelfth-century handscroll we can deduce still more of its architectural aspects and emotional impact. In a time-sequenced vignette, like those of the Tamamushi Shrine *jātaka*, a pilgrim nun is shown several times during her night at Tōdaiji. The colossal, gilt-bronze Buddha towers benignly over her as she prays for divine guidance. The eleven bays have slatted door-panels which open inwards and are taller than the four-square door-panels of today's reduced edifice of seven bays. The total impression of the original structure was horizontal, not square, and the impact of the statue must have been more immediate when it was placed, as illustrated here, dominating the central bay with little to hinder the spectator's view.

Japanese and continental tastes

At this point we should perhaps consider the remarkable speed with which the Japanese assimilated continental cultural stimuli, particularly Buddhism. It was not a matter of sudden and overwhelming contact; there had been frequent contacts for millennia. Tremendous cultural receptivity in the Asuka period, therefore, may reflect a new Japanese sense of cultural inferiority in the face of an urbane, continental culture and a concommitant yearning for international parity. In the Tempyō period, the Japanese wholeheartedly adopted Chinese culture, Buddhism and statecraft. Administrative and court rituals were regulated on continental models; court wear changed from Korean to Chinese; palaces were built in continental style with tiled roofs, bright crimson pillars and slate floors and, at back-breaking cost, to continental scale.

All these imports were, however, no more than an external covering draped over a Japanese framework. Not all parts fitted. The original eleven-bayed Great Buddha Hall of Tōdaiji, for example, based as it was on Chinese imperial scale, and requiring the removal of entire hills to provide the site, must have been drastically out of proportion with the surrounding Yamato hills. In spite of the new regard for external prestige, when it came to personal habits, native preferences triumphed. In particular, Chinese food and eating habits were rejected; later, even within the Chinese-style palace compound in Heian-kyō, the Emperor's private quarters (*dairi*) retained Japanese traditions of cedar-bark roofs and pillars of plain, undecorated wood.

The same contrast can be seen in the Tōshōdaiji Kondō and Kōdō built in the latter half of the eighth century. The Kondō shows Chinese solidity, symmetry and grandeur. (Its present roof

35. Tōdaiji scene showing the
Great Buddha in the *Shigisan
Engi*. Narrative handscroll.
12th century.

soars some fifteen feet higher than the original, however, destroy-
ing the previous impact of blocky, horizontal weight and vigour.)
Across the court stands the Lecture Hall (Kōdō) whose simplicity
and horizontality, stressed by the slender pillars, are typical examples of japanization. Originally part of the Heijō Palace, it was
donated to Tōshōdaiji and moved there in the late eighth century
when the fortunes of that monastery waned. Although now tiled,
the ridge is extended to run nearly the entire length of the roof (a
Shintō characteristic) and is gabled at each end to soften the drop
of the eaves.

Even in the face of persistent continental influence, such
examples of indigenous traits persevered. It is obviously possible
to import major aspects of another people's material culture but it
is not possible simultaneously to import its engendering social
and spiritual attitudes. (The same situation exists today, where
intensive efforts are made to assert Japan's 'international image' in
the art world. Artists with an 'international image' are sent to

36. Kondō (Golden Hall) of Tōshōdaiji. Tang style. Late 8th century. (Roof has since been raised 15 feet.)

37. Kōdō (Lecture Hall) of Tōshōdaiji, more Japanese in its horizontal emphasis. Late 8th century.

38. Ganjin seated in meditation. Dry lacquer. H. 79.7 cm. Late 8th century.

international exhibitions, but those whose works are free of overseas influence, however accomplished and original, are ignored at home and excluded from publicity abroad.) This need for parity with external powers may have its genesis in the Tempyō period of self discovery and self assessment.

The Tōshōdaiji is a major symbol of the reforms instigated by Emperor Shōmu. The Buddhist clergy of the time had become too lax and he sent Japanese monks to China to find a leader who would purify and revitalize religious practice. After years of searching they approached Master Ganjin (Jianzhen in Chinese) who, when his disciples showed unwillingness to travel such distances to an undeveloped land, took on the mission himself. In 753, after a disastrous seven-year journey during which he was blinded, he arrived in Japan, aged sixty-seven. Nine years later, in 762, Ganjin ordained a group of monks and nuns in the courtyard of Tōdaiji, in the presence of the Emperor and the imperial court.

A remarkable dry lacquer sculpture of the time shows the aged and learned Master Ganjin in profound meditation. The naturalistic depiction of such physical features as the blind eyes, the mouth resolute yet kind and the aged but firm cheeks and chin, is matched by an extraordinary expression of emotion and spirituality. This combination of realism and expressiveness in sculpture was to become one of Japan's major contributions to world art.

38

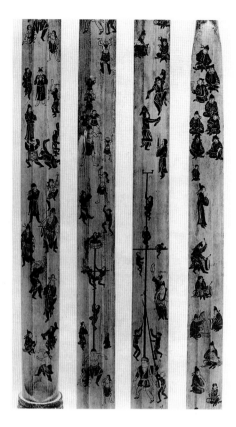

Tempyō secular art

In 756, Emperor Shōmu's widow dedicated all his treasures to the
Great Buddha. They are still in the Shōsōin repository of the
Tōdaiji monastery and give a lively and detailed picture of court
life in the first half of the eighth century. There are imperial clothing, prayer beads, swords and ornaments; musical instruments
include lutes, flutes, the double-reeded *xiao* and *sheng*, the trans-
verse flute and the plucked string instrument called *qin* in Chinese;
board games such as *go*; bows, arrows, quivers, armour and sad- 39, 40
dles. Inner chambers were hung with textiles and furnished with
mirrors, standing screens, portable shrines, masks for musical performances, baskets, cabinets, flower vases and hanging incense-
burners, brushes and writing tools. Examples of calligraphy by
the Emperor and Empress after China's 'Sage of Calligraphy'
Wang Xizhi (303–379) were also dedicated and are preserved to
this day. Many of these objects are of native manufacture and their
motifs and materials reflect assimilation of diverse influences.

39. Ink painting of entertainers
on a long bow. Lacquer on
catalpa wood. L. 162 cm. From
Emperor Shōmu's treasure, before
756.

40. Knives in Persian-style
jewelled, silver scabbards, with
a dedicatory tag by Shōmu's
widow. 8th century.

Glass ware suggests Mediterranean origins; objects of tooled gold and silver, adorned with Persian motifs, are similar to the cache buried near Xian, the Tang capital in 756 (and excavated in 1970). Silk and hemp are woven, or resist-dyed, in symmetrical patterns in the manner of Persian hangings. Elaborately inlaid and evenly distributed designs on lacquer objects ranging from boxes to lutes attest to Central Asian influence. Although Chinese artists absorbed all kinds of Central Asian, Indo-Tibetan and Persian ideas and continued for several generations to produce works in the cosmopolitan amalgam known as the Tang style; in Japan the Tang fad seems to have lasted less than three generations. Almost none of Shōmu's imported styles survived in subsequent arts.

Amid the new and exotic influences on the objects in the Shōsōin, there are clear indications of native Japanese discrimination, i.e. selection and rejection. For example, the mother-of-pearl inlaid Chinese lute, called a Genkan (*Ruan Xian*) after the Chinese 41 musician of that name, is decorated with a pair of pearly pink parrots flying in a circle round a central medallion of kaleidoscopic and radiating roundels. The instrument and the Middle Eastern technique of mother-of-pearl inlay have since become part of Japanese tradition, but the purely decorative roundel motif, the symmetry, and the predictability in design, had gone by the next generation.

In another example, an early ninth-century ash-glazed pot 42 from the Shōsōin repository, while fairly centred and well formed (according to Tang canons) is glazed naturally by the falling ash settling on the shoulders, producing a mottled and uneven

41. *Ruan Xian* (4-stringed lute). Wood with mother-of-pearl inlay. Early 7th century.

42. Covered medicine jar. Ash-glazed clay. H. 18.5 cm. An inscription dates it to 811.

transparent green glaze. The Chinese potter would have considered such a glaze imperfect, even unacceptable; the Japanese saw in it another dimension of beauty. The potter neither controls nor wishes to control every inch of the surface decoration and lets both the material and the firing process play a part in the finished work. Although ninth-century Japanese potters did make Tang-style 'three-colour' (Tang *sancai*) glazed wares, these found little favour with later generations. By contrast, later natural-glazed Japanese pottery, such as Tamba and Bizen wares, achieved worldwide renown for the potters' empathy with the beauty of chance accidents.

Over ten thousand objects were donated to the Great Buddha of Tōdaiji during the eighth and early ninth centuries by the court. It is a treasure house of the arts to be found along the Silk Road whick linked Japan to the Mediterranean, and offers the present-

43. Plectrum guard of *biwa* lute. Shitan wood decorated with marquetry and painted. Before 756.

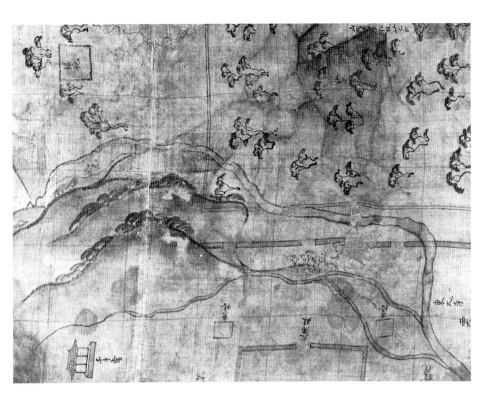

44. Map of Tōdaiji precincts (detail). Ink, light colours on hemp. (North is at the bottom.) Note the *Yamato-e*-like hills in contrast with Chinese pinnacles of Ill. 43. 756.

day observer clear examples of those styles which Japanese artists accepted, rejected or modified. Another example is the painting (which shows clear Chinese influence) on the plectrum guard of a *biwa* lute. Two gentlemen have paused momentarily, one in the midst of writing, to gaze upon the cliff to the left and are lost in a state of communion with nature. The image has faded; only drawings made from infra-red photography now reveal the basic outlines. The scene is typical Tang, with emphasis on the awesome, vibrant scenery. The peaks are adorned with trees, their ornamental forms spread out against the sky and cliffs. The painting is fluid, with few straight lines or harsh forms, and successfully suggests harmony between the two contemplating figures and natural forces.

43

A large map of the precincts of Tōdaiji, painted in 756, offers another glimpse of how knowledge of Chinese landscape painting was used. The sharply rising cliffs of the previous example are here replaced by gently rolling hillocks like those of the Yamato plains. (These gentle outlines later became the hallmark of native *Yamato-e* painting.) The trees on top of the hills do not pierce the

44

sky like those on the *biwa* plectrum and are rendered by thick ink lines in soft curves. They do not cover the entire hill but are scattered irregularly over the central portions. On the Chinese-style plectrum painting the trees are evenly spaced in a Middle Eastern manner, whereas the Tōdaiji map disperses the elements in an irregular and naturalistic manner. The map incidentally shows us the main buildings of Tōdaiji in 756: two L-shaped red brackets show the front of the Main or Great Buddha Hall; two squarish ink outlines at the sides are the East and West Pagodas, placed like imperial twin watch towers, attest to a radical change from the original temple plan that embodied psycho-physical interaction between pilgrim and sacred 'energy field' in the single, central pagoda. Focus has shifted from spiritual vitalization to worldly, political power. To the east, a Chinese building with tiled roof and four posts on a platform, is the Senjūdō or Thousand Armed Kannon Hall. The Kaidanin or Ordination Hall is indicated to the north-west.

Japanese figure painting is characterized by a striking, lively interpersonal link, that acutely observed emotional tension which charges figure painting of all styles, from the most formal to the most profane, even to this day. While Chinese figure painting has since become more impersonal (all the more due to the large number of forgeries), the Tang Chinese origins of this psychological dimension in Japanese art can be seen in the set of deftly painted ink figures on the inside of a bow with ninety-six acrobats, jugglers, musicians and dancers caught in mid-action. Their faces reveal different personalities and moods. The strong man balancing four children on top of his head stands with eyes closed in concentration, while the children look warily down. The man balancing four other children on a cross-barred pole has just taken a step; his effort is clearly visible. While the children show absorption in what they are doing, the onlookers express emotions which range from curiosity to concern. Lower down, musicians accompany a dance. The artist has exploited the narrowness of the format by diagonally linking the last person from one group with the first person from the next by eye contact. The development of this style was carried to extraordinarily expressive heights in the succeeding Heian period.

39

Chapter 4:   Heian (794–1185)

Towards cultural identity: a new capital and new Buddhism

The imposition of Chinese institutions upon Japanese society was too swift and widespread and proved unworkable. The Confucian system of statecraft required learning centres with examinations, designed to foster a meritocracy that was essentially democratic, providing the potential for upward social mobility to one and all. A Japanese National University was founded, with about four hundred students in the capital and fifty in each regional centre. However, entrants were restricted to the hereditary aristocracy and examination administration was lax. The entrenched interests of the regional nobility prevented the proper functioning of a government built upon ethical practice. While high-minded scholars often called for reforms, their memoranda carried little weight with an idle aristocracy.

The great monasteries grew to unwieldy proportions. Tōdaiji, for example, owned more than 12,000 tax-exempt acres, burdening farmers and impoverishing the national treasury. The monks of Nara became cosmopolitan and worldly, and often involved themselves in Court intrigues, to the detriment of proper administration. In China, the government had occasionally suppressed Buddhism, even persecuting the Church in order to defend imperial authority. The Japanese solution was quite different: in 784 Emperor Kammu and his court fled from Nara. After several abortive attempts to settle in Nagaoka, work began in 793 on the site for an entirely new capital. This was called Heian-Kyō (Capital of Peace and Tranquillity), present day Kyoto, which remained the seat of the imperial court until the Meiji Restoration of 1868. Significantly, the great monasteries remained in Nara.

The establishment of a new capital ushered in an era based on the newly introduced Buddhist principles which stressed inner spiritual discipline unhindered by mundane considerations. Two great religious leaders, Saichō and Kūkai, established schools of Buddhism which were to have lasting effects on Japanese life.

Saichō (767–822) grew up under Chinese monks in Nara. He disliked the spreading decadence and spiritual laxity among the clergy there, however, and left to found a small monastery on Mount Hiei. (Small mountain retreats were common in Chinese Taoism and Buddhism.) When Emperor Kammu arrived at Heian-Kyō he found Saichō already practising a systematic spiritual discipline nearby. According to Chinese geomancy, the mountain was the *kimon* or demon entrance to the capital; hence Saichō's presence protected the city. Reverences he paid to the gods of Mount Hiei, in a genial amalgam of Buddhism and Shintō practices, were thought to protect the city. Kammu was impressed by Saichō's rigorous discipline and in 804 sent him to study in China. When Saichō returned, a year later, he brought back new learning from Mount Tiantai.

The Tiantai School was a native Chinese development – that is, without Indian precedent – which sought to reconcile all aspects of Buddhist doctrine in a single discipline, and, significantly, to provide solace for the common man. Salvation was no longer the prerogative of the rich or learned, and would not be achieved exclusively by scriptural study, charitable works or religious practices, but from a dedicated combination of all three. Saichō advocated the reading of the *Lotus Sutra* (subsequently one of the most influential texts in Japanese Buddhism). It assured the salvation not only of men, but also of women, and stressed the importance of the arts.

Licensed by the Emperor, Saichō founded the Tendai Lotus School on Mount Hiei. In time it became a national centre of culture and learning, with some 300 buildings spread over the summit and flanks of the mountain. A connection with the court was prominent from the outset, and continued until the monastery was destroyed in 1571. Kammu was a Confucian by training and admired Saichō's moral calibre; Saichō, for his part, was extremely loyal to the throne, even requiring his monks to swear an oath which included a moving declaration of indebtedness to Kammu. This was a major step in the japanization of Buddhism.

The second reformer was the brilliant master Kūkai (774–835). He excelled as a spiritual leader and as a calligrapher, poet, scholar, inventor and explorer. Born into an aristocratic family, he showed remarkable intellectual precocity. At the age of seventeen he wrote a treatise analysing the teachings of Confucianism, Buddhism and Taoism; revised in 797, it remains a major theoretical work. In 804 he sailed to China to study with the great Huiguo (746–805). On his return, in 806, Saichō begged him for lessons. In 816 he built a monastery on Mt Kōya, establishing the Shingon (True Word or Mantra) School of esoteric Buddhism,

45. Womb Mandala (detail), showing Tibetan colour schemes. Ink, colours on silk. Heian, 859–880.

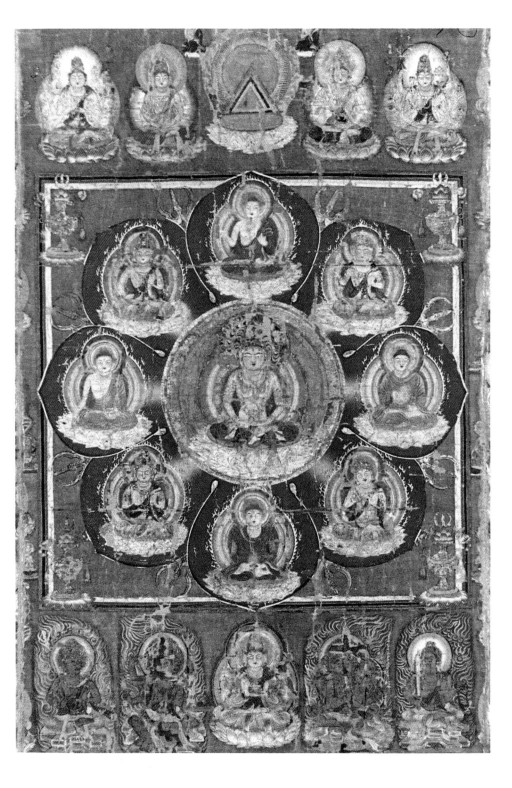

a system whose mysteries, including the mantras themselves, were taught privately, orally and directly, but never written down. In 822 Kūkai was appointed Abbot of Kyōōgokokuji, Monastery for the Salvation of the Emperor and Protection of the Realm, called Tōji for short, the East Temple commanding the main entrance to the capital.

Shingon and the Mandalas

The teachings of Shingon focus on the essential unity of the noumenal and the phenomenal (or the spiritual and the physical worlds). These are represented by painted or sculpted illustrations of the Diamond and Womb Mandalas respectively, the universe of Dainichi Nyorai (Great Sun or Mahāvairocana), greatest of all Buddhas. The mystery and aestheticism of Shingon held great appeal for Heian courtiers. From their rich colours and schemata spring many subsequent formulae in Buddhist and secular art.

The Womb (phenomenal) World is represented by a series of concentric squares, the innermost of which contains an eight-petalled red lotus with a Buddha seated on each petal. As Yanagisawa Taka has shown, the mandala here illustrated is one of the earliest Shingon polychrome mandalas painted in Japan; it is a copy of the pair commissioned by Emperor Montoku and produced in Tang Changan under the supervision of the prelate Faquan and painter Diaoqing, and brought back to Japan by the Japanese monk Enchin in 859 CE. They retain the strong shading and high colour contrast typical of Tibetan painting, as the region around Changan had been under Tibetan occupation between 786 and 843. Already in this copy we see several signs of japanization and departure from the Sino-Tibetan model: in particular, the way in which the faces of the deities exhibit a variety of expressions and gaze in different directions showing an interest in individual particularities that persists in subsequent Japanese art involving diverse groups present at any common situation. Dainichi Nyorai is in the centre; the bodhisattvas Myō-ō (Acalas), Ten (Devas) and other deities are ranked, in decreasing size, about the central square. The Mandala of the Diamond (noumenal) World has nine equal-sized square mandalas forming a single large square. The believer's task was to contemplate aspects of the mandalas and by means of such meditation and special mantras, to realize Buddhahood while in this human realm.

Kūkai designed his monastic buildings to conform with the plan of the mandalas. The sculptures are arranged according to

45

46. Yakushi Nyorai. Painted
cypress wood. Early 9th century.

47. Shaka Nyorai. Painted wood.
Late 9th century.

their relative positions in the mandalas and the schemata of the
Diamond and Womb Mandalas form the groundplan of the twin
pagodas.

Jōgan Sculpture

The new sculptures of this era are dark and heavy, with an air of
mystery and inward absorption, but so powerful as to seem forbidding. The 'Jōgan style', named after the reign-era between 859 and
877, is used to designate all the heavy-set, brooding sculptures of
the early Heian period. Many large works are carved from single
blocks of Japanese cypress, and Indo-Tibetan and Tang (Chinese)
influences are marked. A typical example is the awesome Yakushi
Nyorai of Jingoji in Kyoto. The massive, elongated head reveals
deep chisel marks around sharply bevelled features of forbidding

46

48. Shingon deity Blue Fudō and his *dōji* child attendants. Detail of Fudō. Colours on silk. Mid-11th century.

49. Amida Buddha on a cloud,
the central panel of the Amida
triptych. Colours on silk. Early
11th century.

power and severity. Intentionally larger than life, the neck is styl-
ized (three rings of equal size), and the shoulders are four-square
and high. The symmetrical folds of the drapery serve to induce the
viewer's concentration as in hypnosis.

More conservative is the magnificent Shaka Nyorai, central
image of the Murōji in Nara. The figure is also markedly fleshy, the
torso broad, solid and powerful. But the face harks back to late
eighth-century style such as that of the Fukūkenjaku Kannon also
in Nara. The sensuous mouth, rounded chin and high, arched eyebrows radiate compassion and benevolence; the expression is out-
going and welcoming, in marked contrast to that of the Jingoji
Yakushi.

The Shingon School found room not only for Indo-Tibetan
deities but for indigenous Shintō gods as well. From the start of
the Heian period, Shintō shrines appear within Buddhist
monastery compounds and Buddhist buildings in Shintō
precincts. Shintō deities were identified as local manifestations of
Shingon's universal truth, and were represented alongside
Buddhist icons. As time went on, Shintō began to lose its identity
and became a convenient intermediary between the new religion
and the native population.

One of the major deities in Shingon teaching, Fudō Myō-ō
(Acalanā-tha, the King of Light), is widely depicted in painting
and sculpture. As a bringer of light and wisdom, he became a popular household icon, particularly as his spectacular powers could be
invoked by prayer. He looked ferocious, with protruding teeth,
glowering eyes and furrowed brow, poised amid billowing flames
holding a double-edged sword in his right hand and a lassoo in his
left; no earthly evil could match him.

The glowing world of Pure Land Buddhism

Sir George Sansom characterized late Heian culture as a 'rule of
taste' which extended into nearly every facet of daily life and made
'religion into an art and art into a religion'. An outstanding example of this is the belief in Amida's Western Pure Land Paradise, a
belief which inspired some of the most beautiful art traditions of
Japan. This was largely due to the Tendai priest Kūya (903–72)
and to the pilgrimages he made all over Japan. He was called 'the
Amida saint' because of his *nembutsu*, a ceaseless recitation of the
name of Amida, Buddha of the Western Paradise. Of the four basic
types of meditation, *nembutsu* (thanks to Kūya's proselytizing
example) became that chiefly practised by the laity: Amida's name
was soon on everyone's lips. And images of a Western Pure Land

Paradise were conjured into being in paintings, sculptures and architecture.

Another Amidist leader, Genshin (942–1017), recommended a dying nobleman on a distant frontier to intone Amida's name while fixing his eyes on a *raigō-zu* (an image of the Welcoming Amida Buddha and His Host bringing the new soul to Paradise). This practice became widespread, and resulted in a dramatic increase in *raigō* paintings throughout Japan. Like the Fudō Myō-ō, the *raigō* was originally one of many subsidiary scenes in a mandala. Now it became important as an object of contemplation, inspiring works of great beauty in a new and distinctly Japanese pictorial style.

One of the earliest and most sublime *raigō* paintings is the central panel of the Amida triptych in Hokkeji in Nara. The composition is symmetrical and frontal. Amida's eyes gaze directly downwards at the beholder, as if to draw his soul up into the Pure Land Paradise. The ethereal quality is enhanced by gradual, high contrast shading of the lotus petals and the aureole. The Amida is rendered in sure and sensitive lines and simple colours. Discreet dark red swastikas pattern the robe and delicate green shading beneath the eyebrows lends an aristocratic air. The style of the face and the close colour harmony speak of the emerging native aesthetic that was to dominate the courtly arts and permeate Japanese consciousness to the present day. This luminuous and transparent image absorbs the believer with a quiet mystery and magnetism.

The Fujiwara period (897–1185)

By the end of the ninth century, Shōtoku's Sino-centric bureaucracy of the meritorious had virtually vanished. The emperor's function was now merely to preside over fossilized state rituals, whilst actual power fell into the hands of the regent (*sesshō*) and chancellor (*kampaku*). From the mid-ninth century onwards, Japan was ruled by the powerful Fujiwara clan, who strengthened their position by regularly marrying their daughters into the enfeebled imperial family. Government schools, originally meant to train future civil servants, were now open only to those of court rank, and clans close to the ruling family. Courtiers amassed vast wealth from grants of land; conspicuous consumption accompanied rank and prestige. The new ruling class had regained the powers held prior to the seventh-century reforms. But in time, courtiers in the capital became an élite, far superior to their provincial equivalents. Late Heian culture was centred on the capital and dominated by the Fujiwara family. For the next millenium, the role of emperor was to be that of a figurehead.

The Phoenix Hall

The regent Fujiwara Yorimichi (994–1074) demonstrated his power and influence by converting his residence into an earthly copy of the Pure Land Paradise itself, as represented in the Taima Mandala imported from China in the late ninth century. The exquisite park in Uji, outside Kyoto, is a perfect setting for the *Byōdōin*, his private chapel, completed in 1053. With its harmonious fusion of religious fervour and aristocratic splendour, the *Byōdōin* is the ultimate expression of the age.

Fujiwara Yorimichi's master sculptor was Jōchō, whose father Kōshō had worked for Yorimichi's father, Fujiwara no Michinaga (966–1027). The conversion of the Fujiwara estate into the *Byōdōin* Pure Land Paradise both introduced and consolidated several aspects of japanization. Its main building, for example, is not of colossal proportions but built on a human scale, at once enveloping the seated Buddha Amida with a tangible closeness and warmth that form and characterize the clarity and immediacy of Fujiwara art. Although Chinese-style tiles, pillars and white-washed walls remain, the raised angle of the eaves, enhanced by the reflection in the surrounding water, gives an impression of imminent, graceful flight.

The Amida Hall (called the Hōdō or Phoenix Hall because of the phoenixes crowning its rooftop) was built on a small island in the middle of an artificial lake. The central image of Amida, of

50. View of *Byōdōin*, in Uji, Kyoto, showing front portico. Completed 1053.

51. (*opposite*) Jōchō's masterpiece, the Buddha Amida. Gold leaf and lacquer on wood. H. 295 cm. 1053.

50

51

52. Celestial bodhisattva on a cloud, school of Jōchō, from the background of Ill. 51. Painted wood. Heian, 1053.

53. *Raigō* Kannon Bosatsu, one of twenty-five figures. Gold leaf and lacquer on wood. H. 96.7 cm. 1094.

gilded and lacquered joined wood-blocks, is 2.5 metres high, and is seated on a golden lotus in *dhyānamudrā* of concentration or absorption. It is Jōchō's masterpiece, with proportions of the perfect human ideal: the rounded head, poised on a graceful neck, is balanced by gently sloping shoulders and softly articulated knees. The awesome mystery of Jōgan sculpture gives way here to mercy and compassion. The deity is approachable; the chapel envelops one in a feeling of intimacy, of earthly aspiration raised to sublime and lyrical heights.

On entering the Phoenix Hall, our gaze is immediately drawn to the shining Amida, and then upwards to the dazzling openwork canopy which is gilded, lacquered and inlaid with mother-of-pearl. The entire ceiling consists of elaborately painted and latticed woodwork. Behind the Amida is a flame-like golden aureole, adorned with gilded apsaras flying on descending clouds, in worshipful attitudes. On the walls, murals show the Western Pure Land Paradise in four seasons, with descending Amida *raigō* and attendants coming to receive the soul of the faithful. On the south door is a particularly striking *raigō* image of *Amida and the Celestial*

54. *Raigō* of *Amida and the Celestial Host*. Detail from a Phoenix Hall mural. Colours on wood, 1053.

Host. It shows Amida gazing down at an unseen soul in the lower right of the painting. His hands are in the *mudrā* of welcome (the right thumb and forefinger joined and the hand raised up, while the open left hand is extended downward towards the dying believer). The mural depicts not only a host of celestial beings playing musical instruments and monks absorbed in prayer, but also a new element emerging; that of Japan's rural landscape – the serene, low-lying hillocks and meandering streams of Yamato. The reassuring familiarity and ethereal clarity of these images suited the new *nembutsu* Amidist practice far better than the complexity of the earlier Tantric Shingon school.

Above the murals, over the whitewashed upper register of the walls, fifty-two monks and bodhisattvas descend on clouds. In high relief, they are dancing, playing instruments and praying. The great variety of mid-eleventh-century sculptural techniques is clearly visible, as only small traces of gilt and paint remain. The most advanced technique is used for the central figure of Amida. Single-block sculptures of great size had been found to split, warp and crack, even if the core had been hollowed. Jōchō and his craftsmen prevented this by revolutionary *yosegi* and *warihagi* techniques where the main block was cut into front and back halves, hollowed and rejoined for carving. Additional pieces were added to the sides, back and front where necessary. These techniques ensured strength and stability and were favoured through the Kamakura period. They also enabled Jōchō and his workshop to mass-produce Buddhist sculpture in assembly-line fashion. This School prospered and one branch later moved to Nara where it produced the Kei School of sculptors during the Kamakura period.

Very much in the manner of the Jōchō School are the endearing *gokuraku* or paradise sculptures made in 1094 for the Sokujōji monastery in Kyoto. They were sculpted from Japanese cypress in the multi-block technique, then lacquered and gilded. An extra fifteen attendants were added to the original ten during the Edo period. Here the bodhisattva Kannon (Avalokiteśvara) is kneeling forward, holding a lotus pedestal to receive the newly ascending soul.

The effects of court taste are even more pronounced in twelfth-century art. The perception of celestial beings, such as the Water Deva (*Suiten*), one of the twelve in Tōji, for example, closely reflects courtly ideals. Their expression is aristocratic and dream-like. Compared to the robust Devas charged with the protection of the realm in the ninth-century *Womb Mandala*, the stress is now clearly on aesthetics, and less on spirituality. Compared to the Hokkeji Amida of the early eleventh century with its diaphanous luminescence, the Water Deva is even more gorgeous and more sensuous, and the use of many more layers of colour allows for subtler colour-harmonies and contrast. The impression of absorption given by the earlier image is here replaced by one of beatific tranquillity.

By the thirteenth century, Kamakura Buddhist painting exudes a new spiritual vigour. There is a new *raigō* form where the Buddha Amida and his two or more attendants appear over the mountains. Amida looms large over the landscape, as if parting the hills and coming directly towards us. Kannon (right) and Seishi (left) are standing on clouds in reverential and welcoming positions, fronted by the Two Children and the Four Celestial Kings reduced in hierarchical scale. The landscape is relatively realistic but the superimposition of the heavenly host is dramatically out of scale, compelling, immediate and imminent. The sweetness of the

55. *Suiten* (Water Deva), one of twelve. Colours and gold on silk. 1127.

56. *Descent of Amida over the Mountains*. Hanging scroll; colours and gold on silk. Kamakura, early 13th century.

Water Deva, and the innocence of the Jōchō images are here superceded by an alert spirituality, simple and vigorous. The Yamato landscape is quickened with a sense of urgency.

In *The descent of Amida and his host* (popularly known as *Haya Raigō* or 'Rapid Welcoming Descent'), the Buddha Amida and twenty-five bodhisattvas on a white cloud descend at a steep angle above a precipitous mountain towards the priest below, who sits

57. *Haya Raigō* of Amida and bodhisattvas. Hanging scroll; colours and gold on silk. Kamakura, 13th century.

upright at the very moment of his death. This is an example of the painting style known as *kubon raigō-zu* (Nine grades of Amitabha's descent), of which we have seen an earlier (mid-eleventh-century) example in the Phoenix Hall mural. Comparison at once shows an increased urgency in the later work. The Paradise itself, usually the focus of gorgeous achitectural painting, is here reduced to a symbolic palace in the upper right corner; instead, the landscape of *this* life looms large. The figures are all standing, their attention focussed on the new soul. Gold is liberally used and the lacy intricacy of Heian decoration here gives way to flat application of unmixed pigment. The landscape is sombre and vertiginous compared to that of the Phoenix Hall; emphasis has shifted from an idyllic conception of Paradise to the moment of death and rebirth itself; dream has given way to action.

Fujiwara secular arts

In their secular arts, although Heian courtiers enjoyed Chinese poetry and painting, the arts, even when in the Chinese manner, increasingly showed Japanese qualities. In 894, as the much admired Chinese Tang empire was disintegrating and voyages to China were fraught with danger, the Japanese court decided to stop diplomatic missions altogether. This isolation served to trigger an unparalleled outpouring of Japanese splendours from deep within the native psyche.

Like its temporal Chinese counterpart (Northern Song, 960–1126), this late Heian or Fujiwara period (897–1185) was one of introspection and self-discovery. Both cultures were settling down after the ebullient and extrovert phases of Tang and Nara. During those cosmopolitan centuries, both China and Japan had been flush with the power of newly consolidated realms. Japan had assimilated a host of spiritual and visual stimuli which had swept from Central Asia, India and Sassanian Persia. In the tenth and eleventh centuries, however, both the Song and Heian cultures turned inward; political unassertiveness enabled them to discover their respective aesthetic identities and release the unfolding of their greatest artistic glory. Song China produced landscape painting and the Heian court *Yamato-e*. At this time, Japan's own calligraphic form, *kana* writing, also reached its zenith. And the profound differences between the two cultures became manifest; in Japan, many aesthetic preferences which were to become hallmarks of Japanese art now found full expression. (Modern scholarship, however, has traced the subdued colour tone, the use of bird's-eye perspective and the frequent stress of the diagonal back to Song sources, which in turn derive from Tang Buddhist painting. Curiously, in retrospect, we may say that while Song aesthetic ideals did not prevail, Heian artistic sensibilities once having flowered, took root in the very fabric of Japanese perception and can still be felt today).

The growing apart of the two cultures can be seen in a comparison of painting techniques. In Northern Song, the flat,

58. *Early Spring Landscape.*
Door panel in Phoenix Hall,
Byōdōin. 1053.

colourist tradition of Tang painting was replaced by a linear modelling technique called *cunfa*, where depth and texture are defined
in brush strokes rather than shading. This eventually gave way to
an ink monochrome landscape tradition which was enthusiastically adopted by scholars and academy painters alike, spawning a
host of contending schools. In Japan, however, the poetic, colourist
Tang style was retained and its emotive potential was developed
so far that eventually *Yamato-e* painting had little in common with
either its Chinese contemporary style or its Tang sources.

The culmination of japanization may be seen in the 1053
Byōdōin Phoenix Hall murals. *Yamato-e* landscape paintings were
greatly influenced by the highly developed Japanese literature of
the time, that is, poems on the four seasons, on famous scenic spots,
on *mono-no-aware* (the pathos, literally the 'ah-ness', of things).
Departing from Chinese aesthetic preferences, for example,
indigenous new poems on Spring replace the snow prunus with
cherry blossoms, majestic mountains with cosy paddy fields. The
world of Japanese imagery shimmered with wisteria, the seashore,
spring rains, spring moon and spring mists, in poetry and painting
alike. An example is the *Early Spring Landscape* on a door panel of
the Phoenix Hall. A gentle river scene combines lushness and a

58

sense of intimacy typical of Japanese landscapes with favourite details: the meandering river, the sand shoal with its few reeds remaining from last year still covered in snow, the pine-clad hills and the thatched roofs of the cottages. The colours are applied in flat layers, with volume suggested by discreet intensification of the greens and whites. The only sense of motion is provided by the rippling lines of the river bend. The native predilection for laterally spreading motifs is hinted at here in the gently swollen silhouettes of the pines.

Alluding perhaps to one of the Famous Places so often mentioned in Heian literature, the simplicity of the scene belies the sophistication of its evocative and poetic rendering. This tenderness, poignancy and vulnerability becomes the emotional hallmark of so many later coloured screens. To perceive them as merely decorative would be to blind us to the emotive impact or the quintessence of Japanese art. Decorative art is passive and static, with visual elements evenly disbursed; this scene is vibrantly alive and invites an emotional response from the spectator. (See, for instance, the free-floating cloud forms, where the pigment is sprinkled on, rather than brushed. The clouds seem to breathe, and so seem charged with motion and emotion in the otherwise still space. They function as emotional indicators henceforth, releasing this quickening and poignancy. We may call this unique device the 'emotive cloud'.) The Heian artist may have chosen this scene, and this way of depicting it, in order to express the first quivering of New Year's joys: he may even have been inspired by a poem in the recent anthology *Gosenshū* (951 CE):

mizu no omo ni	The breezes of spring
aya fukimidaru	Are blowing the ripples astray
haru kaze ya	Along the water . . .
ike no kōri wo	Today they will surely melt
kyō wa tokuramu	The sheet of ice on the pond.

(Ki no Tomonori, trans. Donald Keene)

The Heian preoccupation with minutely identified emotion found expression in poetry which led to painting, diaries, letters, screens and narrative handscrolls. Even in gardens of the period, both real and those shown in screen paintings, plants, shrubs, streams and stones were deliberately arranged to evoke specific emotions, or to recreate Famous Places identified with specific poetic associations. A unique feature is the cloud-form island covered with white sand which appears in pond gardens and garden manuals of the time. The free-form, emotive, 'cloud form' or *kumo-gata*, seen as islets or reflections of the sky, evoked in sprinkled pigment on paper a subtle confirmation of the indefinable, the transient and the moving. In Heian art, nature motifs functioned to express human emotions. Not only did Heian architecture encourage maximum integration of interior space with garden, but the sliding door panels (*fusuma*), which often surrounded three sides of a room, were themselves adorned with evocative landscapes.

But the dichotomy between the public and private senses persisted. Official, public architecture was termed *hare*. It had tiled roofs, slated floors and red lacquered pillars in the Chinese manner. The Emperor's private residence, however, was emphatically in the domestic mode termed *ke*, with thatched roof, wooden floors and pristine, unpainted pillars. In a scene in the first scroll of the *Ban Dainagon E-kotoba*, where Fujiwara no Yoshifusa is shown advising the Emperor, the double standard is apparent: in the outer vestibule the mural is in the public, Chinese style, while murals in *Yamato-e* style decorate his private chambers. In general, art for public places and ceremonial events were in Chinese mode. In the palace, the *Screen of Sages* shows Chinese sages, and the *Lake Kunming* screen has Chinese references. Because they were associated with the pomp of High Tang or the much admired Confucian tradition, Chinese-style paintings carried great prestige. In time, such paintings came to be called *Kara-e* or Chinese (theme) painting, in contrast to *Yamato-e* or Japanese (theme) painting.

Handscroll painting

The *Yamato-e* painting of Japanese subject-matter developed some unique features in the illustrated narrative handscrolls, or *emaki-mono*, significantly an art form practised by members of the court. Handscroll painting or calligraphy is an intimate format. The handscroll is unrolled (30 to 80 cm at a time) over a desk and perused at leisure: artist and viewer communicate one to one. Work for such a project was divided among a great number of painting masters (*eshi*, often members of the aristocracy), who selected the scenes, laid down the drawing for the compositions and indicated the colouring; artisans then mixed the pigments and filled in the colours.

Most celebrated of aristocratic artworks are the narrative handscrolls illustrating *The Tale of Genji*, a romance of Japanese 59, 60 court life written in the late tenth century by Lady Murasaki

Shikibu. The earliest set of illustrations on this theme comes from 1120–30 and only survives in fragments: nineteen segments of illustrations and twenty of narrative in elegant *kana* calligraphy by at least four great calligraphers of the day. (Today, these fragments are divided between the Tokugawa and Gotō museums.) The writing of the text is considered as important an art form as the paintings themselves.

The novel of fifty-four chapters originally must have covered at least twenty separate scrolls with hundreds of illustrations and thousands of sheets of calligraphy. Tokugawa Yoshinobu suggests that the story had been completely changed since the publication of the novel, and that the original illustration comprised twenty scrolls made during the Hōan era (1120–1123), at the latest by 1147. He identified three of the many calligraphers: Minamoto no Arihito, Fujiwara no Tadamichi and Fujiwara no Koremichi, among others. The paintings were done by court ladies, including Ki no Tsubone and Nagato no Tsubone. The influence of court women over the entire Heian cultural sphere has given the world the first full-blown fulfilment of feminine aesthetics since the spiritual and lyrical culture of Bronze Age Crete. The surviving illustrations are mostly from the last, so-called 'ten chapters of Uji', and our understanding of the style and techniques of the whole work is necessarily incomplete. Unlike didactic Buddhist illustrations aimed at common folk, the Genji paintings and calligraphies are works of art that were circulated among aristocratic

59. *Kashiwagi I*, detail from *The Tale of Genji* scrolls. Ink and colours on paper. Early 12th century.

60. *Suzumushi II*, detail from
The Tale of Genji scrolls. Ink
and colours on paper. Early
12th century.

connoisseurs. It should be stressed that these paintings reveal a
twelfth-century nostalgia and melancholy for the passing of the
old Heian order of poetry and peace. Here each illustration depicted the emotional tensions of a given moment in the textual narrative, thus freezing it, as it were, in high relief.

In the scene *Kashiwagi I*, the retired Emperor Suzaku, now a
monk, is full of concern for his daughter Princess Nyosan, and is
quietly weeping. His daughter, stricken with guilt and remorse at
having Kashiwagi's child, is insisting upon taking the tonsure. She
is prostrate on the tatami on the left, unable to tell her father the
truth or to face her husband Genji (seated below centre). Genji, for
his part, is full of compassion for his wife and tries to dissuade her
from her vows. In the text Genji is described as regretting his own
inability to give up the worldly life, and envying his father-in-law's
resolution. To the right, behind the curtains, ladies-in-waiting
share in the sorrow.

Nowhere in this painting is there characterization or facial
expression. The mask-like faces are painted in the technique
known as *hikime kagihana* (line-eye hook-nose), which indicates
features but does not identify individuals. (Reading the calligraphy portions, one would be familiar with the text, and would
recognize the characters by their relative positions and postures.)
Characteristically, such scenes show the tension just preceding an
action, not the action itself. The ancient Tang Chinese technique,

with examples surviving only in Danhuang Buddhist cave illustrations, called in Japan *fukinuki yatai*, a bird's-eye view with the ceiling and often wall partitions removed, is used to great effect in the surviving Genji fragments, nearly all of which show indoor scenes. The many narrative devices developed to astonishing effectiveness in Japanese painting without exception have prototypes in Chinese Dunhuang Buddhist paintings many of which, in turn, may have Central Asian derivations.

In this apparently tranquil scene emotional turbulence is revealed by subtle and effective means. The psychological isolation of the characters is symbolized by the silk room-dividers which are here placed to form cells of separate emotion. Elegant black ribbons hang from the curtains, in disarray, between the princess and her father and beside the ladies-in-waiting: this allows the artist to show strong emotion without giving his characters unseemly gesticulations. The tension is further heightened by the sharply tilted ground-plane.

In *Suzumushi II*, the painter has combined two episodes from the narrative. Genji has been unexpectedly invited by the Emperor Reizei, his supposed half-brother, for a moon-viewing party. Genji and his friends immediately set out for the palace, delighted that the spontaneous call promises a lessening of court formalities, at least on this occasion. In fact Reizei, here facing Genji who is seated against the central pillar, has just renounced the throne upon discovering that Genji is not his half-brother but his actual father. In the text, flutes are played on Genji's way to the palace; but in the painting the artist has depicted an idyllic, moon-lit flute concert on the Emperor's verandah.

In this scene, the tilt of the ground-plane is less steep than in *Kashiwagi I*, and the parallel lines formed by the balustrade, tatami mat borders and exposed beams provide a sense of relaxation and harmony. The meeting of Genji and his son is a poignant moment where the men are shown with heads inclined towards each other, prevented by stringent court etiquette from direct utterance of emotion. (Language, conduct and posture were so rigidly regulated in the eleventh and twelfth centuries that courtiers developed uncanny sensitivity to the slightest nuances of behaviour and situation allowing court paintings to depict scenes of great psychological intensity in compositions of apparent physical inertia.)

The articulate Lady Sei Shonagon, a contemporary of the author of *The Tale of Genji*, remarked that certain things suffer when given visual form, particularly some species of flowers and 'characters in fiction who have been praised for their beauty'. (Any

60

attempt by the artist at interpretation of an idealized person or deity interferes with the spectator's own concept.) This widely held view accounts for the abstracted faces in the *Tale of Genji* scrolls, a convention also recognizable in Heian Buddhist painting and sculpture. However, the *hikime kagihana* technique allows the suggestion of extremely subtle emotional nuances. In *Suzumushi II*, for example, the characters' eyebrows and eyes are built up from many fine, straight lines into thick layers, with the eyebrows high on the foreheads; the pupils of the eyes are single dots, exactly placed along the eyeline. Reizei's pupil is placed towards the centre of his face, to indicate warmth and humility.

The 'rule of taste' also developed colour consciousness to a high degree. The art of combining colours in daily wear revealed one's breeding as surely as taste in poetry, calligraphy, incense and even paper for love letters, or as the way one conducted one's amorous affairs. The following passage from Lady Murasaki's diary (trans. Ivan Morris) makes this clear:

The Empress was wearing the usual scarlet robe, under which she had kimonos of light plum, light green and yellow rose. His Majesty's outer robe was made of grape-coloured brocade; underneath he had a willow-green kimono and, below that, one of pure white – all most unusual and up-to-date in both design and colour . . . Lady Nakazukasa's robe, which was also of grape-coloured brocade, hung loosely over a plain jacket of green and cherry.

On that day all the ladies in attendance on His Majesty had taken particular care with their dress. One of them, however, had made a small error in matching the colours at the openings of her sleeves. When she approached His Majesty to put something in order, the High Court Nobles and Senior Courtiers who were standing nearby noticed the mistake and stared at her. This was a source of lively regret to Lady Saishō and the others. It was not really such a serious lapse of taste; only the colour of one of her robes was a shade too pale at the opening.

It is a pity that the colours in Heian painting and scrolls have changed with time so that we are unable fully to appreciate the original tones and hues. The subtlety and refinement of colour-matching in Heian art is among the highest achievements of any ancient society. Even so, we can still easily see and respond to the strong sense of *mono-no-aware* which suffuses Heian perception of nature, people and art. It is an emotional shorthand, instantly leading from the perception of beauty to a melancholy consciousness of the transience of human life.

Onna-e or feminine painting

As we have seen, there was in the Heian period an acute awareness of the distinction between public formality and private emotion. The public world was associated with the masculine (*otoko*) principle and seen in such public or *hare* manifestations as Chinese-style architecture and *kanshi* poetry in Chinese script. The inner world is expressed in the feminine (*onna*) mode, and with indigenous arts such as the Japanese syllabary script *kana* which perfectly suits polysyllabic Japanese poetry. Heian courtiers took pride in their command of Chinese *belles lettres*; but they reserved native styles for their most intimate thoughts and feelings. It is likely that this dichotomy caused the emergence of the terms *onna-e* feminine painting and *otoko-e* masculine painting in Heian writings. Some scholars have interpreted these terms as describing the gender of the subjects or of the artists or as referring to the style itself. But given the dramatic contrast betwen the exterior and interior worlds of Heian courtiers, it is possible to identify *onna-e* with introvert, emotional feelings and *otoko-e* with extrovert, physical action. (*Otoko-e* are often associated with historical narratives including the founding of monasteries, or wars where the focus is on actual events.) Each style of painting uses different techniques.

Onna-e (the style of the *Tale of Genji* scrolls) achieves pictorial stillness through subtle compositional devices such as those described earlier. The style is equally effective with or without colour. For particularly sumptuous scenes, whether in *onna-e* or *otoko-e* style, a laborious colouring process known as *tsukuri-e* was often used: the underdrawing was covered up by applications of colours in thick, flat layers with little gradation, after which the outlines were redrawn in a delicate, unbroken line. The precise, complex designs on costumes and crests were painted by specialists, with attention paid to the women's hair and the lacquered headgear of the men. Architectural features such as beam-lines, tatami mat borders, and curtains of state were ruled, and the visual impact was enhanced by manipulating the groundplane tilt and the viewer's vantage-point. The calligraphic sections were inscribed in fully developed *hiragana* script; the paper was often dyed in many shades and decorated with tiny shapes, cut from gold foil, called *kirigane*. Other examples of *onna-e* painting, including many of the frontispieces of the sumptions *Heike Nōgyō* described below, combined the *tsukuri-e* technique with *kirigane* decoration in lavish opulence. In the following Kamakura period the monochrome *hakubyō* style emerged, using only fine ink lines with tiny red lip-accents.

61. Yakuō Bosatsu Honjibon, detail from *Heike Nōgyō* handscrolls. Ink, colours on paper, with *kirigane* decoration. c. 1164.

About fifty years later than the *Genji* scrolls, but clearly influenced by their style and techniques, came the *Heike Nōgyō* (the *Lotus Sutra* scrolls) commissioned by members of the Taira clan (Hei-ke in their Chinese reading.) By this time, Taira no Kiyomori controlled almost half of Japan by force: his power matched only by his immense wealth. Among Fujiwara courtiers, the military were still stigmatized as uncouth and uncultured and it may have been to counter this reputation that the Taira warriors undertook this project of simultaneous conspicuous piety and extravagant expense. The ascendancy of the Taira clan in fact marked a cultural shift from a courtly aristocracy, such as that described in *The Tale of Genji*, to one of martial overlordship. Kiyomori's sutra offerings, begun about 1164, are both a nostalgic glance at the past and proof of a strong desire to beat the aristocracy at their own high-culture game.

The *Lotus Sutra*, which preached the salvation of both women and men, had long been a favourite with court ladies. Sutra copying often involved joint efforts on a single scroll, through the writing out of which the copyists established karmic relationship with one another; it could also be done by hiring specialists in sutra-style calligraphy and paper decoration. In the case of Taira no Kiyomori, a total of thirty-three scrolls (five more than the twenty-eight chapters of the *Lotus Sutra*), was commissioned for dedication to the principal deity of Itsukushima Shrine, the Kanzeon Bosatsu (Avalokiteśvara) of the Thirty-Three Manifestations. Each member of the clan undertook the preparation of a scroll and tried to outdo the others. The result was the most lavishly decorated sutra collection ever produced, as can be seen from the frontispiece to the twenty-third chapter. This states that women who receive the teaching of Yakuō Bosatsu (Bhaisajya rāja) and live by it, will be reborn on a lotus flower into the Blissful Amida Paradise. In the illustration, a court lady leans against her black lacquered armrest, holding a sutra scroll tied with a red sash, her hair in disarray, billowing over a garment of at least six layers, suggesting the *jūni hitoe* or twelve-layered court robe. Her youthful, pear-shaped face is turned towards golden shafts of light radiating from the aureole of the Welcoming Amida Raigō, descending on a purple cloud. The clouds are sprinkled with silver-white pigment; *kirigane* as well as pieces of silver foil of various sizes are liberally used. (They were applied individually, by rubbing a stiff brush through the hair to produce static electricity, then using the brush to pick up each foil piece and deposit it precisely. The metal dust was applied by flicking the brush, charged with gold or silver pigment, against one finger.)

Words from the sutra are camouflaged as part of the painting. The word 'born' is emerging at the top, as the new soul arrives, on the lotus pedestal. This technique of hidden writing is called *ashide*, and was often used in *Yamato-e* painting, particularly in *onna-e*. If this frontispiece had been painted in the *otoko-e* tradition, the heavenward journey of the dying woman would have been physically shown and not symbolized in this subdued but pregnant manner.

Otoko-e or masculine painting

The robust, action-filled narrative painting known as *otoko-e* is in dramatic contrast to the static and emotion-filled *onna-e*. Historical events are realistically depicted and uninhibited emotions are plainly shown in physical movement and facial expressions. Even the brush-strokes of landscape are charged with action; they swell and shrink and dramatic and varied strokes are used simultaneously to define as well as to accent the pictorial composition.

An exemplary group of three painted scrolls, known as the *Shigisan Engi*, depicts miracles performed by the devout ninth-century monk Myōren of Mount Shigi. (Scholars are puzzled by the lack of a prior, complete, source-text on which the narrative might have been based.) In the section shown, the painter depicts a 63 miracle worked by the alms bowl which Myōren sent to be filled at the granary of a wealthy townsman. One day the servants left it in the granary, whereupon the magic bowl slipped out, dipped under the building and carried the entire store of rice back up the mountain. Here townsfolk are seen rushing after it, with wild gesticulations. The vantage-point is high; the illustrations describe events in a continuous narrative with the painting spreading over the entire scroll without a textual break in a remarkable exploitation of the handscroll format. The second and third scrolls each have two sections, written narrative and painting. (One wonders whether the first scroll also had a calligraphic narrative, now lost.) The paintings date from between 1156, when the palace shown was rebuilt, and 1180, when it burned down. The anonymous artists would have been either *eshi* or imperial court painters familiar with obscure details of Buddhist inconography, or else *ebusshi*, Buddhist painters based in Nara, with access to the imperial palace and with knowledge of court customs, a factor which makes even more striking the liveliness and veracity with which ordinary folk are observed. This reflects a twelfth-century aristocratic interest in everyday matters, a characteristic of the new age.

Instead of heavy, opaque *tsukuri-e* style, the *Shigisan* scrolls show how the artists used transparent colours, and sparingly, to highlight the dynamic brushwork. Lively brushwork had been used since the Nara period for underdrawing, but now surfaces as 'legitimate' art in its own right. Another segment from the *Shigisan* scrolls, this time from Scroll III, can be seen on p. 51. It shows Myōren's sister, a nun, arriving at Tōdaiji, and uses six 'exposures' to show consecutive actions, a characteristic of narrative painting thus incorporating time into space. In this illustra- 35 tion, reading from right to left, the nun is seen praying to the Great Buddha, begging for a dream to lead her to her brother, the monk Myōren. She steps out to sleep and dreams she is inside again before the Buddha and is told to 'go toward the southwest and the mountain overhung with purple clouds'. She thanks the Buddha and is seen again, at daybreak, standing confidently on the steps of the Buddha Hall, facing the southwest ready to depart. (The sixth 'exposure' showing the nun left of the steps and on her way is not included in our reproduction.) Note how the Great Buddha and its magnificent Hall are depicted in their original proportions before they were burnt down in the Taira war of 1180.

In the *Ban Dainagon E-kotoba* the lively brushwork of the *Shigisan* scrolls is combined with gorgeous colouring, which places the work stylistically somewhere between the courtly *onna-e Genji* scrolls and the lively *otoko-e Shigisan*. *Ban Dainagon* uses thick *tsukuri-e* colouring in some courtly interiors, and some aristocrats are abstractly depicted in the *hikime kagihana* manner, on the whole both facial expressions and gestures closely reveal minute emotions. *Genji* is a tale of social and emotional affairs, whereas *Ban Dainagon* is about political intrigue. It is a penetrating study of human motives and behaviour and is a valuable reference source on manners and textile patterns, in the twelfth century.

The story is based on actual historical events of the ninth century. In 866 the evil minister Tomo no Yoshio (better known by his court rank Ban Dainagon) set fire to the main gate of the imperial palace and accused his rival Minamoto no Makoto of the deed. As

62. *Ban Dainagon E-kotoba*: the children's quarrel. Handscroll; second of three scrolls; ink and colours on paper. Late 12th century.

63. *The Flying Granary* (detail)
from *Shigisan Engi*, first scroll.
1156–1180.

Minamoto was about to be sentenced for the crime, the Prime Minister pleaded with the Emperor to suspend proceedings for lack of evidence. Several months elapsed. In the autumn of that year a quarrel broke out between the son of a butler in the metropolitan guard and the son of Ban Dainagon's accountant. The latter, presuming on the high rank of his employer, thrashed the butler's son, whereupon the outraged butler shouted that he knew the secret evil doings of Ban Dainagon. Gossip spread on this note and the butler was summoned to court for questioning. He said that he had personally seen Ban Dainagon and his son set fire to the Gate but had not dared to report the deed because of Ban Dainagon's power. Ban Dainagon was sentenced to banishment. The scrolls are replete with noblemen and commoners, and vividly characterize both types.

In the illustration shown, multiple exposure technique (with consecutive actions running clockwise) is used to depict the pivotal scene of the children's quarrel. In the upper right, surrounded by curious townsfolk, the butler's son, wearing a short, blue robe with polka-dots, is having his hair pulled by the accountant's son, as, meanwhile (upper centre) we see the accountant rushing to the rescue, fists at the ready. He shields his son (below left), who sneers triumphantly as his father kicks the other boy, sending him stag-

62

gering to the left. Then (upper left) we see the accountant's wife dragging her reluctant son home to be chastised. Again, architectural details give clues to the date and creator of the work. The accurate representation of the Kaishō-mon Gate, which was burnt down in 1177 and not rebuilt, gives the latest possible date for the scroll. As the Seiryōden Imperial Residence is inaccurately drawn, we may assume either that the artist did not have access to the innermost recesses of the Palace or that the place shown was a temporary residence of the Emperor. On the other hand, the artist has represented the metropolitan police force with an impressive and rigorous accuracy which suggests intimate familiarity with that agency.

A unique and splendid set of scrolls in the ink monochrome *hakubyō* tradition and in the *otoko-e* manner has also survived from this period. The four scrolls are collectively known as *Chōjū Giga* (Frolicking Animals). The first two can be dated definitely from the first half of the twelfth century, while the third and fourth scrolls, of lesser quality in brushwork and slightly different in content, date from the mid-thirteenth. The *Chōjū Giga* scrolls have no accompanying, or even a separate, text; they are the work of Buddhist monks and their often hilarious content has been the subject of much remark. The first scroll shows human games, rituals and other activities performed by animals in human dress. The second scroll shows some fifteen kinds of real or fantasy animals. The third scroll shows monks and laymen at play, while animals parody their actions. The fourth (notably inferior) scroll continues the satirical theme.

This gentle clerical caricature is filled with humorous and compassionate observation of human foibles during the moral decay of the twelfth century. In the example from the first scroll, a monkey dressed as a monk is offering a peach branch before the Buddhist altar; his ceaseless chant is shown by wavy ink lines issuing from his mouth. The simian offering is solemnly accepted by a corpulent frog in the Yakushi Buddha's healing mudra, proudly seated on a lotus leaf, with a giant banana leaf as his aureole. He is framed by leafless branches of a gnarled tree, sketched with a few swelling ink strokes. Beyond the horizon, autumnal grasses sway in the wind as three clerics (two foxes and a monkey) show various states of mortification and *ennui*. Nearby, a fox and a hare, clutching Buddhist rosaries, join in the incantations.

Elsewhere in the scroll there are scenes of animals wrestling, riding, picnicking and taking part in archery contests and water sports. Whether or not they refer directly to the annual court fest-

64

64. *Simian prelate worshipping frog Buddha*, from *Chōjū Giga* scrolls. Ink on paper. First half of 12th century.

ivals and sports, such as those arranged in the *Nenjū gyōji* scrolls, cannot be proven, but there is no mistaking the whimsical caricature of humanity. The Japanese were never Confucian prudes or censorious at heart, thus unlike in China, their acute yet compassionate observations of human foibles, down to the most 'unmentionable', were appreciated without false modesty. Caricature was thus able to develop its own cultural environment and evolved over the centuries into various genres, including the *manga* cartoon that in the late 18th and 19th centuries reached its zenith in the hands of the woodcut master Hokusai.

The two Japanese linear traditions, the discreet, unwavering 'iron-wire' line used in *onna-e* and the oblique swelling and diminishing line of *otoko-e* painting, were both basic to Chinese figurative painting. The Chinese largely used figurative painting to exemplify general moral precepts, and descriptions of specific events or physical traits highlighted the universal values of an ethical society where the arts served to inspire the beholder. The Japanese artist, by contrast, guided only by courtly standards of taste, was free to explore the smallest detail of our human condition. It was not improper to express personal feelings; in fact, such expression was encouraged and the remarkable acuity of observation so developed spawned some of the most masterly narrative paintings the world has seen.

Illustrated narrative handscrolls grew in popularity in the Kamakura period. They had been the oldest means for Buddhist proselytizing among the masses since Tang Chinese story-tellers held up painted scenes to illustrate their market-place narratives.

Japanese religious education continued the practice. *Ebusshi* illustrated not only the glories of Paradise but the frightful torments of Hell. This type of didactic Buddhist painting is known as *rokudō-e* (Painting of the Six Ways) and its subject matter was drawn from the subjects intrinsic to the six realms of illusory existence. Its purpose was to warn those who did not ceaselessly recite Amida's name that they were risking disease, deformity and all the horrors of Hell. *Hungry Ghosts*, for example, now in the Tokyo National Museum, graphically shows how attachment to worldly things in this life leads to similar bondage in the future. After death, former gluttons experience insatiable hunger pangs. Here they are seen feasting on the fecal matter of unwary slum dwellers. The realistic rendering of the bloated stomachs and the

66

65. *(below)* Zemmyō transformed *into a Dragon*, detail from *Kegon Engi* handscrolls by Enichi-bō Jōnin. Early 13th century.

66. *(opposite)* Hungry Ghosts, from the *Gaki Zōshi* scroll (Kawamoto version). Ink, colours on paper. Late 12th century.

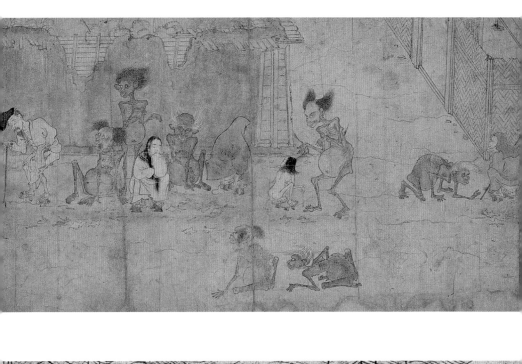

frightening expressions on the ghostly faces illustrate the medieval Buddhist teaching, 'Leave the table when six-tenths full!'

Myōe in mediation

In 1206, the monastic reformer Kōben (a.k.a. Myōe Shōnin, 1173–1232) re-established the forested mountain retreat Kozanji, southwest of Kyoto, as an active part of the Kegon School of Buddhism of which Todaiji in Nara was the centre. Kozanji became known for its remarkable paintings. Myōe is said to have imported many Chinese Song paintings and they may have influenced the new Kozanji painting style. The first were produced by Myōe's favourite disciple, Enichi-bō Jōnin. This famous and remarkable portrait of Myōe is a lasting tribute to the affection between the painter and his subject. It also introduces a new freshness and clarity in coloration. The abbot, in deep meditation, is portrayed three-quarter face, sitting in a tree. His eyes are closed, his smile-wrinkles are emphasized and his resolute, shaven but bristly chin is depicted with striking realism. This outstanding portrait signals the new spiritual vigour of the Kamakura period, when aristocratic and aesthetic indulgence would give way to a new sense of dynamism and moral purpose.

After a long period of diplomatic isolation, Japan was now receptive to Southern Song Chinese works with their new spirit of lyrical introspection, a contrast to the previous opulent extravagance of Tang. Reflecting a shift of power in China from the courtly aristocracy to a scholarly bureaucracy, inner spiritual qualities were stressed rather than external details. Transparent colour-washes were preferred to heavy pigmentation. The development of modelling strokes had replaced colour shading.

The portrait of Myōe is a Japanese interpretation of these Song innovations. The brushwork is firm but supple; the forms express inner tranquillity; the rocks are built up with parallel contour lines and occasional dark accents; finely sketched tree outlines are fortified by lines of broader wash.

The *engi* (founding history) of the Kegon School was produced at Kozanji at Myōe's request. The six illustrated scrolls of the *Kegon Engi* are widely considered to have been painted by Enichi-bō Jōnin. They feature the seventh-century patriarchs of the School, Gishō and Gengyō (Korean: I-sang and Won-hyo), who introduced Kegon (Korean: Hwa-on) teachings from Silla. The first four scrolls are devoted to Gishō (624–702), who studied Buddhism in China and was there adored by a beauty named Zemmyō (Chinese: Shanmiao), whom he converted to the

67

67. *Myōe Shōnin meditating*, by Enichi-bō Jōnin. Hanging scroll; ink, colours on paper. Early 13th century.

68. Burning of the Sanjō Palace in Kyoto by the rebel Minamoto forces. Detail from *Heiji monogatari* scrolls. Ink, colours on paper. Late 13th century.

Buddhist faith. As Gishō's boat was about to sail for Korea, Zemmyō plunged into the ocean herself, whereupon she was transformed into a large dragon and carried Gishō's boat on her back safely to Korea. (Zemmyō thereafter was deified as patron goddess of the Kegon School.)

In the detail shown, her transformation has been accepted by the passengers who are listening as Gishō, in the centre, expounds the Law. As in the Myōe portrait, the painting is relaxed, the brushwork is clear and supple and although every space is full there is no sense of crowding. On the contrary, the soft colour gradations, as the waves turn from blue to white, give a sense of spaciousness. There is none of the drama found in the assertive brushwork of *Shigisan Engi*, and none of the emotional intensity of the *Genji* scrolls. Instead we find a sparkling clarity in concert with the shift from emotionality to spirituality.

War tales

A later, major category of narrative handscrolls tells of heroism and loyalty in battle. The illustrations are based on literary tales or historical chronicles of specific engagements. This development marks the start of military overlordship in Japan, where the

65

bakufu form of government began in 1185 with Minamoto Yoritomo's seizure of power and the establishment of his government in Kamakura. From then to the end of Tokugawa rule in 1868, interest in the code of the warrior (*bushidō*) was reflected in the vast production of war tales, both in literature and in all kinds of fine art: fan painting, album leaves, screens and hanging scrolls as well as narrative handscrolls.

Like a film, the handscroll depicts action in sequence, one segment at a time. The pace of each narrative is masterfully planned. Each scroll painting has its own tempo, fast or slow, which engages our viewing to the extent of conditioning the speed at which we unroll the scroll. In the *Genji* scrolls, for instance, the pictorial sections are separate paintings interleaved with a continuous calligraphic narrative. This 'internal', *onna-e*, style makes the viewer pause at length over each 'frame' to savour every detail of its meaning, whereas the *otoko-e* style of many battle scrolls is more explicit, with continuous action scenes and no textual interruption. The tales of *Shigisan Engi* and *Ban Dainagon e-kotoba* and the *Kegon Engi* are examples of this type. With the growing interest in battle techniques, the detailed depiction of each stage in combat became a crucial feature of handscroll painting. The urgency of tactical manoeuvres brings to the military narrative a dramatic new dimension.

An early, important set of scrolls, the *Heiji monogatari*, describes the crucial battle of 1159 in the civil war between the Minamoto (Genji) and Taira (Heike) clans. The scrolls are based on a novel of the same name written in 1220. Another novel, about a similar conflict in the Hōgen era (1156), called the *Hōgen monogatari*, was written in the same year. Both of these use a new, plain-spoken language where the battle scenes are recounted in a direct and epic manner. Today three scrolls from at least fifteen describing the Heiji wars have survived.

Our illustration shows the burning of the Imperial Palace at 68 Sanjō in Kyoto, as the rebel (Minamoto) forces try to seize power by capturing the Emperor. The instigator of the revolt was Fujiwara Nobuyori, who had conspired with Minamoto no Yoshitomo. The *coup* was staged in December of 1159 and the retired Emperor Go-Shirakawa taken prisoner. Here we see the Imperial Palace in flames, while Minamoto forces the Emperor to board the cart waiting to take him to captivity. Other soldiers are shown charging on horseback, beheading imperial guards and spearing royal retainers as ladies weep helplessly or flee.

The scene is packed with multiple actions some of which are simultaneous, some sequential. It is a far more complex conception than the crowd scenes in *Ban Dainagon* or *Shigisan Engi*, where focus tended to be on a single action. The pace is more urgent and the action moves purposefully from right to left, in spite of vignettes (like film 'freeze frames'), which face right. The figures are grouped in triangles or in lozenges which culminate in a point; single figures lead from each group to the next. This spatial organization allows swift visual comprehension and thus quickens the pace. Unlike twelfth-century scrolls which often resort to exaggeration and caricature, thirteenth-century narratives stress physical realism. Like its literature, Kamakura painting was action-packed and spirited, dealing with real moments. The fire, for example, is seen in several time-lapses, from its explosive outburst to the tongues of flame licking the adjoining roofs and then to the smoke-filled, red clouds, bringing a fall-out of burning cinders. (These last were made by flicking a paint-charged brush across the wrist, covering the paper with red dots.) At the centre of the fire the heat is most intense and the flames are painted sharp and straight, devouring the charred beams. Patronage has changed from the courtly Fujiwara to the martial Minamoto, and the arts sensitively reflect the shift in aesthetics.

Kana calligraphy: onnade

The Japanese regard the development and perfection of their indigenous calligraphy style as the quintessence of Heian contribution to art. This achievement is all the more remarkable because of the unbridgeable differences between Chinese and Japanese speech, poetry, and attitudes towards the written script. Between the ninth and eleventh centuries an ingenious system of adapting Chinese characters was derived, and in the hands of courtiers developed into an expression of the highest order.

Since prehistoric times, the Chinese had shown a need and respect for the art of writing. Ideographic units, either pictographs or ideographs, evolved, each representing a specific idea. They are monosyllabic and were first used by diviner-scribes of the priestly shaman kings of the Shang dynasty (fifteenth century BCE) to communicate with ancestral spirits. Later, the deeds of Zhou nobles were recorded and writing was widely adopted as a means of recording such things as military orders, history and poetry. Chinese verse uses couplets or quatrains of four, five or seven syllables; symmetry is bilateral: that is, nouns, verbs or adjectives, contrasting or paired, appear in comparable positions in the respective phrases and thus, when inscribed, occur side by side in vertical columns, written from top to bottom and ranging from right to left. By the time Chinese script appeared in Japan in the fifth century CE, by way of Korea, it was twenty centuries old and standardized.

The Japanese, on the other hand, throughout their millennia of ceramic pre-history, had been content with an oral transmission of poetry and legends in songs and dances. The need for written documents was felt only with the advent of a centralized government and its diplomacy. In the fifth century, Chinese books on Confucian classics, the histories and literary selections, began to enter Japan and from the sixth century onwards, Buddhist sutras, written in Chinese, also became known. In the late sixth century, Prince Shōtoku had the articles of state of his newly constructed government written down in Chinese, which was learned by the ruling classes. China had come to be regarded as the source of all civilization.

Chinese is linguistically alien to Japanese and its mastery by an adult required then, as it does now, prodigious effort. To use the Chinese writing system to transcribe the Japanese language was an even more formidable task. Chinese is monosyllabic and non-inflected while Altaic-Tungusic Japanese is polysyllabic and agglutinative, with a great variety of suffixes required for different classes of verbal forms, tenses and moods, varying greatly according to the gender and social status of the speaker, in relation to the addressed. In the first written history of Japan, Chinese syntax prevailed. In the histories compiled in 712 and 720, Japanese names were transcribed syllable for syllable, using Chinese characters of close sound value, just as the Chinese themselves had once transcribed the Sanskrit names of Buddhist deities. But whereas the Chinese remained faithful to their original transcription of alien sounds, the Japanese delighted in the myriad visual puns made possible by substituting one of several (visual) Chinese characters for the same (aural) syllable. At first they resolutely refused to standardise the fifty-one syllable sounds of the Japanese language to fifty-one fixed Chinese characters.

This method of transcription was based on the first of two methods of character-transcription devised in Japan: *on-yomi*, the phonographic system of transcribing sound values. Here the Chinese pictograph for fish woud be read *wu* (the contemporary reading along the South China coast) and served as the phonetic element *wu* in polysyllabic Japanese words. The second ideographic system was called *kun-yomi*, and here the pictograph for fish would be given its Japanese sound value, *sakana*, and would mean fish. Early Japanese writing used both systems, as seen in the first poetry anthology, the *Manyōshū*, which contains 4,500 poems written prior to 760 CE. But due to the complex and deliberately irregular method of transcription, some of the poems remain unsolved textual puzzles to this day.

From the ninth century, Japanese writers began to replace this cumbersome method with a syllabic system in which certain preferred Chinese ideograms were reduced to a few strokes and pronounced only for their respective sound values, thus transforming Chinese ideograms into Japanese syllabic phonograms. Its angular *katakana* form was derived from the formal Chinese *kaishu* script and was used in Japan for official documents, Buddhist sutras and printing; its cursive, *hiragana* form, came from the informal Chinese draft script, *caoshu*. This was a tremendous step forward. The Japanese language with its polysyllabic cadences and long vowel stresses, so conducive to recitation and singing, was at last provided with a written equivalent based on phonetic value alone.

The *katakana* syllabary was used for phonetic glosses to Chinese texts and for Japanese written in the Chinese *kun* system but needing suffixes, while the *hiragana* system was developed for use in transcribing Japanese poetry (*waka*), for the writing of

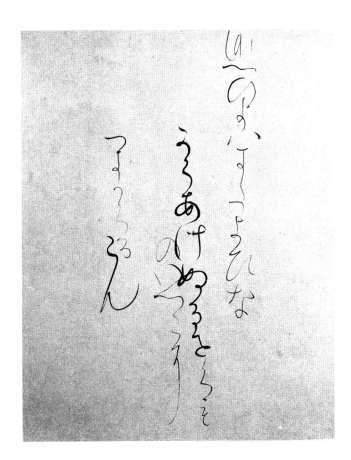

69. *Onnade* calligraphy from one of the *masu-shikishi* set of calligraphies. *Shikishi* album leaf. Late 11th century.

personal letters and new literary forms such as romances and diaries. Men thought it was unbecoming for women to struggle with Chinese learning and it became a tacit social taboo for women to be seen reading Chinese books. Thus men engaged in Chinese studies and used Chinese script for their Chinese and Japanese poetry, whereas women wrote only in Japanese. Their *hiragana* style of calligraphy came to be called *onnade* (feminine hand). By the late eleventh century, as Fujiwara culture was reaching its peak, *onnade* achieved unsurpassed internal balance and grace. The example shown here is the so-called *masu-shikishi* calligraphy, and recalls the pristine purity of the sculpture and murals of the Phoenix Hall. There is no trace of Chinese architectonic script or of the extravagant flourishes to come. The writing was inscribed with a finely pointed brush usually held upright. The diagonal swings do not detract attention from a steady vertical axis which is never actually touched. Balance and dynamic energy are main-

69

tained in elements of different sizes, in the contrast between light and dark, in column alignment and in the density and openness of the internal spirals. Furthermore, the work shows creative originality and expressiveness which are never allowed to interfere with legibility.

The thirty-one syllable poem by Kiyohara no Fukayabu is transcribed below, line by line, as it appears in the calligraphy:

natsu no yo wa mada yoi na-	summer night still dusky and
gara akenuru wo kumo	yet day breaks: oh! clouds
no izukoni	somewhere among them
tsuki kakuru	the moon is hiding
ra-n	perhaps

The thin night air of summer is expressed in the fine lines of the first column. The artist breaks the word *nagara* (and yet) to gain power and momentum in the second column, where his brush tip is freshly charged with more ink and applied with firmer pressure. The letters *a-ke-nu* of the word *akenuru* (daybreak) literally expand, breaking apart, the *ke* occupying about four times the width of the preceding *nagara*. 'Daybreak' thus actually overlaps the *no izuko* (somewhere) of the next column, recreating the clouds which cover the moon at dawn.

This poem demonstrates simultaneous confidence in verbal and visual imagery. Not only are the phonetic elements, the *kana*, in a non-uniform size, but the inscription does not even conform to the internal metre of the poem. An oral recitation of it would produce the following linear arrangement:

natsu no yo wa	summer night
mada yoi nagara	still dusky but already
akenuru wo	dawn breaks. Oh!
kumono izukoni	somewhere amidst the clouds
tsuki kakuru ra-n	surely the moon hides

However, the calligrapher has treated his task in visual, not aural terms. This freedom from extraneous considerations is an essentially Japanese quality. In Chinese calligraphy, the column length, once established, must be maintained. If a Chinese poet had written out the above poem in Japanese *kana* script, he would have either used columns of equal length and broken the metre or he would have reproduced the recitation pattern shown above. The Japanese poet has broken the metre for visual effect. The V-shaped silhouette with serrated edges represents the clouds parting, with the short, lowest (third) column rising and bursting at the top in a moon-like circle.

This poem was one of a pair written in an album format and later mounted separately on cards (*shikishi*). Such creative inscriptions of poetry took various forms. These included *tsugi-shikishi* where two contrasting sheets of paper provided the background for two poems and large or small *shikishi*, boards mounted with plain or decorated paper, which by the early twelfth century came to rival *tsukuri-e* painting itself in sumptuousness, as in the textual passages of the *Genji* scrolls.

Eleventh-century calligraphy paper was usually white or light blue; sutras, exceptionally, were done in Chinese block script, in gold paste on an indigo ground. Japanese paper designs, for poetry or prose, became ever more sophisticated. The material could be dyed before manufacture; the paper itself could be dyed or painted with colour and then sprinkled with cloudy, misty shapes. Other methods included the imprinting of ink figures, gold or silver patterns, *kirigane* metal flakes, hair-fine metal slivers (*noge*) and metal dust (*sunago*). Colours included various hues of red, violet, indigo, blue, white, yellow, brown and green. Heian calligraphy paper often adopted Chinese Tang and Song patterns and used the same woodblock printing techniques.

The high, bird's-eye-view perspective of vast expanses with low-lying hillocks and meandering streams, often associated with Heian landscape painting and paper decoration, had been long considered a Japanese contribution. Egami Yasushi has pointed out, however, that such perspective is rare in Japanese works prior to the importation in 1073 of a set of Buddhist commentaries written out by the Chinese Emperor Song Taizong (he reigned 976–997) and illustrated by fifty Northern Song artists, and then made into woodblock printed editions. The imported book is a Korean copy but faithfully preserves the Song perspective and marked diagonality. While these features were abandoned in later Chinese painting, they took root in Heian Japan and became characteristic elements of the *Yamato-e* tradition that perseveres to this day.

Chinese motifs on calligraphy paper included the so-called 'Chinese grasses', waves, bamboo, sparrows and lions, but soon Japanese motifs appeared, including rabbits in autumn grass, deer, flowing water (a motif traceable to Yayoi times), cherry blossom, peaches and wild chrysanthemum. Collage attained unparalleled splendour where sheets torn or cut on the diagonal formed colourful designs. Some were further decorated with colour pigments or metallic dust. This provided the underdrawing for aristocratic calligraphy.

Almost all Heian secular arts, picture scrolls, screens or lacquer decoration and fan paintings contain direct or indirect literary references. Calligraphy is naturally the most literature-based form of all. The *Sanjūrokunin ka shū* (Anthology of the Thirty-Six Poets) was produced in the early twelfth century and marks the highest achievement in calligraphy and also in the craft of paper making. It is thought that this collection of hundreds of poems, inscribed by twenty calligraphers, was intended as a tribute to the retired Emperor Shirakawa on his sixtieth birthday in 1112. The following example is by Minamoto no Shigeyuki (died 1000):

eda wakanu
haru ni a(h)edomo
mumore
gi wa
Moemo masarade
toshi he-
nuruka-
na

Although the buried log encounters Spring, when branches emerge undivided How many years has it passed without greening!

The poem may refer to a mature woman, symbolized by the buried log, who has seen yet another spring come and go, bringing a loveless summer. It is painted in mica and ink upon collage-decorated paper. In the centre, an abandoned boat (a standard summer subject) is half hidden by reeds. It is painted on a torn fragment of paper inserted between two lighter coloured pieces, as if it were a dream apparition. Above turbulent mica waves, tiny ink birds scatter and a small boat carrying two figures heads toward a minuscule island. The calligraphic alignment of the poem follows the speech cadences, and complex Chinese characters reveal the author's name, Minamoto no Shigeyuki, ending the piece with a firm masculine flourish. In weighted and measured wrist pressure the calligrapher inscribes the secret agonies of the poem as if writing an official edict, less sensitive to emotional nuances than a generation previously in the *Masu-shikishi*.

The calligraphy here differs in several respects from that of the previous example. It is not in the *onnade* or *hiragana* form of phonetic symbols, but in the more Chinese-oriented *sōgana* form, where syllables are mostly made of cursive forms of fuller Chinese characters. Secondly, the calligrapher presses down on his brush from time to time to change the width of the strokes, and uses more oblique strokes than in the previous example. There is no longer

70. Calligraphy fragment from the *Shigeyukishū* collection from the *Sanjūrokunin ka shū. c.* 1112.

the continuity and flow of the late eleventh century nor the sublime perfection of internal balance. The writing reveals self-conscious linkages between words and tight turns around the loops. The calligraphy occupies slightly more than half the double album-leaf format on the right, to be counter-balanced by the weight of the author's name in full Chinese ideograms in the last column on the left. However, the Chinese characters are written with the same flowing quality and emphasis on lateral movement along the writing surface as Japanese *kana* syllabary. The extensive decoration of the paper poses a challenge to the calligrapher's creativity when 'adding' brush to paper. There is a link with the heightened, indirectly expressed emotion of *onna-e* painting. At first glance, the calligraphy is stately and calm but the agitation betrayed in the second line, *haru ni aedomo* (though encountering Spring), shows that it is not a straightforward summer boating song but is redolent with unfulfilled emotions. The harsh breaks within *eda – wa – kanu* in the first column and in *haru – ni – a(h)edomo* in the second are stark and sudden like thunder on a rainless summer day.

Lacquers

A remarkable development in both the technique and design of lacquer making is seen toward the latter part of the Heian period.

71. *Flowing Stream* with small birds. *Maki-e* on wood *koto*. 12th century.

Although scholars have not been able to reach a final conclusion on the origins of the technique (*maki-e*), where colour, gold and silver dust or particles are sprinkled on to still tacky lacquer, its widespread use during the Fujiwara period was indisputably wedded to Japanese taste. The subtle shading of the dust creates nuances previously unseen in lacquers. In the earliest form of the process only the design is lacquered (*hira-makie*). In later and more complex processes like relief motifs (*taka-makie*), the entire surface of the utensil was covered with several applications of lacquer and colour or metal dust. Each lacquer layer was carefully sanded to even the surface and bring out the lustre, with main motifs rising above the surface. Mother-of-pearl inlay (*raden*) was also widely used.

In decoration, relatively crowded, evenly spread Persian-Tang Chinese motifs gave way to a new taste for asymmetrical arrangements and an increased fluidity in the empty space. Whether these tendencies can all be traced to Song designs remains to be studied, but their integration with the form of the utensil is as purely Japanese as the calligraphy described above. In one of the most beautiful examples of *maki-e* designs, gold and silver are finely wrought to create flowing streams of ever-changing width and direction, a poignant hymn to the vissicitudes and inconstancy of life.

71

Chapter 5:   Kamakura and Muromachi (1185–1573)

By the mid-twelfth century rivalry between the Taira and
Minamoto clans erupted in open warfare. Epic battles were fought
in 1156 and 1160 and the land was devastated by famine and
plague until the final triumph of Minamoto no Yoritomo at the
tragic sea-battle of Dannoura in 1185. From then until the
restoration of imperial control in 1868, a succession of military
dictators governed Japan in the Emperor's name.

This military culture was unlike anything Japan or China had
ever produced. It was founded on fealty and honour for which one
was always ready to die a violent death. Unlike the ceremonial
swords of Heian courtiers which were usually sheathed, and within delicately crafted scabbards, the new warrior's sword was a
lethal blade of unsurpassed lightness and strength. Made of two
layers of iron and steel which were subjected to repeated folding
and beating, then to fire and immersion in water, Japanese *samurai*
blades were marked by a unique vapour imprint called *ni-e*, much
prized by connoisseurs. The warrior developed a close relationship with Shintō shrines, as Heian aristocrats had done with
Buddhist temples. The swordsmith's work thus took on a sacred
aspect with extended rites of purification and abstinence before
each new blade was forged. The swordsmith also wore pure white
garments, an echo of the white vestments of the Shintō priest.
Each sword was thought to take on its own spiritual life; success or
failure in battle was attributed to the spirit in the sword.

Gifts of stunning workmanship were made to Shintō shrines,
beginning with the Taira clan's donation of the *Lotus Sutra* scrolls
and of the armour of Taira no Shigemori, Kiyomori's son. Each
military commander identified himself with a particular shrine
where he prayed for victory and offered thanks after battle. Thus,
the Minamoto clan in Kamakura had links with the Tsurugaoka
Shrine where Yoritomo made numerous gifts. His wife Masako
patronized the shrine at Mishima and there offered up her exquisite lacquer toiletry box. The early thirteenth-century sword called
Masatsune was used for warfare until the early eighteenth century
when the Shōgun Tokugawa Yoshimune made it a votive offering.

Military overlordship: the Shōgun and his bakufu

When Minamoto no Yoritomo seized political control in 1185, he moved the seat of power from Kyoto northward to the rugged eastern sea-coast of Kamakura. He instituted the *bakufu* form of government which ruled in the name of the nominally revered Emperor. Yoritomo's military government ruled with spartan resolution and vigour until 1333, demanding unquestioning obedience and rigorous discipline. In 1192 the Emperor confirmed Yoritomo's authority with the title of Barbarian-Subduing Supreme General – Shōgun. The Minamoto family continued in this position until their line died out when their regents, the Hōjō, took effective control. Government administration was in their hands, and the Shōgun himself (no longer of the Minamoto clan) became a puppet like the Emperor. None the less, fierce loyalty to the 'Lord of Kamakura' lived on in generations of faithful vassal families and maintained the integrity of the *bakufu*: even after the Mongol invasions of 1274 and 1281 when finances were low and internal corruption had loosened the *bakufu's* control, when loyalist supporters of Emperor Go-Daigo (1288–1339) twice attempted revolt, but only managed on the contrary to trigger the Emperor's banishment to Oki. In 1333, after the Kemmu Restoration, rival warrior clans supported different pretenders to the throne, creating a northern court in Kyoto and a southern court in Yoshino. The schism lasted for fifty-seven years until the southern Emperor Go-Kameyama abdicated in favour of Emperor Go-Komatsu (1377–1433). In 1392 the country was once more unified.

Kamakura sculpture

The great Tōdaiji and Kōfukuji monasteries of Nara which had supported Yoritomo's cause in 1180 had been thus totally destroyed by Taira forces. Now their reconstruction began. In 1183 the Chinese sculptor Chen Hoqing was brought to Nara to recast the head of the Great Buddha of Tōdaiji but most of the restoration work was undertaken by Japanese artists, particularly those of the illustrious Kei school, descended from Jōchō, master sculptor of the Byōdōin sculptures. Jōchō's sons had established branches in Kyoto and Nara; it was one of the Nara descendants, Unkei (died 1223) who most strongly influenced Kamakura sculpture.

The restoration project at Tōdaiji, which lasted for several generations, involved close study of Tang models and Tang-inspired works for repairs to the sculptures. This study, combined

72. Armour with blue yarns from Taira clan. 12th century.

with the new, stimulating contact with Chinese Song models, led to heightened realism and simplicity; colouring became more subdued and new, emphatically human iconological types appeared. The spirit of reform in Buddhism, with its mass appeal, has already been noted in connection with the Kozanji paintings.

Early works of the Unkei school usher in the last highpoint in Japanese sculptural history. At first sight, these sculptures appear to revive the eighth-century Nara style of realism; but whereas that was idealized, generic and impersonal, Kamakura realism captured both the physical characteristics and the essence of the subject's particular spiritual likeness; dark-centred crystals were now introduced to quicken the eyes.

While the major arts, perfected during the Heian period, continued to flourish under martial rule, the new social structure of society as well as the brisk new *Weltanschauung* created new artistic demands. Yoritomo distanced himself from debilitating court life, and promoted a virile, martial simplicity that stressed inner spiritual alertness rather than exterior grace. He wanted his own Pure Land Paradise enshrined in Kamakura – but not in the effete beauty of the late Fujiwara style. He consulted with Seichō, Unkei's uncle, then leader of the Nara sculptors, and with Tamehisa, a painter working in the new Song brush manner like that of Enichi-bō Jōnin. Unfortunately, the repository for this new art is no longer extant; but we know that Unkei was in eastern Japan, either as Seichō's assistant or on his own, during the shrine's construction.

A group of massive and compelling Buddhist images, some of Unkei's early works, are now to be found in the Ganjōjū-in in Shizuoka Prefecture. In 1752 an inscription was found inside one of them, stating that Unkei began work on the project in 1186, sponsored by Hōjō no Tokimasa, Yoritomo's father-in-law. It is likely that Unkei's years in the invigorating atmosphere of Kamakura contributed to the extraodinary vitality and intensity of his later works.

These works herald the birth of Japanese portraiture. There is little doubt that Unkei was influenced by Song sculpture. Dry lacquer and pottery works produced in the eastern Chinese Liao-Jin dynasties between the tenth and thirteenth centuries show lifelike people with distinct personalities. This reflects an interest in capturing inner essence through faithful outer modelling. None of this was lost on the young Unkei. His father, Kōkei, had assumed leadership of the Nara school when Seichō died and Unkei returned to Nara to work on the Tōdaiji and Kōfukuji projects.

73. *Furuna* (one of Ten Great Disciples). Painted dry lacquer. H. 149 cm. Nara, c. 734.

74, 75. (top) Basū-sen,
(above) Mawara-nyō, both by
Tankei. Painted wood. Early
13th century.

76. (opposite) Muchaku, by
Unkei. H. 188 cm. Kamakura,
1208–12.

Muchaku portrays the Indian patriarch Asanga in carved   76
painted wood. It represents both Unkei's mature style and the best
in Kamakura sculpture. The holy man stands life-size, his weight
on the left foot, turning an intellectual and kind gaze slightly to
the right. Unkei does not carve an idealized representation but
portrays a real individual, probably a particular Japanese Zen master known to him. *Muchaku* is one of the principal figures in
Kōfukuji's North Octagonal Hokuendō Hall, and was produced
between 1208 and 1212. Compared to non-iconic figures of the
Nara period, such as the beautiful dry lacquer standing figure of
Furuna in the Kōfukuji which had doubtless impressed Unkei with   73
its expressive force, *Muchaku* shows a fuller understanding of form
and use of *contraposto*. The sculpted figure is not poised as if about
to fly, like the eighth-century figure: but stands balanced and
relaxed. Song realism has here been heightened by the spiritual tautness peculiar to early Kamakura.

The work of Unkei's six sons and other disciples combines Song
influences and indigenous developments in a similar way. These
include the deep-cut and fluttering drapery in soft curves, more
realistic hand and feet positions, more pronounced but not exaggerated musculature, crystal eyeballs with dark pupils set in the sock-
ets and, above all, palpable spiritual intensity. These characteristics,
however, are only hinted at in the principal icons without changing
their configuration. The further Buddhist iconography is moved
from its source, here India and China, the more rigid and conservative it becomes, allowing little artistic individuality.

The eldest of Unkei's six sculptor sons, Tankei (1173?–1256)
was among his most remarkable followers. In the Rengeō-in,
popularly known as the Hall of the Thirty-Three Bays
(Sanjūsangendō) in Kyoto, Tankei and other Kei School masters
left a seated senjū (thousand-armed) Kannon and a thousand
smaller standing thousand-armed Kannons, all worked in bright
gilt. Among images of the twenty-eight lay followers of this
Kannon, two works by Tankei especially reflect the ardour and
intensity of Kamakura popular Buddhism. *Basū-sen* is shown as an   74
old hermit of frail body but powerful features. Gaunt and bearded,
he leans on a staff. As he stoops forward his right shoulder-bone
protrudes; he holds a sutra scroll in his raised hand. The wrinkled
face and swollen finger-joints show his age and deteriorated physical condition, but faith, piety and benevolence transform the lined
face, with its sunken eyes and long curved nose, into a thing of
beauty. Perhaps most compelling in its simplicity and single-
minded faith is a companion piece, *Mawara-nyō*, who stands erect   75

112

with folded hands. Her neck muscles are taut; her mouth is firmly closed; her large eyes are wide and unblinking; her thoughts are focussed on inner spiritual realities, oblivious of passers-by. There is little here of such Heian qualities as *mono no aware*. Kamakura was not a time to indulge in self-centred fears or regrets, but to cultivate instead the samurai values of asceticism and selflessness. This tendency was given a great boost with the arrival of Chan Buddhism from China.

Zen Buddhism

As contact with China was resumed, increasing numbers of Japanese reformist Buddhist masters like Eisai (1141–1215) and Dōgen (1200–1253), studied there and brought back the self-reliant teaching known as Chan (or Zen in Japanese). Ascetic and pragmatic, Zen eschewed external rituals. This no-nonsense approach held a strong appeal for the Japanese warrior class and soon found official patronage. Zen monasteries in Chinese style were founded from south to north, with the Kenninji (1202) and Tōfukuji (1243) in Kyoto, and the Kenchōji (1253) and Engakuji (1282) in Kamakura.

A genre of patriarchal portraiture, *chinzō*, flourished with the proliferation of Zen monasteries charting a master's active life, usually that of the abbot. *Chinzō* represents the essential personal and direct transmission of the Law. A portrait of the master, with an appropriate inscription of dedication, was given to the disciple who had achieved a measure of enlightenment. It acknowledged the Karmic bond between master and disciple which formed an important part of the seeker's spiritual path. Many portraits of famous Chinese masters were brought back by grateful Japanese disciples; the personal messages 'from Mind to Mind' strengthened the disciple's spiritual penetration and absorption. Jan Fontein and Money Hickman have observed that 'there is perhaps no other form of Chinese and Japanese art in which painting and calligraphy are so intimately connected in their purpose and meaning.'

In 1246 the great Southern Song Chan master Lanqi Daolong (1213–78) arrived in Japan. Two years later he went to Kamakura and converted the Hōjō regent Tokiyori. A magnificent monastery, Kenchōji, was built on the slopes just north of the city and was inaugurated in 1253 with the master as its founding abbot. This was the first purely Chinese Chan ritual held in Japan. With shōgunal patronage Zen quickly spread throughout the land. A portrait of Lanqi Daolong in the Kenchōji, by an unknown 77

77. Portrait of Lanqi Daolong (1213–1278) (detail). Silk hanging scroll, with colophon by Daolong the sitter dated 1271.

Japanese painter, shows the founder about seven years before his death. He is seated in the master's high chair, feet tucked under his habit, holding his *keisaku* disciplinary rod and observing the world attentively with benign yet stern eyes. He looks young for his age, nearly seventy; despite his slight and bony frame, his skin is clear and firm. The fluid, undulating ink brush-strokes show direct Song influence as does the coloration in transparent washes of dark and light browns. A new era of Chinese culture is launched, in spite of strict Chan injunctions against attachment, even attachment to culture.

Kamakura portrait painting

The clear-sighted Zen view of the world injected a striking new realism into Japanese portraiture of the period. Some early examples are the set of portraits in Jingoji temple in Kyoto, attributed to Fujiwara Takanobu (1142–1205). The portrait of the Shōgun Minamoto no Yoritomo is still tinged with some Heian opacity and formality. It had been considered rude in Heian times to copy a person's likeness. But here the artist has not hesitated to bring out

79

115

78. (*below*) Portrait of Emperor Hanazono, by Goshin. Hanging scroll; ink, colours on paper. 1338.

79. (*opposite*) *Minamoto no Yoritomo* by Fujiwara Takanobu (1142–1205). Hanging scroll; ink, colours on silk. 12th century.

his subject's thick lips, protruding mouth suggesting buck teeth, small ear-lobes and slighty rounded, narrow nose and, above all, a determined and possibly ruthless character. His steady, thoughtful gaze, through eyes partially closed, reveal certain inner dimensions of the man, touching his very spirit. The black figured brocade, red inner collar, gold scabbard, ivory tablet of state and gold-encrusted front sash are still opaque, in conformity with Heian practice, but the eyelids, nostrils, ears and lips are discreetly shaded to suggest real dimensions.

Takanobu was famous for realistic rendering; he painted only the faces of his subjects, leaving the rest to craftsmen. In 1173, a courtier recorded in his diary that Takanobu's mural of the Emperor and his court was so life-like that he, the courtier, was able to recognize everyone and thanked the Gods that he himself had been absent at the occasion – a clear example of the Heian aversion to life-like portraiture. It is significant, even so, that this same group-portrait was commissioned by the Emperor Go-Shirakawa-in himself. Although opposition courtiers described the painting as coarse and dreary, and closed the building in which it was housed, the allure of realism proved irresistible. By the early thirteenth century, many more painted records of this type had been commissioned by the palace and courtiers were even identified on the paintings by their names and ages.

Another example of the informal but penetrating quality of such painting is the revealing fourteenth-century portrait by Goshin, a descendant of Takanobu, of the Emperor Hanazono (1297–1348). It is painted in ink on paper and washed in transpar-

78

ent colours. The emperor abdicated in 1318 and took Buddhist vows in 1334. A highly erudite man, he is shown here at the age of forty-two, in a grey monk's habit, holding a rosary and a fan, gazing wearily at the world. A patchwork brocade mantle, with a golden chrysanthemum and grasses on a white ground, offset the clerical habit. The scholarly face is sensitive and effete; Hanazono himself paid tribute to the realism of the painting by inscribing on it, left, 'My deplorable nature, painted by Goshin in the Autumn of 1338.'

Muromachi ink painting
Through patronage of Zen monasteries and associated cultural activities, the martial rulers in Kamakura sought to produce a cultural legacy to rival that of the aristocratic Fujiwara, and thus to establish legitimacy. The new Zen monasteries were centres of Chinese learning and, in time, some Japanese monks became so absorbed in Chinese literature, scholarship and arts that they came to be chastised as *bunjinsō* or '*literati* monks'. Many spent long years in China and the quality and character of their artistic output often approached that of Chinese Chan monks and *literati*. Although Chan teachings held a profound appeal for the Japanese, the Chinese language, script and ink monochrome painting were alien at best, anathema at worst, and shōgunal promotion of Chinese culture proved to be, for Japanese artist-monks, an unenviable task.

Throughout the Yuan dynasty in China, the Chan School was an international community with frequent and enthusiastic exchanges across the China Sea. Chinese abbots were invited to found Japanese Zen monasteries and Japanese monks went to study in China, some eventually becoming abbots there. Chinese poetry and calligraphy by Japanese monks such as Sesson Yūbai (1290–1346) were highly regarded in both countries. Another painter-monk, Mokuan Reien (*fl.* 1330s–1345), who went to China around 1329, became primate of a Chinese monastery.

In the *Four Sleepers*, Mokuan portrays a favourite Chan theme: the legendary eccentrics, Hanshan and Shide, with Fenggan and his tiger, all soundly asleep. The younger men, Hanshan and Shide, have been identified in later writings as avatars of the bodhisattvas Mañjuśrî and Samantabhadra. (The Chan School added the mounted Fenggan and created its own trinity.) Mokuan's style reveals a full grasp of Chinese ink-wash techniques in fluid descriptive lines, wet areas where darker ink is allowed to blur, the extremely dry brush in shading Fenggan's face and belly, and the

80

老豊干抱虎睡捨得
寒山打作一團做湯火
夢裏風流依々老樹
寒巖辰

祥寿紹密拜手

80. *Four Sleepers* by Mokuan
Reien, inscribed by Xiangfu
Shaomi. Hanging scroll; ink on
paper. 14th century.

use of fine, almost invisible, lines for the facial features. This style
is a development of the Southern Song Chan ink painting tradition, 'apparition painting', *wanglianghua* (Japanese *mōryōga*) since
lost to China.

While Mokuan was in China, the seat of power shifted from
Kamakura. In 1368, Ashikaga Yoshimitsu (ruled 1368–94) from
the Muromachi district in Kyoto became the new Shōgun. Unlike
Minamoto no Yoritomo, who disdained court life, Yoshimitsu was
determined to rival it in both culture and opulence. In the
Kamakura period, the restoration of Buddhist monasteries

destroyed in the civil war had held priority. In the Muromachi period, the Shōgun promoted Chinese-style ink painting, pavilions, gardens and tea-houses as aesthetic alternatives to the imperial taste for native expression.

In the wake of despotic Ming policies, Japanese missions to China were severely curtailed and Japanese monastic artists now carried on without direct guidance from Chinese masters. This, and the alien feel of China's inherently unequivocal deployment of black and white to the finely graded sensibilities of Japanese aesthetics, accounts for the peculiarly unfulfilled character of Muromachi ink-wash painting. Although, through most of the fourteenth century, Zen traffic to China had been brisk and scholarship intense, Japanese monasteries had not established Chinese-style *ateliers* to ensure proper transmission of Zen-related art – understandable in a philosophy which eschewed sutras and icons. The Chan repertory of Yuan China had consisted in general of strong input from the then exile *literati* community who introduced intimate formats featuring highly abbreviated ink monochrome representations of men, orchids, bamboo, pines, landscapes or iconographic figures which summed up well-known Song manners in a few strokes. Japanese artists were thus confronted with the pictorial equivalent of shorthand but without recourse to the fuller script. This first serious encounter with China's ink painting coincided with its evolution towards yet further abbreviation, verging on formal dissolution. Chan works of a wide range of quality now entered Japan, from poor to sublime. The Japanese artist could either slavishly copy his continental model or adapt it.

The latter option, though more suited to the creative impulse, was restricted by the need for iconographical fidelity. Since Chinese Chan works expressed spontaneous exhilaration or insight, the Japanese artist had to enliven his version with a degree of inspiration and freedom but could not inject any different vision of his own. His artistic inclinations could not fully surface, but were inevitably routed through the medium of incompatible Chinese models. This was particularly true after the Ming restoration of 1368, when travel to and from China was curtailed.

While outwardly adhering to the continental vocabulary, to comply with iconographic or shōgunal demands, Japanese Zen ink painting was nevertheless slowly evolving into a more poetic and indigenous expression. This was achieved by altering the morphology and expression of the models but without changing compositional elements. Thus, Muromachi ink painting was deprived of the complete artistic freedom which had marked the

81. *Orchids and Rocks* by Gyokuen Bompō. Hanging scroll; ink on paper. Late 14th century.

development in the Heian period of Tang blue and green styles into *Yamato-e*. And for viewers today, it may lack the totality of transformation and fulfilment so apparent in *onna-e* painting, *onnade* calligraphy, *raku* pottery, *Rimpa* painting and calligraphy or *ukiyo-e* woodblock prints, genres where Japan's artistic genius was given unhindered expression.

However, rearrangement of Chinese elements in a Japanese manner was not only possible, but inevitable. In *Orchids and Rocks,* Gyokuen Bompō (1348–1420) demonstrates that a poetic version of China's philosophical prototype can be successfully made without changing motifs or technique. (Bompō was a *literatus* or *bunjinsō* and once served as abbot of Nanzenji in Kyoto. He was celebrated as a poet and calligrapher but above all for his orchid paintings.) In this painting, the standard rocks and plants are depicted; but instead of radiating outwards to penetrate and dominate space, as is often the case in Chinese orchid paintings, Bompō's elements, in gentle and fluid strokes of graded ink wash, enfold an open and mobile space which is charged with peculiar psychic energy.

82. *White-robed Kannon* with flanking landscapes by Ue Gukei. Hanging scrolls; ink on silk. Late 14th century.

83. *White Heron* by Ryōzen. Ink on paper. Mid-14th century.

While the genre of orchids, bamboo, etc., in ink derived specifically from Yuan *literati* and Chan sources, other Japanese works produced under Zen influence are of diverse origins and show a marked degree of eclecticism and syncretism. A good example is the triptych by Ue Gukei (*fl.* 1361–75), showing a white-robed Kannon flanked by landscapes. Although landscapes were known to form the backdrop of patriarchal and *arhat* paintings, this is the earliest example of a triptych where landscape is brought forward in such a dramatic manner. There is an ebullience, perhaps inspired by Korean models, and the abbreviated brush technique suggests familiarity with the work of the Southern Song master, Yujian. In the central panel the ingenuous Kannon floats placidly on a rock which fairly erupts from the water, while to the right and left mountains, trees and rocks rush, uprooted, towards the figure in the central panel. The artist's interest here is not in stability, solidity or spatial clarity; instead, he shows an illusionistic landscape swirling with gravity-defying motion, while each of the three figures, the Kannon, woodsman and fisherman, is utterly absorbed, oblivious of the commotion.

One of the most accomplished monk-painters was Ryōzen (*fl.* mid-fourteenth century) who may have come from Kyushu. All his works are of Buddhist subjects and suggest a busy, professional painter of considerable attainment, surprising in a monk thought to have held high ecclesiastic rank. One of his best known paintings is of a white heron. Although ostensibly a secular subject, various bird species were used symbolically in Zen painting. Here the heron, painted in white upon the ink-washed paper, is caught mid-step just as it stoops forward, recoiling its long neck in preparation for the lunge at an unseen fish. In the right foreground a few reeds and leaves balance the tension created at the left. Ryōzen's brushwork in the fine, fluid water lines, the white feathers and dark beak, as well as the more impulsive upward strokes of the reeds is ever decisive. In this simple picture, doubtless based on continental models, Ryōzen has achieved the intensity and purity that characterize Zen meditation.

84. Penglai, the immortals' isle. Rock arrangement in the pond garden of Tenryūji, Kyoto. Completed by 1265.

Gardens and landscape painting

By 1265 Tenryūji temple had been completed on the site, to the northwest of Kyoto, of an ancient garden which had been a favourite retreat of courtiers since the tenth century. A remarkable rock arrangement in the pond, suggesting the Chinese isle of immortals, Penglai, may well have been constructed by visiting Chinese craftsmen. The seven stones create a three-dimensional Song landscape – a soaring central pinnacle flanked by subordinate peaks – and may be the only extant example of Song rock-garden art.

84

The collection of Chinese works and their reinterpretation, hitherto purely a monastic activity, was now enthusiastically encouraged by the Shōgun. Ashikaga Yoshimitsu (who died in

85. Golden Pavilion, Kyoto, 1398. (The original was destroyed by fire in 1950 and rebuilt in 1964.)

1408) bought an ancient estate renowned for its garden and built a splendid study now known as the Kinkaku or Golden Pavilion, which he used as a library and the site of his art collection. The Heian pond garden, originally designed to be viewed in changing perspectives as one moved about in a boat, could now be seen in its entirety and from a single vantage-point, his three-storey pavilion. The emphasis has shifted from the Heian ideals of boating parties to one of quiet, one-pointed Zen contemplation.

The Shōgun collected and displayed Chan-related art originally imported by and for Japanese monasteries. He also made a collection of Southern Song court-related academy works in an attempt at parity with the Emperor. (In 1382, for example, Yoshimitsu ordered the building of the Shōkokuji monastery, and employed its painter-monks to decorate his own manor as well.) In this way Zen-related art works, once creations of spontaneous exhilaration of erudite clerics for mutual appreciation, came in Japan to assume a secular and ornamental function.

For their training, Zen clerics used the traditional corpus of Tang Chinese conundrums (Jp. *kōan*) to jolt the disciple's mind out of his accustomed perceptual habits and into spiritual one-pointedness. Now there arose a type of poetry composed at literary gatherings, and often inscribed in groups on an inspirational painting ordered for the occasion.

In the late fourteenth century, reflecting the secularization among Chan monks in China and Korea where literary accomplishment was displacing spiritual quest, a form of poem painting (*shigajiku*) evolved in Japan; in it, a landscape painting complements the group of poems composed during monkish literary gatherings. This largely remained an art form exclusive to the learned clerical community until a Shōgun, probably Yoshimitsu, specifically ordered such a work to be produced as a backdrop screen for his dais. He asked distinguished monks from Kyoto to compose poems, and commissioned Josetsu (*fl.* early fifteenth century) of his Shōkokuji monastery to paint in the 'new style' (of the Southern Song academician and Chan painter Liang Kai). The theme of the painting was the Zen riddle on catching the slippery catfish with the smooth-skinned gourd. Josetsu's compelling work is largely in monochrome, with a touch of red to accent the gourd. Faint echoes of the Liang Kai manner can be seen in the angular lines and hooks of the drapery. The sweep of the bank is remarkable, from the dense confluence of streams on the left to the grand opening up on the right (in a reversal of the customary narrative flow from right to left). The gentle curves of bank, bamboo,

86. *Catching Catfish with a Gourd* by Josetsu. Hanging scroll; ink, colour on paper. Early 15th century.

catfish, gourd and flowing water are offset by the bristling intensity of the reeds on the right, and by the extraordinary absorption of the aspirant. The screen was subsequently remounted in its present hanging scroll format.

'Studio paintings' which portray an idealized mountain retreat also appeared as *shigajiku*. *Reading in the Bamboo Studio* is by 87, 88 Josetsu's pupil Shūbun (*fl.* 1423–58), who in turn taught the great Sesshū. Shūbun further developed the current monastic 'mind-landscape' style. He retained Southern Song and Yuan elements which enhance the sense of expanding space (houses and boats sunk deeply among trees and reeds, mists which separate planes, reduced figures walking hunched over), and thus 'archaized' the Chinese models then becoming available. Just as Bompō transformed the orchid, so Shūbun turned the increasingly solid forms and closed space of late Yuan and Ming works in the Xia Gui tradition into evocative, almost transparent forms embracing a fluid space that appears to breathe and expand in the mist. The scholar-monk looks out from his thatched hermitage on to the real subject of the painting: poetic space/time (here enfolded by langorous pines and, on the other side of the lake, by the outjutting banks and

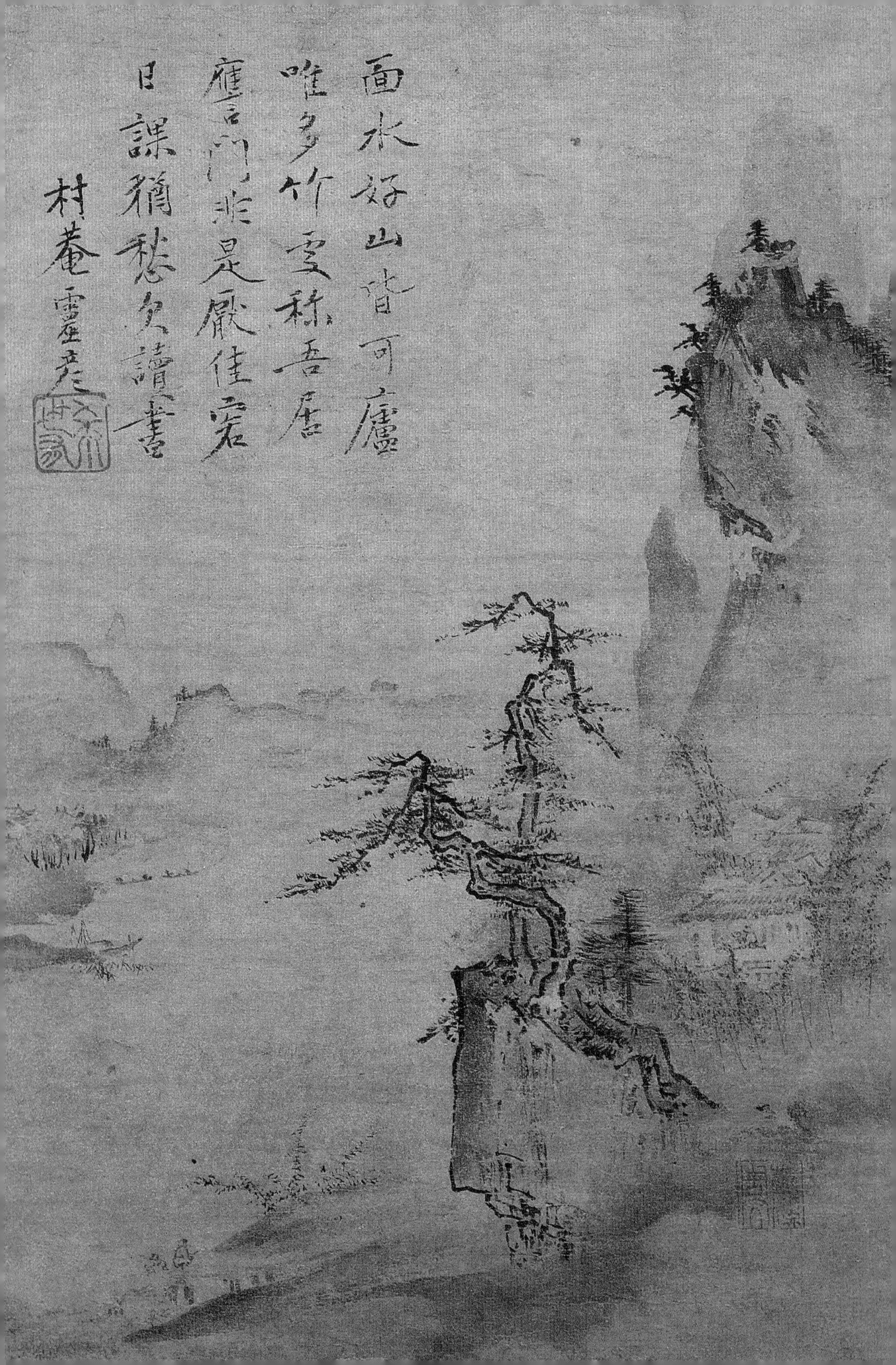
面水好山皆可廬
唯多竹處稱吾居
雁門非是厭佳客
日課猶愁久讀書
村庵靈彥

ring of misty mountains). Ming motifs of affluence are given an eremitic Yuan spatial handling of emptiness and Japanese selectivity is brilliantly displayed.

Poetic spatial expanse achieves dramatic dimensions in the *Small Lake Landscape* by a follower of the Shūbun School, Shōkei Tenyū (*fl.* 1440–60). More assertive brushwork, however, here robs the motif of some of its dreaminess, and the elegant gold coloured lake-side pavilions contrast with Shūbun's rustic mountain huts, in a direct reflection of the rising materialism emerging in early Ming painting. The water expanse is more vast, opening to the left and right and merging with the sky in the upper left. 89

One of the most lyrical extant works of the period is *West Lake* by Bunsei (*fl.* 1460s), a mature statement of the Shūbun Yuan-based 'mind-landscape' ideal. Like Tenyū and Shūbun before him, Bunsei worked with Yuan and Ming works in the Xia Gui style, keeping the Southern Song and Yuan notions of scale, but rearranging elements from diverse sources in a Japanese formal and spatial relationship. As good Chinese models were scarce and spanned some 250 years, and as the Shōgun often requested Chinese styles from Southern Song to contemporary Ming, it became common practice among Muromachi painters to produce highly eclectic works incorporating not only vignettes from various Chinese sources, but also the structural changes engendered through time. It is also noteworthy that while most of the Chinese sources were in intimate formats of fan paintings, album leaves or horizontal handscrolls (favoured in Southern Song and Yuan), Japanese works of the time were mostly narrow vertical hanging scrolls (based on Yuan Chan-*literati* traditions since lost in China) or transposed into large-scale sliding door paintings (*fusuma-e*) and screens (*byōbu*) with specific and fixed functions for Japanese architectural milieux. In Bunsei's reworking of vignettes from different Chinese compositions into a coherent vertical format, we see Japanese genius at work. In the quiet, contemplative space of the mind-landscape we see the scholarly equivalent of the 'emotive cloud' born in Heian *Yamato-e* painting. Not so passionate, the mood is nature-oriented and more profound, the space flowing in a generous S-curve to the middle left and then up to the right. Elements from Xia Gui landscape prototypes are laid out along a consistent groundplane. Each group of motifs is consistent within itself, but the diminution of the bridge section in the foreground in relation to the rock and twin pines draws the entire scene together and creates a hush that reverberates from vignette to vignette. 90

87, 88. (*above*) *Reading in the Bamboo Studio*, complete scroll showing the poetic inscriptions by six monks. (*left*) detail by Shūbun. Hanging scroll; ink on paper. Muromachi, mid-15th century.

89. (*left*) *Small Lake Landscape* by Shōkei Tenyū. Hanging scroll; ink, colours and gold on paper. Mid-15th century.

90. (*right*) *West Lake* by Bunsei, inscribed by Zuikei Shūhō and Ichijō Kanera. Hanging scroll; ink on paper. Before 1473.

The Shōgun also collected works associated with the scholar-amateur idealist tradition later called the Southern School in China. Unlike the 'Northern' academic landscapes, which feature jagged rocks painted in slanted 'axe' strokes, the Southern '*literati*' landscapes derive from a tradition of rounded hills and expansive lake vistas, where the texturing was done largely with a more upright brush in ropey 'hemp-fibre' strokes or in wet blobs and graded ink-wash. In Muromachi collections this latter Southern or Mi Fu style is represented by works associated with the Chan monk Muqi (who died between 1269 and 1274), including Buddhist figures, animals, flowers and landscapes. Most Japanese landscapists worked in the Northern Ma-Xia academy style, but one of the Shōgun's curators, Sōami (who died in 1525), was able to produce works in the Southern style, such as the breathtaking *Eight Views of the Xiao and Xiang* still to be seen on the sliding door panels of the Daisenin sub-temple of the Daitokuji monastery. These incorporate major features of the Chinese *literati* traditions related to the Song masters Juran and Mi Youren. (The Ami family had for generations acted as curators, conservators, appraisers and connoisseurs for the Ashikaga, and Sōami had grown up in the sinophile milieu of Yoshimasa's court, acquiring intimate knowledge of Chinese painting styles from direct study.) Artistically far more accomplished than the 'Northern style' works above, this large work, spanning over twenty panels, demonstrates Sōami's understanding of the Chinese *literati* mode, and attests to the greater suitability of the Southern mode for Japanese expression. None the less, shōgunal preference for more angular Northern academic styles (based on the more difficult oblique brushwork) precluded the development in Japan of a Southern style. This development had to wait till the Tokugawa period when independent painters took it up on their own.

In the detail shown, originally on one of the western sliding doors but now remounted in hanging scroll format, Sōami achieves a fine synthesis of Chinese Southern imagery and technique with Japanese formata and expression. Low-lying, rolling hills swathed in rising autumnal mists yield to marshy grasslands where boats are moored and geese descend in formation. There is a striking parallel to the half dormant, half waking mood of the *Early Spring Landscape* among the Phoenix Hall murals. The houses tucked beneath the mountain are wrapped in quiet; only the occasional wild goose breaks the silence of the chilly air. Two boats are moored among reeds in the middleground and two fishermen by the lowest bank are all but lost in the vast, evening calm. 91 58

132

91. *Eight Views of the Xiao and Xiang* by Sōami. Detail of one of 23 sliding door panels in Muqi style. 1509.

Like an emotive cloud, the expanding mist is free-form, rising, all enveloping. Sōami's composition is mid-way between the void-centred works of the Shūbun School, and the mass-centred works of the Sesshū School to follow. In his mastery of the Southern idiom with soft, pliant wash and minimal use of texture strokes, his wet, inky one-line tree trunks, and consummate use of ink-wash in the evanescent mists, we see in this earliest example of *nanga* or Southern-style landscape created in Japan, one of the master-pieces of Japanese ink painting of all time.

Decorated space served a peculiar social function in Japanese secular and monastic architecture. Wrapping a room up as it were in an enlarged handscroll painting of landscape of various types by way of all-around *fusuma* panel paintings, each entire room exuded a particular mood which suited a particular class of visitor or activity. In monastic architecture which used mostly landscapes (sometimes reflecting the actual pond-scapes outdoors), ranking of the space was conditioned by the formality of the painting style, or the strictness with which four-season paintings conformed in their situation. This had to do with the relative cost of producing each room, where the more elaborate styles required longer hours and more pay for the artisans. A room painted in the Chinese academic Ma-Xia style was equated with the formal script in calligraphy, the Muqi-style with semi-cursive and the Yujian style with the cursive script; thus *shin*, *gyō*, *sō*-styled rooms were ranked in decreasing formality. Four-season panel paintings showed Winter and Summer to the north and south respectively, Spring and Autumn to the east and west respectively, thus according the whole space with a veritable feeling of the seasons' progression. Rooms less strictly or less completely adhering to scheme were assigned less formal status. Thus rooms were known as 'Bird and Flower Room', 'Xia Gui-style Eight Views Room', 'Sun Junze-style Room' etc., by the title of the paintings that dominated them. Most expensive was the *goshō no ma* for receiving military leaders or aristocrats, which was sumptuously fitted with colourful 'Flower and Bird' painting.

The client supervised the construction, and decided on the nature of each space and the manner in which it was to be decorated. Here budgetary considerations entered, affecting the degree of lavishness each space was assigned. The painters like the carpenters, were paid by the day; the most elaborate paintings required the largest number of working days, making the room the most expensive, the most valued, and hence reserved for the most honoured. Consequently, clients ordered the most laborious painting styles for the most important rooms.

But with the sixteenth century came a gradual change in evaluation of relative merits among artists, where famous masters were paid far more per day than their apprentices, thus spurring a new evaluation of room-design and function.

Portraiture, meanwhile, continued to be vigorously realistic. The great Zen master, Ikkyū Sōjun (1394–1481), was of royal birth and began Buddhist studies as a boy. He attained advanced spiritual learning, and refused the abbacy of the Daitokuji because of its administrative corruption. In this portrait by Bokusai, painted during his lifetime, he is depicted with economy of line and great sensitivity. Bokusai highlights the worn, thoughtful face and, in particular, the Master's penetrating mind. 92

The intense cultural activities of Kyoto were not lost on provincial rulers, *daimyō*, and the later fifteenth century saw the growth of regional patronage and art collections. The greatest master of Japanese ink landscape, Sesshū Tōyō (1420–1506) came

92. Portrait of Zen master Ikkyū Sōjun by Bokusai. Hanging scroll; ink, colours on paper. Before 1481.

from this regional tradition. Having studied Zen painting at the Shōkokuji in Kyoto under Shūbun, he founded the Unkoku-an studio in Yamaguchi at the south-western tip of Japan's main island, close to the Chinese trade route. From 1467 to 1469, he accompanied a trade mission to China, where he plunged into activity, painting large works for hanging on the walls of the examination hall in Peking, visiting monasteries and directly experiencing Ming academic painting. This exposure to the massiveness, solidity and relative self-sufficiency of Chinese painting *in situ* profoundly altered Sesshū's own vision. On his return to Japan, he replaced the spatial ambiguity and inconsistencies of scale which had characterized the poetic Shūbun style with a substantive, rational order. In a very late work, however, paying tribute to his Japanese teacher, he nostalgically returned to traditional Shūbun motifs. But the focus of the work has moved from empty space to solid masses. The dominant feature is the central mountain. The viewer's response is no longer to drift in reverie but to follow the measured steps of the travellers. They wend their way from the stone path, lower left, around the foreground boulder, past pavilions tucked beneath the road, to the rocky promontory and pavilion on the left where they will gaze past the jutting peaks on to the lake. However, the twin pines which used to enfold Shūbun's space now obliterate the lake expanse with their central

93

position and assertive, upward surge. By the time of this work Sesshū had already startled the world with his virile granite forms (such as the famous *Autumn* and *Winter* landscapes) in his personal version of the Xia Gui style, the explosive renditions of the splattered ink landscape works after Yujian (*fl.* thirteenth century), in all re-working the Song-Yuan repertoires with new virility and coherence.

Sesshū's legacy flourished in various styles. His favourite pupil at the Unkoku-an was Sōen (*fl.* 1489–1500), who received the master's famous *haboku* (splattered ink) landscape as certificate of his proficiency in the style. In Sōen's own *haboku* landscape the handling of brushwork and ink is far closer to Sesshū than to Shūbun or the original Southern Song master Yujian. More poetic than Sesshū's work, the organization of space is nevertheless dominated by mass and motion. The mist-engirdled central range twists into the picture plane in an S-curve, while an arrow-straight boat heads for the centre from the left, and a firm plank bridge brings in (potential) motion from the right. All forces converge at the central foreground in a dynamic thrust of jet black strokes. This Ming 'behaviour' is in direct contrast to the dispersing nature of Yuan-based Shūbun School works.

Another follower of Sesshū, Tōshun (*fl.* 1506–42), echoes the master's sense of turbulence in a splattered ink version of Yujian's views of the *Xiao and Xiang*. Instead of the Southern Song master's inwardness and quiescence, Tōshun's work verges toward Sesshū's in both brush-technique and expression. The snow mountain on the left is reserved in white, while a waterfall flows from a crevice over snow-covered rocks. A wintry gale is blowing

94

95

93. (*left*) *Landscape* by Sesshū Tōyō, inscribed by Ryōan Keigo in 1507. Hanging scroll; ink and light colours on paper. Early 16th century.

94. (*above*) *Haboku* landscape by Sōen. Ink on paper. Late 15th or early 16th century.

95. (*right*) *Evening Snow* from *Eight Views of the Xiao and Xiang* by Tōshun. One of eight hanging scrolls; ink on paper. Early 16th century.

96. *Hawk on Pine* by Sesson Shūkei. One of a pair of hanging scrolls; ink on paper. Mid-16th century.

97. *Dry Landscape* garden in Ryōanji, Kyoto, constructed in the 1480s.

snow towards the mountain across a darkening sky. No poetic contemplation here where mass and motion rule.

With the waning of Ashikaga fortunes and the rising restlessness of regional rulers, art works of the later fifteenth century charge the sense of motion with a foreboding of violence, and increasingly reflect an autocratic mien. Sesson Shūkei (c. 1504–89) was active largely in north-eastern Japan; his famous *Hawk on Pine* perfectly captures the aggressive mood of the time. Done in rapid ink strokes, the work centres on the bird of prey; bristling tension galvanizes the entire space down to the last pine needle. In a late work, *Landscape in Wind*, Sesson depicts a solid world in turmoil. His mature style is brilliant in its total fusion of modelling strokes (which had erstwhile merely adhered) to the forms. His remarkable integration of description with expression reveals a new, idiosyncratic vocabulary of volatile forms where rocks resemble solid projectiles that pierce the space with new violence. Here a startling contrast of stillness and motion, perhaps of peace and war, is evoked by the juxtaposition of the moonlit islet jutting from tranquil waters on the left, with the mighty central rocks whose energy charges at gale force, bending the trees and grasses and virtually dissolving the mass in the process. The fisherman seems incongruous, quietly angling in all the commotion.

The *Dry Landscape* garden in Ryōanji, Kyoto, though a monument to stillness, sums up all the artistic tensions of the

98. *Landscape in Wind* by Sesson Shūkei. Hanging scroll; ink on paper. Late 16th century.

Muromachi age. This Zen garden, framed by a wall and meant to be viewed from the veranda of the adjoining building, creates a seascape using only rocks (for mountains) and white pebbles (sea). Seventeen rocks are arranged in five groups amidst the raked (wavy) pebbles to produce maximum visual tension. Viewed from the entrance, the largest group is in the foreground while the others decrease in size as they increase in distance: in a brilliant use of built-in perspective the modest space thus organized appears far larger. To change the position of a single rock would dissipate the pulsing psychological energy. This supreme statement of reality/illusion has been the despair of successive generations of garden masters who have tried in vain to repeat the effect in other settings, and has remained a major challenge for scholars of the history of Japanese gardens.

Chapter 6: Azuchi-Momoyama and Edo (1576–1868)

Castle murals

In 1576, Oda Nobunaga (1534–82) seized control of Japan, and
made Azuchi into a stronghold centred on a walled castle, the
whole completed in 1579. (In these times, many ambitious men
built fortified castles on enormous stone ramparts, their stone
walls pierced by tiny musket apertures and crossed with massive
timbers.) Interior walls of the Azuchi castle were decorated by
members of the prolific studio led by the Kanō atelier of professional painters, among them Kanō Eitoku (1543–90). Completion
of the Azuchi castle marks the start of the Azuchi-Momoyama
period, named after the castle-towns of the contending warlords.

The Kanō painters had been in the service of the Shōgun for
several generations, and by the Edo period were creating the official style for the Tokugawa shōgunate. Although most of the great
castles have now long been destroyed, Kanō Eitoku's work can
still be seen in monasteries such as the Jukōin sub-temple of
Daitokuji in Kyoto. The sliding door panels *Pine and Crane* display   99
the young artist's virtuosity in brushwork, in the handling of
form; they also demonstrate the ebullience and martial vigour
characteristic of the age. Eitoku transforms the Southern style
of Muqi (once so perfectly japanized by Sōami) using Northern
academy style handling that converts soft modelling strokes and
gentle moss dots into bristling, angular configurations of rocky
shores and massive craggy pines that electrify the space. The
crackling tension is virtually audible. His hoary, overarching
forms fill the large sliding doors and extend implicitly beyond
them.

The small windows of castles such as Himeji engendered gold-   100
ground screen painting to reflect light into the dark rooms: entire
walls and ceilings were glowing, decorated in this way. Kanō
masters spent much time creating imposing, heroic designs in
impasto, such as the magnificent *Great Pine* murals. These are by   103
the hand, or school, of Kanō Tanyū (1602–74). Room after room,
hall after hall, was decorated with paintings of Chinese curly-
maned lions, Zen dragons and tigers, the four seasons, moored

99. *Pine and Crane* by Kanō Eitoku. Sliding door panels; ink on paper. 1566.

boats and curved bridges, gardens and peonies, all executed in encrusted pigments and lavishly finished in gold foil. To convince the masses that he was there to stay, Toyotami Hideyoshi (1537–98), the new warlord, exploited every means of self-aggrandizement: on one occasion he threw a tea party, lasting several days, with no less than five thousand guests, flaunting the traditional Way of Tea, the quintessence of which was minimalism, *wabi* or rusticity, and contemplation.

The Japanese art of mural decoration is deeply rooted in tradition. Professional painting on a large scale had begun in the early eighth century with the decoration of Hōryūji. Heian domestic architecture included many large paintings on screens which functioned as movable walls and which became a firmly established interior feature with the invention of the sliding door (*fusuma*). Almost nothing of these early works remains apart from a few landscape screens and, if it had not been for the meticulous detail of interior scenes depicted in narrative hand scrolls surviving from each century, the modern viewer could suppose that mural painting was a late phenomenon in Japan.

Momoyama wall coverings were sumptuous paintings of flowers, landscapes or figures upon gold foil walls or sliding doors. In *White Peonies* by Kanō Sanraku (1559–1635), even the petals and

101

leaves show the characteristic glitter, ostentation and extroversion of the age.

One of the most remarkable painters of the Edo period was Kanō Tanyū, grandson of Eitoku. He worked in both Edo and Kyoto and produced paintings for the imperial palace and for the Shōgun's castle in Nagoya. The green and gold pines in Nijō castle in Kyoto are generally thought to be his work. In 1636 he painted *Legends of the Toshōgū Shrine* at Nikkō, handling the delicate Tosa hand scroll style with ease. Tanyū helped reinvigorate the court-favoured Tosa tradition which was then on the point of dissolution from a half millennium's recycling of the same motifs.

Tanyū's insatiable interest in all manners of painting, whether Chinese or Japanese, resulted in the first collection of art-historical records of works he had seen. Scroll after scroll contains concise notes and reduced sketches (*shukuzu*) which not only reproduce general outlines but also accurately reflect the original brushwork. This tradition of recording works was continued by Tanyū's followers and 'Kanō *shukuzu*' are an invaluable resource for art historians today.

In the mural *Night Fishing with Cormorants* Tanyū casts a keen 102 and sympathetic eye over his contemporary world. It is night and

101. *White Peonies* by Kanō Sanraku. Detail of sliding door panels; colours and *impasto* on gold foil. Early 17th century.

the scene is lit by torches from boats forming a semicircle in the bay. A rich merchant, top left, sits enjoying the lively scene of rippling water, diving cormorants and busy fishermen, while an elder regales him with stories. The interest in this scene is in the diverse poses of this activity; the surrounding rocks and reeds are sketched economically, in gentle hues, in contrast to Tanyū's usually more formal style.

Tanyū's incomparable visual experience comes from easy access to imperial and shōgunal collections of ancient and contemporary works, both Chinese and Japanese. As their study-sketches

102. *Night Fishing with Cormorants* by Kanō Tanyū. Six-fold screen. Mid-17th century.

103. *Great Pine* murals (detail), Nijō castle, Kyoto. School of Kanō Tanyū. 1624–26.

104. *Landscape with Sun and Moon*, anonymous, Tosa school. Right-hand screen (detail) of double six-fold screen; ink, colours and gold on paper. Mid-16th century.

of works included those by Chinese masters of the Southern *literati* School, he and his followers could have produced works in this idiom had they wished, but the orthodox shōgunal style had long been set either in the formal four-square Ma-Xia idiom or in the nearly brushless, abbreviated Yujian style in ink wash.

Meanwhile a lively native movement had been developing among the aristocracy and upper merchant class (*machishū*) during the fifteenth and sixteenth centuries. Town painters, anonymous screen decorators of the late Muromachi period were producing great numbers of large-format landscapes based on

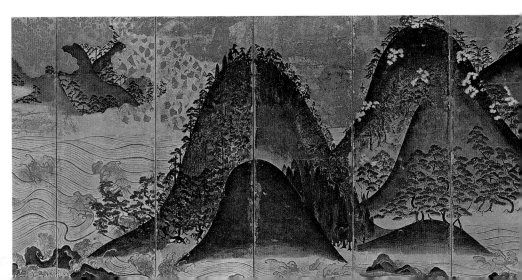

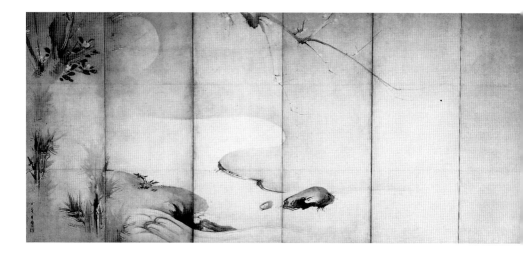

105. *Pine and Plum by Moonlight* by Kaihō Yūshō. Pair of six-panel screens; ink and light colour on paper. Late 16th century.

Yamato-e painting. The subjects included the eternal Japanese themes: famous places with poetic associations, the four seasons, pines, reeds and boats. Anonymous sun and moon screens with rounded mountain isles are among the most remarkable works of all time. In an unsigned work of the Tosa School, for example, the four seasons are worked into a unified screen format with the winter scene appearing third in the sequence. On the right, a full, noon sun, golden over tall, round mountains bright with spring blooms, is the favoured opening. The second group of mountains is shown in summer; at their feet the waves are turbulent. In the third section, the snow-covered folds of hills are contoured to balance the misty autumnal mountains further left. This layering of mountains in a frontal manner, an old *Yamato-e* device harks back to Pure Land landscapes like the thirteenth-century *Yamagoshi Amida*. Eighteenth-century Japanese theorists called this Japan's own blue-green landscape style. It had always survived in both monastic and secular painting, in spite of all the periods of Chinese dominance, and must be numbered as an 'essential' Japanese image.

Evocative screen painting
Tawaraya Sōtatsu (who died in ?1643), the greatest master of evocative screen painting, was bred in this delicate, archaizing tradition. Sōtatsu created innovative variations on the centuries-old themes. The *Matsushima* screens in the Freer Gallery, Washington DC, are among his most striking works. This compelling image of a turbulent sea crashing on to small, pine-covered

104

56

106

146

islets may be a view of Ise, home of Japan's imperial shrine. However, Sōtatsu's rendition is less a rearrangement of well-worn forms than a completely new perception of their latent possibilities.

The theme of waves, rocks and pines had long been treated expertly. The favourite Muromachi arrangement was to align the pine-topped rocks along the foreground, leaving the upper two-thirds of the painting surface for the waves, interspersed by two or more protruding rocks. Sōtatsu's arrangement, three rocky isles and three sandy shoals across two screens, dramatically exploits these Heian motifs. Here, however, each element is seen from a different perspective. The largest rocky islet, which leads in from the right, is seen from an elevated vantage point, while the second and third islets, in diminution, are shown from increasingly lower perspectives where the middle one is seen frontally. The left-hand screen shows three sandbanks, the largest one on a flat, gold ground, extending into the right-hand screen, where it changes into a cloud. On the left-hand screen it is in fact shown from directly overhead and its two giant pines are laterally spread in a bird's eye perspective. Above and below, two shrub-covered sandy islands are depicted in an unprecedented mixture of ink, gold and silver paste. These islands too, seen from overhead, appear at the same time like floating clouds. Once drawn into the picture, the viewer is taken on a somersault flight proceeding from the right where we dive into the waves but are then in the left screen hurled skyward over the beaches. We dive and soar, literally like the playful plover (*namichidori*) conspicuously absent

106. *Matsushima (Pine Island)* by Tawaraya Sōtatsu. Double six-panel screen; ink and colours on gold paper. Early 17th century.

here but kinesthetically implied. The waves are rendered throughout from the same 45-degree elevation; their whirlpools and rushing crests are in stark contrast to the stillness of the rocks and trees.

Inkwash screen painting

Japanese artists had long struggled with uses of inkwash to render atmospheric mist in fine gradations, and the use of long, curving lines over a large area. The Azuchi-Momoyama period saw the final triumph over this latest of Chinese artistic imports in the thorough japanization of ink monochrome painting. Artists now covered entire palace and monastery walls with continuous screen

107. *Pine Forest* by Hasegawa Tōhaku. Pair of six-panel screens; ink on paper. Late 16th century.

painting, as if wrapping the halls in giant hand scrolls. It was a common practice for rooms to be surrounded by lake-views like the *Eight Views of the Xiao and Xiang*, by giant trees, magnificent flowers, or by stormy seas.

91

Pine and Plum by Moonlight is a superb example of the late style of Kaihō Yūshō (1533–1615), an outstanding artist of the age. Twin curving streams emerge from the thick mists which function as emotive clouds creating an evocative, expansive space. Pine and prunus trees flank the moonlit scene; half hidden by mist and branches, some dandelions and spring grasses can just be seen. In spite of the economy of line and the abbreviated rendering of forms, unctuous brushwork gives the scene a striking, almost

105

Opposite

108. *Myōkian*, tea house by Sen no Rikyū, 1582. Embedded stones lead to the entrance and the windows are framed by bamboo and wistaria.

109. *Tai-an* tea room of *Myōkian* tea house. (Notice recessed *tokonoma* alcove.)

110. *Katsujishi*, *raku* ware tea bowl by Tanaka Chōjirō. Black slip glaze. H. 8.8, diam. 10.9 cm. 16th century.

tactile reality. *Pine and Plum by Moonlight* is not only an eclectic synthesis of *Yamato-e* and *Rimpa* styles (see below) but an original masterpiece.

Perhaps the most extraordinary mastery of the ink monochrome idiom is the double six-fold screen *Pine Forest* by Hasegawa Tōhaku (1539–1610), most of whose surviving works are of the colours-on-gold genre of the Kanō school. Having made extensive studies of the style of the Song master, Muqi, and particularly of his paintings of monkeys and cranes now in the Daitokuji, Tōhaku achieves in his *Pine* screens a superb synthesis of Chinese media and techniques with Japanese expression. Four groups of beach pines, *hamamatsu*, are placed across the twelve panels. Nearly eighty-five per cent of the painting surface is left blank and yet the entire screen is suffused with a sense of the mists and stillness of an autumn dawn. Whereas *Yamato-e* painters usually showed the pines in twisting, curving forms, Tōhaku shows them tall and gaunt, using a straw brush on thin, coarse paper, varying the intensity of his ink from faint to dark in swift, sure strokes. Although of the period of jousting warlords, the spirit here is of the Way of Tea, the new medium for contemplation which formed such a striking contrast to the gaudy splendour of the feudal court.

The Way of Tea

Perhaps to balance this extravagance, Hideyoshi engaged as his mentor the most distinguished tea-master of the wealthy Sakai merchant class, Sen no Rikyū (1521–91). Rikyū's spartan views on the Way of Tea have since had a profound influence on both 'tea architecture' and on Japanese aesthetics as a whole.

Drinking tea in quiet surroundings had been instituted by the fifteenth-century tea-master Shukō in the time of the aesthete Shōgun Yoshimasa. He invented the ceremony of tea as an art form to be enjoyed in a small room specially designed for it, containing selected 'tea' paintings, calligraphy scrolls or Chinese celadons. Sen no Rikyū eschewed the jade-like perfection of the Chinese porcelains and favoured a rough-textured and irregular ware first discovered in Korean peasant kilns. He promoted spiritual ideals of 'harmony, respect, purity and tranquillity' and in 1582 built his tea room, the Tai-an, in a hut in his native Yamazaki. This small and rustic cedar structure is based on a complex synthesis of asymmetric and irregular forms, with rough-textured earthen walls, unpolished, exposed beams, a cedar-board covered ceiling of two levels and papered windows of singular shapes set at different heights. The guest was invited to leave his worldly con-

cerns outside with his sword, to crawl into the tea house by the waist-high wriggling-in-opening (*nigiri guchi*), and to enter the warm, dark and intimate atmosphere within. In this timeless world, friends commune, collected, at ease and in close proximity where the tea master's every move becomes one's own. In a recessed alcove, the host might choose to focus attention on a specially treasured art work or on an allusive floral arrangement to induce 'spiritual one-pointedness'. To this day tea men maintain that it is a unique aesthetic experience which integrates the spirit of Zen, the beauty of art and of mundane things.

109

For his tea bowls, Rikyū commissioned the tile maker Chōjirō (1516–92) to produce *raku* ware. His rejection of Song celadons and fine porcelains in favour of simple peasant earthen and stoneware produced the aesthetic that Okakura Tenshin has termed 'Japan's worship of the imperfect'. The irregular glaze, shape and decoration of *raku* was intended to echo the asymmetry of the teahouse as a whole; it was also felt that dazzling decoration on pottery would break the contemplative mood. Chōjirō's celebrated tea bowl *Katsujishi* is typical. It has a straight edge but an irregular mouth and foot, tapers slightly at the sides and rises upwards from the base to allow a clear view of the foot-rim. The entire bowl is covered in a dull matt black slip of irregular density, permitting

110

111. Yōmei-mon (Sunlight Gate),
Tōshōgū in Nikkō. Early 17th
century.

the body's buff colour to lighten the tone in certain areas and to
highlight its rough, pitted quality.

Although the smallness of Rikyū's Tai-an tea room did not
have lasting influence, the *sukiya* style of architecture based on its
aesthetic developed into a major tradition which eventually
extended to domestic architecture, with or without a teahouse.
Like *onna-e* painting, *onnade* calligraphy and *waka* poetry, the tea-
house was a personal art form, catering to the intense Japanese
need for the preservation of the private self as distinct from the
public face. Both demand expression in art forms as in life styles.
(Hideyoshi himself reflects the extremes. At one moment he
would indulge in public displays of wealth and in the next he
would crawl humbly into the darkness and intimacy of Rikyū's tea
house.)

The contrast between public and private architecture is

nowhere better seen than in the ostentatious vulgarity of the shōgunal Nikkō Tōshōgū on the one hand and the pure taste of the detached imperial villa *Katsura* on the other. Both date from the seventeenth century. The first Tokugawa Shōgun ordered a family shrine-mausoleum to be constructed in mountainous Nikkō. Every surface of this monumental project is lavishly decorated in painted relief or in lacquer and gold work. By contrast, the aristocracy having rarely felt the need for self-assertion, Prince Hachijō Toshihito and his son Noritada created in the *Katsura* imperial villa an idealized private world: cedar-roofed buildings, ponds and a garden to be walked in and enjoyed from different vantage-points at different seasons. Like the Tai-an, structural elements are exposed but never lacquered, echoing the effect of rusticity and airiness which integrates the interior and exterior space. Critics have suggested that the continual stressing of rusticity and creative innovation (*sakui*) of tea men sometimes itself borders on artifice. But in works such as this villa, it is clear that even when such effort is discernible it is directed away from showy confrontation and towards harmonious union.

111
112

112. *Katsura*, villa and garden of Prince Hachijō Toshihito. 1642.

External influences and the arts

The Ōnin wars (1467–77) ended Ashikaga power and the subsequent decades of civil strife saw the emergence of several dictator-warlords. During the same period, a new merchant class arose whose fortunes lay in brewing and money lending in Kyoto. This rising upper merchant class (*machishū*) and the increasingly impoverished aristocracy (*kuge*) converged on similar political interests. The crude and often violent methods of the provincial military upstarts provoked resistance among those who had hitherto enjoyed luxury and freedom. The aristocracy often depended on the *machishū* to bail them out of financial difficulties and the latter, through frequent contacts with the court, soon developed similar cultural preferences.

Oda Nobunaga, who destroyed the Muromachi *bakufu* in 1573 and burnt down northern Kyoto as a reprisal for alleged insubordination, was assassinated in 1582 and his successor, Hideyoshi, took over control of foreign trade which had spawned Japanese mercantile colonies in Manila, Siam, and other ports of Southeast Asia. Hideyoshi exacted punishing levies to finance his disastrous Korean campaigns of 1592 and 1597. He died in 1598 and his remaining forces were vanquished by Tokugawa Ieyasu who instituted a central government in Edo (Tokyo). Ieyasu eventually gained complete control and subjected all potential rivals to severe regulations. The most effective of these was a system of hostages and attendance at the Shōgun's court in Edo, where the families of all the *daimyō* (provincial feudal lords) had to live, while the *daimyō* themselves spent alternate years in Edo and their own domains. In time the *daimyō* began to vie with each other for bigger and more splendid mansions in Edo; this rivalry kept their economic strength in check and stimulated a diverse and lively phase of artistic production in the new capital.

Contact with Europeans also affected Japanese culture at this time. By 1580 there were over 150,000 Christians in Japan and double that number fifty years later. European traders were quick to follow the Christian missionaries. Portuguese traders came to western Kyūshū by 1543 and were followed in 1593 by Spanish Franciscans. Protestant Dutch set up their trading post in Hirado in 1609 and were joined by the English in 1613. The Protestants convinced Ieyasu that foreign trade did not depend on missionaries, and that allegiance to God above all posed a potential threat. By 1617 the Christian faith had become so strongly rooted that Ieyasu banned it on penalty of death. Tokugawa Iemitsu expelled the Spanish and the Portuguese and in 1636 decreed that no

Japanese was to leave the country and no 'foreigners', not even the thousands of Japanese colonials then living abroad, were to set foot on Japanese soil. This left Japan's foreign trade to Chinese and Dutch ships, which were allowed to dock at Nagasaki and its small island of Dejima respectively. Despite this isolationist policy, foreign trade with China, Korea and Southeast Asia flourished. Korean trade was conducted by the Sō clan, lords of Tsūshima. The Chinese trade remained in the hands of Ming loyalists sailing from resistance centres in Fujian, and until the 1680s, decades after the Manchu conquest of China, the Tokugawa court held debates on the loyalists' request for military aid in arms and in personnel.

However, once passion for western knowledge, or 'Dutch learning', had been fired it could not be extinguished. In spite of Japan's politically isolationist stand, European trade continued under Dutch auspices. Astronomy, medicine, the natural sciences and foreign languages were eagerly studied. In the arts, perspective drawing and life sketches of flora and fauna became permanently established. Oil painting, which began with the copying of Christian icons, was also practised. A novelty for the Japanese painter was the faithful but often exaggerated portrayal of 'Southern Barbarians' (*Namban*). The Europeans, with their curious, waisted garments and plumed head gear, their sharply chiselled features and curly hair, were portrayed with a keen eye for detail. Their enormous galleons were of special interest. European textile patterns, fabrics and colour schemes found their way into Japan inspiring the brilliant and innovative ceramics of Furuta Oribe and his followers in stunning examples of artistic assimilation.

Flowering of wabi-cha rustic teaware

During Hideyoshi's Korean campaigns, the Way of Tea spread rapidly and *daimyō* in western Japan soon discovered the artless simplicity of Korean pottery and its suitability for the teahouse. Many Korean potters were invited, even abducted, by western lords to set up kilns in various parts of Kyūshū. This artistic immigration led to a dramatic flowering of Japanese tea ceramics, with protracted influences that can still be seen today in Europe and North America.

Tea ceremonies also became popular among the new middle class (*machishū*) in major manufacturing and commercial centres such as Sakai, Kyoto and Hakata. Fresh ceramic styles such as Shino, Oribe and Yellow Seto vied with the original Kamakura

113. *Namban* (Southern Barbarians) screen. Part of six-fold screen; colours on paper, *c.* 1600.

Seto wares, and kilns gradually shifted from Seto in Owari to Mino further west. The warm, cream-white-bodied Shino ware, usually covered with a rich feldspathic glaze, often with simple under-glaze designs in iron slip, is typical of the Momoyama period. The rosy tone of the body glows from beneath the glaze. This heavily potted, thickly glazed ware is still highly regarded for the simplicity of its decoration and the evocative sense of vulnerability and imperfection. The water-jar *Kogan* (Ancient Shore) is hand-crafted in generous proportions and decorated with the childlike rusticity of native potters: three reeds and criss-cross grasses are swiftly but confidently brushed on, and the bottom of the foot-rim is tooled with a sharp knife. It is prized for the cracks and glaze-imperfections which enhance nostalgia for distant antiquity. In another, later type of Shino ware, a grey-toned (*nezumi*) vessel was first covered with a high iron slip, parts of which were scraped off to reveal the cream-buff body. Then the rich Shino glaze was applied and the pot was fired in a reduction kiln which turned the underlying iron to a dark mouse-grey.

114

115

Bizen ware is rich, reddish-brown and unglazed. After the scratching and gouging, the potter allowed natural ash to drift over parts of the inverted mouth and slouching body. Asymmetrical ear-handle loops were added, and indentations caused when removing the freshly potted vase from its wheel were left uncorrected. These details, partly natural and partly devised for the much admired effect of creative ingenuity (*sakui*), were greatly prized by tea masters.

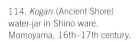

114. *Kogan* (Ancient Shore) water-jar in Shino ware. Momoyama, 16th–17th century.

115. Small dish in *nezumi* Shino glaze. Momoyama, 16th–17th century.

116. Iga ware, *Yabure-Bukuro* (Torn Pouch), water-jar. Momoyama, 16th–17th century.

Iga ware is thickly glazed with deep cracks and a rough texture. The Momoyama water-jar *Yabure-Bukuro* (Torn Pouch) is 116 typical. The coarse clay contained quartz particles which made it difficult to handle on the wheel, so Iga wares were often hand-coiled. When it was fired, the quartz particles came to the surface and, with the flying wood ash swirling in the kiln, fused into a blue-grey glaze with scorched and greenish spots. Since the late twentieth century it has been easy to accept such pots as 'art objects'. Indeed, contemporary ceramic art around the world is still deeply influenced by Bernard Leach's discovery and emulation of Japanese folk pottery. With complete freedom, the Japanese folk potter prizes expression above technique. Through his wares, Western ceramists learned to transcend the geometric concept of form, and plane-oriented decoration – a major breakthrough in Western pottery design.

At the same time as Bizen and other major tea-ware kilns flourished, Korean artisans were introducing technical innovations such as the climbing kiln and high-fired porcelains. These lustrous, thin, white porcelains with under-glaze blue-line designs were shipped from the port of Imari, hence the generic name 'Imari ware'. In 1616, the Korean potter Ri Sampei eventually found white potting clay in Arita where he built his first linked-chamber climbing kiln. In Europe, Korean and Chinese porcelains were highly prized and were imported in large quantities. The *daimyō* were naturally keen to reproduce such wares locally and many kilns for porcelain were built. By the Genroku era (1688–1704) continental porcelain decoration had been replaced by Japanese motifs.

In 1628 the official kiln of the Nabeshima domain was founded to raise standards and ensure clan control of the proceeds. By 1635 the kiln site had been removed to Ōkawachiyama where the finest Nabeshima ware emerged including plates, bowls, side-dishes and 117 *sake* decanters. Well-centred and fine-bodied, their inner surfaces are smooth and their decoration, often echoing lacquer designs, features the newly mastered technique of filling the underglaze blue outlines in bright overglaze colours of green and yellow, together with an unusually attractive and subdued beige-tinted red. Later, a lovely pale aubergine was added to the palette. The designs treat the entire surface as one continuous ground unbroken by planes; overglaze enamels are carefully applied so as not to spill beyond the underglaze outlines beneath. One of Japan's authorities on ceramics, Mikami Tsugio, complains of Nabeshima ware that 'beauty itself became subordinate to the all-important

117. Nabeshima plate with design of flowering buckwheat. Overglaze enamels on porcelain. Early 19th century.

standard'. This is a typical Japanese observation, reflecting a preference for spontaneity and originality above technical perfection.

As Nabeshima wares flourished, so did their folk counterpart and predecessor in overglaze enamels, Old Imari, also in Arita. 118 These are unabashedly decorated in bright primary colours, often with the addition of gilt. In the southern tip of Kyūshū the Satsuma kilns produced a buff ware with a fine-crackled glaze and distinctive, colourful decorations often marked with gold bosses. During the second half of the seventeenth century, when China was too embroiled in war for trade, the Dutch East India Company turned to Kyūshū and promoted the export of Imari and Kakiemon wares, with their characteristic iron-red lip-rings, from the Arita area.

As well as in pots, Tokugawa foreign trade also dealt in lacquers and metalwork, often completely inlaid with intricate ivory or mother-of-pearl, in manners pleasing to the European eye. The Victoria and Albert Museum, London, for example, has a group of lacquered inlays, imported before the Hirado port was closed in 1623, which includes bowls, chests and other items specifically 121 made to western orders. Europeans enjoyed Japanese ceramics as much as Chinese wares, but developed a special fondness for

159

118. Old Imari *sake* bottle depicting Europeans. Edo, 17th century.

Japanese lacquers, called *japon* in France. The interplay of influences between European and Japanese craftsmen can be seen in European household furnishings and ceramics of this period.

Art of the Machishū

Japanese society enjoyed three centuries of peace and prosperity under the Tokugawa hegemony. Even before this, the nobility and upper merchant class were growing. It was this class which, in the late sixteenth century, had launched the last and most glorious effulgence of Japan's classical traditions.

Hon'ami Kōetsu (1558–1637) was from a distinguished family of sword connoisseurs well known among the wealthy patrician

119. *Fujisan, raku* ware tea bowl by Kōetsu. Momoyama, early 17th century.

120. *Kuro Oribe Chawan*, tea bowl by Furuta Oribe. Momoyama, 16th–17th century.

families in the imperial cultural circle. In 1615 Tokugawa Ieyasu, perhaps as a gesture of appeasement toward the *machishū*, granted Kōetsu a large tract of land in Takagamine, north-east of Kyoto. There Kōetsu established a colony of craftsmen of the Nichiren Buddhist school and inspired and directed the production of art works of unparalleled quality and diversity. Kōetsu had been educated in the Heian-oriented courtly arts and in the early fourteenth-century Shōrenin-style of royal calligraphy. He also studied the style of the fourth-century Chinese aristocratic Wang Xizhi and was himself judged one of the finest calligraphers of his day. He brought his genius to bear on lacquer, painting, gardens,

121. Lacquered wooden chest with floral inlay of mother-of-pearl and gold foil on paper. Early 17th century.

poetry, tea and ceramics: no form of art failed to benefit from his influence. He dazzled Kyoto society by publishing the tenth-century *Tale of Ise* and the twelfth-century *Hōjō-ki*, inscribed in his own elegant calligraphy on specially produced paper decorated with his own designs based on Heian ideals. He also published song-books from the Nō theatre: this too focussed cultural attention on the past.

Kōetsu's colony included not only artists but also paper-makers, lacquerers and brush-makers. These craftsmen, inspired by Kōetsu's guiding spirit, collaborated with the artists and with each other to produce works of a standard unmatched since Heian times. A fine example is the writing box called *Boat Bridge*, which contains inkstone, ink and brush. It is clearly inspired by Heian lacquers such as the twelfth-century *Waves and Wheel of Life*, with its gold and mother-of-pearl inlaid wave design interspersed with a wheel motif. Kōetsu added the common base metal, lead, to gold and silver – a striking innovation – laying it across the convex top and the sides in the form of a bridge, floating over the gold lacquer carved with boats in low relief. Although the box is nearly square, the decoration is entirely asymmetrical. Three boats bob up and down out of phase; the tiny raised-line waves lap in yet another rhythm and the bridge, which gives the box its name, is wrapped

122

123

122. *Boat Bridge*, writing box by Hon'ami Kōetsu. Inkstone case, lead and mother-of-pearl on gold lacquer. Early 17th century.

123. *Waves and Wheel of Life*. Lacquer handbox; gold and mother-of-pearl inlay. Heian, 12th century.

around the entire work at an angle. Balance is restored by Kōetsu's inscription of a *waka* poem, applied in high relief silver over the whole scene.

A man of tea, Kōetsu made many tea bowls. In *Fujisan*, doubtless by his own hand, he created the most superb Japanese *raku* tea bowl of all time. Its taut, straight sides taper slightly towards the bottom, the reddish body is covered entirely in a blackish matt slip with opaque white glaze over the upper half, leaving the darker glaze for the bottom: the effect produced by firing is that of gently falling snow. The vigour and grandeur of Mount Fuji are suggested. There is nothing of the cleverness or cuteness which are so often the downfall of tea bowl makers with too much zest for *sakui*. The impression is of monumentality. In tea ware such as this, Kōetsu echoed the simplicity and purity of Rikyū's time, following the forthright form produced by Chōjirō. His work was in stark contrast to that of his contemporary, Furuta Oribe (1543–1615) who had achieved a lively and remarkable synthesis of free-form *raku* ceramic style and Western patterns and colouring.

119

120

164

124. (opposite) *Lotus and Swimming Birds* by Sōtatsu. Hanging scroll; ink on paper. Momoyama, early 17th century.

125. *Flowers and Grasses of the Four Seasons* by Kōetsu (calligraphy) and Sōtatsu (painting). Detail of handscroll. Momoyama, early 17th century.

Kōetsu collaborated with the sensitive and skilled painter Sōtatsu (who never joined the Takagamine artistic colony but worked out of his Kyoto establishment which sold decorated paper and painted fans to the *machishū* and aristocracy). Sōtatsu produced beautiful designs for Kōetsu calligraphy paper in long handscrolls, fan shapes and square board *shikishi*. He applied them in silver and gold by hand and by woodblock impressions. Both masters were inspired by Heian *waka* inscriptions on decorated paper. In the example shown here, Sōtatsu, with a brush dipped alternately in gold and silver, has painted flowers and grasses of the four seasons in sequence. The ancient Chinese method of 'boneless' painting (without ink outlines) was given a new sense of liveliness by Sōtatsu who combined it with a pooling device called *tarashikomi*. This method of dropping ink or colour pigment on to still-wet areas of the painting surface may well have been invented by Sōtatsu. Here the silver flowers and golden leaves appear in different intensities, seeming to emerge from dense mists.

125

Kōetsu's calligraphy equally reflects classical preferences. Even on relatively unabsorbant paper he fully controls every stroke and dot. The inclusion of cursive Chinese characters among the *kana* syllabary echoes Sōtatsu's effect of leaves and flowers

among stems. Kōetsu alternates between thick and thin, large and small strokes, but the wrist pressure is steady, changing with the column rather than within single morph configurations. Kōetsu's calligraphy is more stately than Heian prototypes, carrying traces of the China-inspired symmetry of the Muromachi period, producing a synthesis of the two styles.

Sōtatsu's association with Kōetsu and *machishū* collectors, with their nostalgia for the art of the past, and his own contact with the finest Heian traditions in painting when he restored the *Heike Nōgyō* and other masterworks, led him to create a new world 61 of poetic imagery in an energetic revival and reinvigoration of Heian motifs. His school came to be known as *Rimpa*. This mode has often mistakenly been called decorative. If 'decorative' means 'serving to decorate' or 'purely ornamental', then we must say that there is hardly anything decorative in Japanese art at all, at least since Shōsōin days. Japanese artists seem incapable of static, purely visual, patternistic decoration. Be it lyrical, contemplative, dramatic or aggressive, nearly all Japanese art is united in one essence: emotion. It may be more appropriate to call the *Rimpa* style evocative.

Everything Sōtatsu created, whether fan and screen paintings, under-paintings for Kōetsu or his own ink monochrome works, such as the *Oxen* in the Chōmyōji in Kyoto, combines visual beauty with considerable emotional intensity. Vignettes taken from Chinese woodblock printed books are radically transformed and japanized. The elements in *Lotus and Swimming Birds* are so placed 124 as to share the space, not to divide it. The forms are not self-contained and permanent, each commanding its sphere; rather, they depend on and interact with each other. The psychological energy typical of Japanese forms is mostly turned outward. The use of watery ink in pooled *tarashikomi*, especially on the leaves, gives a sense of expansion and, as in the 'emotive cloud' device, creates an emotional quickening analogous to a blush or the sound of breathing. But the ebullience of the Momoyama period marks the works of Kōetsu and Sōtatsu with energy and immediacy, in contrast to the dreaminess of their Heian models.

About half a century after Kōetsu and Sōtatsu, the Ogata brothers Kōrin (1658–1716) and Kenzan (1663–1743) consolidated the *Rimpa* style. Their father had been a member of Kōetsu's artistic community and transmitted its spirit to his sons. Kenzan, 126, 127 the younger brother, was a calligrapher and ceramicist. He studied first with Ninsei, then with Kōetsu's grandson, Kūchū, and became a celebrated potter, combining the dignity and nobility of

126. Five small plates signed by Ogata Kenzan. White slip and rust glaze, decorated with grey and gold pigment. Edo, early 18th century.

127. *Waterfall* tea bowl by Kenzan. White slip glaze and rust painting. Early 18th century.

Kōetsu with the inventiveness of Oribe. A Zen Buddhist in his late twenties and thirties, Kenzan felt that beauty of things was seen as such, and had no place for *mono-no-aware* or other associative sentiments. His brushwork is weighty and disciplined, his style compelling and reserved.

If Kenzan was introvert, Kōrin was a determined extrovert. The two brothers lived in the boisterous Genroku period (1688–1704) which saw the eclipse of the *machishū* elite by the lower merchant classes (*chōnin*) and Kōrin entered drunkenly, sardonically into the spirit of the times. Once at a picnic, while the bourgeois displayed their elaborately lacquered gold and silver picnic boxes, Kōrin astounded them by unwrapping his food from plain bamboo leaves which turned out to be gold-foiled on the inside and which he proceeded to toss casually into the river. On another occasion, he engineered a beauty contest so that the winner was a beautiful woman plainly dressed in white with a black wrapper, while her attendant wore sumptuous colours.

Kōrin's work, in textile and lacquer design as well as painting, was notable for its urbane elegance. It is less a nostalgic recreation of Heian style than a deliberate display of virtuosity. Typical of his work at its flamboyant best are the *Red and White Prunus* screens in the Atami Museum, the *Waves* screens at the Metropolitan Museum, New York, and his copy of Sōtatsu's *Thunder and Lightning Gods*. In *Irises* he boldly covers a double six-fold screen with brilliant repetitions of a single motif: blue irises, green leaves. The four groups on the right, in inverted triangle formation, gently descend, while five unequal groups on the left-hand screen increase in size and height towards the left. The rest is gold-foil. There are no plank bridges, rippling waves, meandering earthen banks or emotive clouds: the work is hard-edged and uncompromising. Motion is created in the asymmetrical grouping and the repetition of the motif out-of-phase. It is here, and in his daring and unrelenting use of gold, blue and green that Kōrin displays his supreme self-confidence. Since Heian times, irises had been associated with the eight-fold plank bridge, *yatsu hashi*, zig-zagging over swamps, among wild flowers. In the Heian *Tale of Ise* the hero pauses by a stream banked with irises. Kōrin removed the bridge and the hero, reducing the image to the flowers alone. As Sōtatsu had turned his viewer into an aerobatic sea bird, so Kōrin turns us into the hero of the *Ise* tale, walking enchanted across the eight-planked bridge. By removing all external props, 'framework' or 'borders', both men plunge the viewer into the scene, and create a sense of dramatic immediacy and personal involvement.

128

Throughout his work, Kōrin took the asymmetry of Kōetsu and Sōtatsu to exaggerated extremes. His lacquer inkstone box, for example, uses gold, silver, mother-of-pearl and pewter in another reworking of the *yatsu hashi* bridge-and-iris theme. The bridge is inlaid with lead like Kōetsu's but the angle is steeper. Similarly, in studies of flying cranes, Kōrin's fly upwards at a much sharper angle than those of Kōetsu or Sōtatsu. This tendency to sharpen the angle and to tilt the ground up towards the vertical plane, also present in Kōrin's landscapes, is particularly dramatic in his *Red and White Prunus*. 130

Kōrin's watercolour sketches are quite distinct from the stylish glitter of his other works. *Flowers and Grasses* for example, which probably dates from 1705 when he first went to live in Edo, is relaxed and intimate. He outlines the blue and white flower petals with a fluid, evocative calligraphic brush and the leaves and smaller flowers are 'boneless' and further softened by the use of *tarashikomi*. 129

Textiles

By the middle of the seventeenth century Japan's own silk industry was established, bringing an end to reliance on Chinese imports. The richness of fabric production and variety of design proclaim a time of peace and prosperity.

The creation and decoration of Japanese garments, like ceramics or lacquers, were conceived as a single artistic activity where the design was integral to the garment. Clothes, with long or short but always broad sleeves, appeared in designs of stunning daring, seldom matched even in Paris fashion houses. A robe spread on a lacquer hanger might well be used as a room-divider, like an evocative screen. Crashing waves and diving plovers, a diagonal grouping of wisteria and chrysanthemum, even the aggressive hawk and dragon, are all typical patterns.

Momoyama and Edo artisans were masters of several techniques which included dyeing, embroidery, brocade, appliqué, raised gold-thread repoussé and hand-painting. The demand for innovation in textiles was insatiable, not only in Nō theatre and noble houses but also among the wealthy *machishū* and *chōnin*. This example is from a shōgunal household and shows the sophistication of these techniques; embroidery has been used to accent the flower-and-leaf shapes already created in the dyeing process and the peacock feather loops made of gold repoussé. Another striking robe, made for a courtesan, uses gold-foil for dramatic effect. It features a hawk and a dragon in action and is made of velvet, a 132

131

128. *Irises* by Ogata Kōrin.
Double six-fold screen; colours
and gold foil on paper. Early 18th
century.

129. *Flowers and Grasses* by
Kōrin. Handscroll; colours and
white pigment on paper.
c. 1705.

European fabric, whose novelty coupled with the remarkable design must have achieved the desired startling effect.

Humbler folk wore cottons and, occasionally, silks. They enjoyed a variety of designs with largely Southeast Asian (rather than continental) sources. The ancient Indonesian technique of *ikat* was often used to create bold designs. Cotton yarn was tied in sections and dyed indigo; the result was an alternation of white and indigo in the weaving. Warp or weft yarns, or both, could be partially dyed in this way. Warp-*ikat* fabrics are the most common;

weft-*ikat* is rarer and double-*ikat*, the most difficult to make, requires consummate skill. All three methods were common in Japan during the Edo period, and were called *kasuri*. Another technique with Southeast Asian origins is *batik* (resist-dye) which, using only dark and light indigo on white, nevertheless provided a great variety of designs for peasant wear. Humbler still are the banded and striped fabrics which combine cotton yarns of different colours in a straight weave. Home dyers also used a paste-resist method which seems to have been derived from

133

130. Inkstone box with *yatsu hashi* (eight-fold plank bridge); designed by Kōrin. Edo, 18th century.

131. *Hawk and Dragon*, courtesan's *kosode*. Gold on black velvet. Edo, early 19th century.

twelfth-century China. A mixture of boiled, glutinous rice and rice bran was applied through a tube or poured or stencilled on to the cloth, which was then dyed. The process could be repeated with several colours, giving a splendid polychrome effect. The Art Gallery of Greater Victoria in British Columbia, Canada, has some handsome examples of this folk art; clearly, a strong awareness of beauty and design was present in Japanese society at every level.

Nanga (Idealist painting)

In an effort to promote loyalty towards themselves, the Tokugawa shōgunate established Confucian centres of learning and produced a new class of esteemed but powerless Confucianists. And here, China's contagious love of its own past created something like an identity crisis among Japanese sinophiles. They found themselves yearning for what they had come to regard as the source of their civilization: ancient China. In painting, the ideal of the Chinese scholar-amateur-painter that had been spawned in the eleventh century and consolidated by the fourteenth was now introduced to Japan for the first time. The Japanese were appalled

132. Detail of peacock on *kosode* (short-sleeved robe). Gold thread repoussé and embroidery. Edo.

133. *Rooster and Flowering Tree*, cotton panel, originally a bedcover. Resist-dyed on an indigo ground and mounted as a double screen. Meiji, late 19th century.

that for seven hundred years they had been following the lesser tradition, and had missed the true essence of Chinese painting by pursuing the Northern styles of Southern Song and Ming academies rather than the free expression of lofty ideals represented in the *wenren* painting of Chinese scholar-amateurs.

In China, idealist painting was enjoyed by the leisured class as an activity of taste and cultivation. Originally such paintings incorporated poetry written in a distinguished hand and the works were meant for the private enjoyment of small groups of highly cultivated associates. Japan lacked a scholar-bureaucrat class, and idealist painting became an avenue for departure from traditions of various kinds: it was now taken up by discontented members of the *samurai* class, by the new breed of scholars, by monks, physicians, merchants and professional painters. Late Ming Chinese texts coined the term *Nanzong-hua* (Southern School painting); in Japan it was called *Nanga* (Southern painting) but soon became, like all Japanese arts and crafts, a commercially viable vehicle with its particular patrons. Geographical and technical features distinguish the Northern Academy (rocky peaks, angular brushwork) from the Southern Amateur (rounded hills; long, rope-like brush-strokes) traditions in China; in Japan, the Shūbun, Unkoko and Kanō schools had worked mostly in Northern styles, while Sōami's works alone were often of

134. *Pine Tree and Waves* by Ikeno Taiga. One of a double six-fold screen; light colours on paper. *c.* 1765–70.

134. *Pine Tree and Waves* by Ikeno Taiga. One of a double six-fold screen; light colours on paper. *c.* 1765–70.

135. *Pine Tree at Karasaki* by Yosa Buson. Detail from handscroll. 1778.

Southern origin. But this schism was clearly not understood by Sōami or even by early Tokugawa theorists, and the distinction between the two schools was not fully appreciated till the end of the eighteenth century. The broadly curvilinear brush mode of the Li-Guo School that had been popular in late Northern Song and schematized in early Yuan, was transplanted via diplomatic couriers to Korea where it spawned the genesis of Korean idealist painting of the An Kyon School, whence it was carried forward to Japan. Traces of Korean idealist configurations abound in early experimental *Nanga*, but the Japanese themselves restricted their acknowledgement of inspiration to ancient Chinese masters who alone remained the iconic source of *Nanga*'s heritage.

Japanese painters in the new mode produced some curious hybrids drawn largely from a mixture of contemporary Chinese provincial imports. The Mampukuji monastery outside Kyoto, founded in 1661 under Tokugawa patronage, became the centre of Chinese culture in Japan, and its (largely Fujianese) clergy were granted access to Chinese imports and entirely Chinese lifestyles. Their artistic and utilitarian imports from strife-ridden China were avidly sought after by Japanese fanciers without regard to quality or stylistic origins. The professional painter Sakaki Hyakusen (1698–1753), however, drew upon works of higher calibre from late Ming Suzhou. But Ikeno Taiga (1723–1776) boldly

and radically transformed his models, even though his contact
with Chinese paintings and Japanese collectors was limited largely to the Mampukuji circle, as he did not have the access to the
imperial and shōgunal collections granted to official painters like
Kanō Tanyū. Tanyū's study of Chinese paintings was academic:
precise line copies and learned interpolations of ancient masterpieces in shōgunal and other collections. Taiga interpolated,
mixed and invented, and even produced manual-scrolls of
Southern School methods, playfully attributing Chinese names
without real basis. *Pine Tree and Waves*, done in his forties, displays   134
a thoroughly Japanese use of ink and brush, and transforms what
had been a rather stiff provincial Fujian manner into a comfortable
picture of an ancient tree at ease. The rendering is abbreviated,
with only traces of the Fujian models available to him in
Mampukuji (with notable circular bark strokes) and harmonizes
perfectly with foaming waves so familiar in traditional Japanese
art. By the time of this painting, Taiga had confidently absorbed
and transformed diverse Chinese painting techniques, but his own

vision speaks above them all. The mediocrity of his models was immaterial, as he selected only compositional motifs and technical innovations which interested him, but primarily gave full expression to his own creativity.

Taiga transformed the sedate and introspective Chinese scholar-amateur tradition into something evocative yet powerful, endowing the genre with luminosity and lyricism. A host of pupils and followers carried his vision forwards and made of *nanga* a viable tradition. The celebrated *haiku* poet Yosa Buson (1716–83), who enlivened his verse inscriptions with whimsical *haiga* illustrations, also painted in the newly fashionable manner. His *Pine Tree at Karasaki* was painted in 1778, two years after Taiga's death. Here the giant, ancient pine, resting on wooden supports, dwarfs the small house. The brush is charged with wet colour-wash to such an extent that the image seems flooded with unreal light, as if alluding to some unstated past. In contrast, Buson's calligraphy is crisp, fluid and assured, speaking of the present.

The *samurai* Uragami Gyokudō (1745–1820) served a branch of the Ikeda family until 1794 when, despondent over his wife's death and generally disillusioned, he resigned his post to take up *nanga* painting. His style is notable for its highly personal brushwork. James Cahill points out a resemblance to seventeenth-century Chinese painters who overlaid dry brush-strokes over wet, light strokes over dark, creating a tapestry effect. A critical and profound difference is that Gyokudō applied the stroke series in layers. Thus, a layer of horizontal modelling strokes might be

136
135

covered in turn by a layer of cross-hatching, a layer of wet dots, and a layer of dry black-ink scratches. The result is what had been depicted in Chinese paintings in depth, the strokes intertwining as in a nest and built up perpendicular to the painting surface, was in its Japanese transformation re-ordered along the picture plane, creating lateral tension between the elements; the method, often mis-identified as merely decorative, in fact achieves the visual clarity and luminosity beloved in Japan. A fine example is *High Winds and Banking Geese*, a work from Gyokudō's seventy-third year. The sedate Chinese archaic script in *sarabande*-like clerical *lishu* style, rendered with deliberate awkwardness, contrasts with the explosive energy of the swirling, cyclone-like brushwork. All motion is circular; mountains are reshaped into flying cylinders and rounded rocks. The geese and fishing-boats are incidental; the subject of the picture is energy, direct, raw and exhilarating. 137

Among the most original *nanga* masters is the painter and potter Aoki Mokubei (1767–1833) whose works in diverse media are

137. *High Winds and Banking Geese* by Uragami Gyokudō. Album leaf; ink and light colours on paper. 1817.

138. *Birthday Felicitations* by Aoki Mokubei. Hanging scroll; ink and light colours on satin. 1830.

139. *Sketches of Cicadas* (detail) by Maruyama Ōkyō, from his *Sketchbook of Insects*. Ink and light colours on paper. Mid-18th century.

marked with dynamic inner cohesion and a strong sense of inter-relatedness, both among the pictorial elements and between work and viewer. In *Birthday Felicitations* (1830), he celebrates a friend's seventieth birthday in a scene aglow with serenity and wellbeing. Painted on satin, the swirling mists (done in dry ink lines) suggest a cipher for a dragon, providing the gravity and mystery proper to the occasion. Psychological energy converges towards the centre (and the viewer), from the craggy pine of longevity on the right and from the left from the God of Longevity himself as he ambles towards the centre, followed by his child attendant with the para-sol of state. The focal point is the confluence of clouds, tree energy, dragon–cloud and long life beneath the mountain peak (placed left of centre to balance with the inscription on the upper right).

Diversification of schools

The long peace brought wealth, and its wider distribution brought more patrons, and more art. In Kyoto alone, besides the traditional styles of Tosa, Kanō, *Rimpa* and the newly-established *nanga*, yet another school appeared and was soon to dominate. Maruyama Ōkyō (1733–95) had studied with Kanō masters and then became interested in Western perspective and Chinese paint-ing: his style was a synthesis of all three traditions. Not the least of

his activities was to paint Japanese scenes for the newly-imported Chinese viewing-device, where a picture was reflected and magnified. In China, Suzhou artists had been producing woodblock prints with Western perspectives for such viewing boxes; Ōkyō supplied the demand for new and Japanese views. He also produced scrolls and large screens, combining a gold ground with majestic pines, peacocks on rocks in the Chinese academic style, or wisteria in Japanese-style colour wash. He investigated, in short, every available style, format and subject. He taught his pupils to sketch directly from nature, and produced some of his own most charming works in this genre.

Ōkyō was enthusiastically supported by a former pupil of Buson, Matsumura Goshun (1752–1811) and their combination of talents came to be known as the Maruyama-Shijō school. For a while it was lively and active but in the nineteenth century it declined into saccharine sentimentality.

The most individual of Ōkyō's pupils, Nagasawa Rosetsu (1754–99), possessed a vision which is as fresh and vital today as it must have seemed to his contemporaries. From a warrior family, he changed his name in order to paint rather than be subject to official positions. His first works were in the manner of Ōkyō, but after mastering Western techniques of perspective and *chiaroscuro*, he began to contribute to the eccentric and grotesque modes then fashionable. He worked in ink wash as well as in fine lines and colours, on silk and paper, painting everything from fans to murals. In four to five months in 1786, travelling through Kii, Rosetsu painted no less than 180 wall-panels and sliding doors for four separate monasteries. *The Itsukushima Shrine* from Rosetsu's *Eight Views of Miyajima* (1794) is a bird's-eye view rendered deftly in ink, sometimes very fine and dry, sometimes wet and diffused. The twisting covered walk and the main hall (with its stage-like front for performing sacred dances) rise on stilts from the sacred waters. It is twilight, and stone-and-paper lanterns have been lit to dispel the misty gloom descending upon the pine-clad isle.

Another great individualist was Itō Jakuchū (1716–1800). His works in colours and ink monochrome juxtapose barnyard fowl, vegetables, flowers and trees in elegant distortion, combining foreshortening and perspective techniques with a flat, highly chromatic use of ink and brilliant colours. He turned his animal paintings into still-lifes with a sharp wit, posturing the figures in an exaggerated manner, comically suggesting human behaviour. His strutting male and submissive female birds, for example, strike poses reminiscent of *ukiyo-e* actor prints. Jakuchū was

139

140

140. *The Itsukushima Shrine,*
fifth view of *Eight Views of
Miyajima* (Hiroshima) by
Nagasawa Rosetsu. Album leaf;
ink and colours on silk. 1794.

influenced by several schools: the Chinese Zhejiang style of Shen Nanping (becoming in Japan the Nagasaki school) introduced in the 1730s, the late Ming Fujianese Ōbaku (Mampukuji) techniques of Chen Xian, Japanese Kanō gold screen decoration, as well as the Western ideas mentioned above. The peculiar use of very wet brushes tied in a row and charged with pale ink to create a rapid series of parallel strokes in forming textured shapes such as dragons, feathers and the like, suggests familiarity with the 'trance' type of folk-painting at religious festivals. He also originated a bizarre and laborious painting technique. A double six-fold screen features a phoenix and an enormous white elephant each surrounded by outlandish birds and animals. In this astonishing composition Jakuchū imitates the effects of mosaic in paint. Each screen was underpainted with 310 vertical and 140 horizontal lines making approximately 43,000 squares each measuring 1.2 cm. After the paper was primed with white, each square was separately filled with colour. In the centre of each square was a smaller area of the same or lighter tone. This extraordinary style had no imitators; the few works which survive including a second double six-fold screen like this one, all originate from Jakuchū himself or

141

his atelier. That it had no followers should not surprise us, since in this departure the highly urbane Jakuchū froze his satirical images into concrete, as it were, robbing Japanese painting of its essential inner energy flow and emotionality.

Although Edo (Tokyo) was a new, upstart city compared with Kyoto (Heian), the shōgunal presence drew many talents there; there was a proliferation of artistic schools working for the *daimyō* captive in Edo for part of each year, and it was a centre for Chinese and Western ('Dutch') learning. The Edo master Tani Bunchō (1763–1840) had a typically eclectic style. Often counted among *Nanga* painters, he had also studied Kanō, Tosa, Nagasaki, *ukiyo-e* brush paintings and Western techniques. Born into an established *samurai* family, Bunchō (unlike his fellow *Nanga* painters, who often represented anti-establishment sentiments) moved in prominent political circles. He wrote treatises on painting, and produced a series of wood-block prints featuring famous

141. *Phoenix and White Elephant* by Itō Jakuchū. One of a pair of six-fold screens. Ink and colour *impasto* on paper. Mid-18th century.

mountains. In the later years of his life he developed his well-known spontaneous, abbreviated style.

Among the clergy there were as ever enthusiastic calligraphers and painters. The Zen master Gibon Sengai (1750–1837) was the abbot of Shōfukuji in Hakata from 1790 until his retirement in 1811. His painting was in a simple, direct and spontaneous style; it was widely appreciated, and thought particularly appropriate to the world of Tea. His characteristic *Frog and Snail* was done in a few rapid strokes with the brush only half-charged with wet ink. This results in unevenly inked line-edges, in both the calligraphy and the subject. The seven Chinese characters blend perfectly into the picture. Their meaning, 'Swallow the Three Buddhas, Past, Present and Future, in One Gulp', refers to the innate perfection of all: of frog, of snail, of swallowing. The lowly status but sacred potential of the frog was a common Buddhist theme.

142

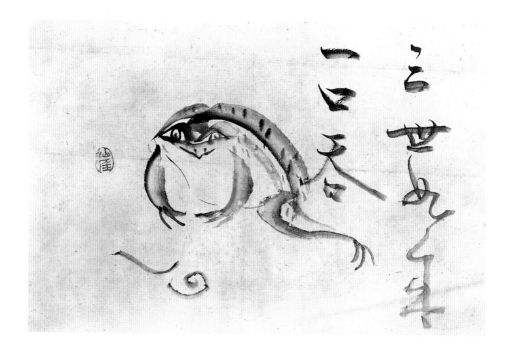

The Zen master Hakuin Ekaku (1685–1768), who more than anyone revitalized and japanized Zen, expressed himself in a particularly bold and powerful style. In a large portrait of Daruma (222.8 by 36.5 cms), he used his brush with such vehemence that the tip splayed in places, producing a dramatically rough-edged effect. Another Zen artist of this time, the sculptor-monk Enkū (1628–95), wandered round the country and left many statues of Buddha and bodhisattvas in rough-hewn wood for peasants worshipping at regional Buddhist temples and Shintō shrines.

Genre painting and the wood-block print
In the Edo period, diversity and elegance in the fine arts was matched by the robust humour and virile self-confidence of the rising lower mercantile class. Anonymous craftsmen working on everyday items such as ceramics, textiles, farm implements, architecture, household furnishings, book illustration and printing catered to mass tastes. For ordinary people, peasants and townsmen alike, this was a vigorous artistic period. And it is this new urban and urbane culture that marks the most notable departure from previous eras. Although the Tokugawa had placed merchants beneath farmers and artisans in the new social hierarchy, this enterprising class nevertheless came increasingly to domi-

142. *Frog and Snail* by Gibon Sengai. Hanging scroll; ink on paper. Early 19th century.

143. *Shō Kannon Bosatsu* by Enkū. Unpainted wood. Late 17th century.

144. *Daruma* (Bodhidharma) by Hakuin Ekaku. Hanging scroll; ink on paper. 1751.

nate life in the land. In cities and in towns, they created a vigorous commercial economy: during this period Kyoto finally regained its importance as a centre for fine silks and ceramics. Enormously wealthy families (such as the Mitsui, who by the early twentieth century controlled one of the largest financial empires) flourished; mass literacy was among the highest in the world; popular and satirical novels were extremely fashionable, and the printing business flourished.

145. *Dancing under the Cherry Trees* by Kanō Naganobu. Detail from double six-fold screen; colours on paper. Early 17th century.

146. *Shijō-Kawara*, one of a pair of bi-fold screens by an anonymous artist. Colours on gold paper. Early 17th century.

Since the early sixteenth century, a favourite art-form among the rising bourgeoisie was genre-painting. These works featured a variety of popular recreations and amusements. Large-format screen paintings depicted entire sections of the city from a bird's eye perspective, interlaced with gold clouds, and burghers delighted in identifying the castles, major temples and pleasure quarters they knew and, for the patron, his own street and manor house. These were called *Rakuchū-Rakugaizū* (Scenes In and Around the City). The affluent commissioned multi-panelled screens depicting entire city zones enlivened with street dancing, festival floats and exteriors and interiors of every kind. They were lavishly covered with goldleaf for both its sumptuousness and for its function as space/time divider. Famous narrative handscrolls (*emaki*) that had been viewed sequentially in a gradual unrolling process, now came to be transcribed onto the screen format where the whole narrative is seen at once, giving rise to a host of artistic devices in organization and in sub-text references that enhance visual effects in space and in time. The knowledgeable burgher could identify not only the setting but episodes where illustration and narration are fused and (often) rearranged. Many such anonymous works provide tantalizing glimpses into the historical city with views of palaces and temples since burnt down. Artists were free to depict existing structures together with glorified versions of what had once been, or they could insert an idealized version of the present. On a simpler scale, scenes such as the anonymous *Shijō-Kawara* 146 are the apotheosis of bourgeois collective (albeit edited) self-portraiture. *Bijinga* or Pictures of Beauties showed elegant, beau- 145 tiful women in leisurely pursuits; with meticulously recorded details of dress. Later versions revealed forms featuring the more down-market activities of lower grade prostitutes, or bath-house attendants working in the 'water-trade', *mizu-shbai.* Towards the end of the seventeenth century, as the appeal of this kind of art increased, it began to be mass-produced. Urban life seemed at its most elegant and extravagant in the demi-monde of Edo, Kyoto, and Osaka: here, as the late Sir George Sansom put it, was 'the world of fugitive pleasures, of theatres and restaurants, wrestling booths and houses of assignation, with their permanent population of actors, singers, story-tellers, jesters, courtesans, bathgirls and itinerant purveyors, among whom mixed the profligate sons of rich merchants, dissolute *samurai* and naughty apprentices'. The Japanese themselves confessed:

Living only for the moment, turning our full attention to the pleasures of the moon, sun, the cherry blossoms and the maple leaves, singing songs, drinking wine, and diverting ourselves just in floating, floating, caring not a whit for the pauperism staring us in the face, refusing to be disheartened, like a gourd floating along with the river current: this is what we call the floating world (*ukiyo*)

(from *Asai Ryōi*, trans. Richard Lane, *Tales of the Floating World*)

These 'floating world' pictures or *uikyo-e*, dominated both genre painting and the now world-famous Japanese wood-block prints.

Printed illustrations had been known in Buddhist circles since the Heian period, but with the Edo boom in communications, the printed book became an independent art-form. The literate bourgeoisie was hungry for printed literature of the outspoken type

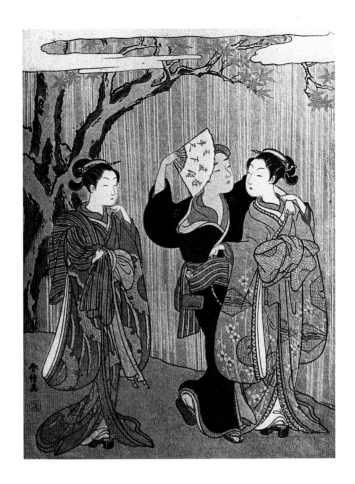

147. *Viewing Maple Leaves by the Waterfall* by Suzuki Harunobu. 'Brocade print' (*chūban nishiki-e*). Late 1760s.

which had long been part of the vernacular tradition. Illustrations, particularly to bawdy tales, were in great demand and astute publishers accordingly commissioned and produced some of the world's most explicit and joyous celebrations of earthy pleasures. Equally, the spread of scientific interest and knowledge resulted in the publication of medical and botanical books containing exquisite drawings of plants and herbs. It was during this time that the woodblock-carver's art soared to unexcelled heights.

In Edo, Hishikawa Moronobu and others began by producing black and white prints, hand-coloured in orange-red. Many of these were overtly and extravagantly erotic, and their style imitated the calligraphic character of the ink-brushed line. By the early eighteenth century, a wider range of colours, including an attractive rose-red and a deep-toned black resembling lacquer, was added. A great many hand-coloured actor-prints of this type

were now produced. In about 1745, a more elaborate and expansive technique of multiblock colour printing (probably learned from China) was used to produce limited editions of calendar prints. Here, since each colour required a separate block, meticulous accuracy in positioning the blocks was achieved by the use of guide marks (*kentō*). Prints of this kind, large or small, were often commissioned by a patron for distribution among friends.

The 'brocade prints' (*chūban nishiki-e*) of Suzuki Harunobu (*fl.* 1765–70) were the first to perfect the new and more costly techniques. In *Viewing Maple Leaves by the Waterfall* a tipsy roué, 147 kimono in disarray, holds a fan inscribed with a line of poetry. (Here artists delighted in inscribing moralistic Confucian adages by way of piquant satire.) He is oblivious to all but the closer courtesan who is leading him by his belt, while the other woman carries his outer garment. The waterfall in the background is in very fine lines, white and pink on grey; the man's face and arms are flushed with wine, in contrast to the white of the girls' faces. The beautiful garments, in pink, orange and lilac, reflect fashions of the time. Harunobu uses an embossing technique to raise certain areas of the courtesans' kimonos; by adding glue to the black, he achieves the intensity of lacquer in the man's garment. Compared with later

148. *The Coquettish Type* by Kitagawa Utamaro, from the series *Ten Physiognomic Types of Women*. Polychrome wood-block print. Late 18th century.

190

prints, Harunobu's work is notable for its qualities of tenderness and innocence.

Later print-masters like Kiyonaga extolled the statuesque elegance of courtesans, highlighting their role as leaders of high fashion; Kitagawa Utamaro (1754–1806) produced many series showing women at home and in the 'licensed quarters'. *The Coquettish Type*, taken from a series published in the early 1790s, shows a close-up view of a woman just out of the bath; although her hair is meticulously piled up, her kimono is carelessly worn and the sash is loosely tied. The background has been rubbed with mica to produce a silvery grey, which highlights the warmth and softness of the fleshtones. Utamaro's prints, spicy, sardonic and psychologically acute, are among the most treasured by Western collectors and connoisseurs. Van Gogh and Toulouse-Lautrec, among others, transformed European ways of seeing and painting as a direct result of their experience of the *ukiyo-e* prints. 148

The actor-prints featured the matinée idols of the time, the Kabuki actors. Prints announcing or celebrating particular performances, or portraying an actor in a certain role, functioned like movie-star posters today. Here was a medium for theatrical panache and irony. Eerie satire is the realm of Sharaku (*fl.* 1794–5).

149. *Sakata Hangorō III as the Villain Mizuyemon* by Sharaku. Polychrome wood-block print with mica-dusted background. 1794.

He may have been a Nō actor; certainly his hardly flattering view of the more popular Kabuki style seems to have offended Kabuki actors, and his publisher dropped him after only ten brilliant months. In his portrait of *Sakata Hangorō III as the Villain Mizuyemon*, the squinting eyes, twisted mouth and contorted arms of the figure set against the ominous, mica-flecked background, show how the designer can convey a sense of the drama by distortion. Now figurative prints, including mythological heroes and actor-prints, became increasingly grotesque; the phenomenon also imbued the paintings of Rosetsu, Jakuchū and others with a sense of suppressed hysteria.

149

Little of this baroque exaggeration is found in the work of Katsushika Hokusai (1760–1849) whose fame grew out of his numerous cartoons (*manga*) or humorous sketches. His landscape prints discovered vigorous new life in an ancient form. Like the great painters Taiga and Tanyū before him, Hokusai drew on a dazzling variety of sources, not the least among them Chinese illustrations, and was fired by extraordinary creative energy. He noted:

From the age of six I have had a mania for sketching the forms of things. From about the age of fifty I produced a number of designs, yet of all I drew prior to the age of seventy there is truly nothing of any great note. At the age of seventy-three I finally came to understand somewhat the nature of birds, animals, insects, fishes – the vital nature of grasses and trees. Therefore at eighty I shall have made great progress, at ninety I shall have penetrated even further the deeper meaning of things, and at one hundred I shall have become truly marvellous, and at one hundred and ten, each dot, each line shall surely possess a life of its own.

(trans. Richard Lane)

150

His famous views of Mount Fuji, so overexposed as to seem banal, remain nevertheless a synthesis of supreme draftsmanship tinged with a remarkably humane view of the world he knows.

Encouraged by Hokusai's example, Andō Hiroshige (1797–1858) perfected a new genre of travelogue prints, with numerous series such as *The Fifty-Three Stages of the Tōkaidō Highway*. Making ample use of chemical dyes newly introduced from the West, Hiroshige provided a more lyrical vision in which the poetry of mood is given memorable expression, as in the feeling of loneliness and quietude in the snow-covered pass at Kambara.

151

Chapter 7: Modern Japan (1868–   )

By the middle of the nineteenth century the conservative and isolationist policies of the Tokugawa *bakufu* had been rendered untenable by several forces: the Confucian notion that the Emperor (Son of Heaven) was the only legitimate source of rule, the presence of Western gunboats demanding trade relations and a growing feeling among the intelligentsia that Japan was socially, politically and militarily backward among the world's nations. With the Meiji Restoration in 1868, the Japanese made westernization and modernization their goals.

The cultural experience of the Meiji, Taishō and Shōwa eras involved a massive ingestion of European and American learning. Japanese students studied in the West and foreigners established universities and colleges in Japan. The young Meiji Emperor and Empress were photographed in formal Western attire. Architecture aped British-Victorian grandeur. Western oil painting was called *Yōga* and students in Europe for long periods were able to effect japanization of its themes and techniques far more rapidly than in the Tokugawa period when foreign travel was banned. Kuroda Seiki (1866–1924) whose 1897 *Yōga* painting (in oil on canvas), *Lake Shore*, shows a woman resting by a lake after bathing, had studied painting for nine years in Paris before returning to Japan in 1893 to open his own art school. (He later became the first Japanese Professor of Western-style Painting at the Tokyo School of Fine Arts.) *Lake Shore* is an ingenious treatment of late nineteenth-century French composition with the aura of Japan's unique courtesan-prints. But here the woman is emancipated, and *ennui* is replaced by intelligence. Kuroda demonstrates a breadth of vision quite beyond the chauvinism or narrow parochialism prevalent among hidebound Japanese image-makers both then and now. For it is only when an artist has lived abroad and has fully absorbed a foreign culture that he can see his own with clarity and objectivity. The inferiority complex in face of technologically more 'advanced' nations dissolves and a true synthesis of old and new, East and West, takes place here.

152. *Lake Shore* by Kuroda Seiki. Oil on canvas, Western-style painting (*Yōga*). 1897.

Another Meiji effort at mirror-parity was to ape the West in having only one religion. To this end, Shintō was disentangled from imported Buddhism. Buddhist monasteries and art treasures were systematically destroyed, and had it not been for the timely appointment of Dr Ernest Fenollosa (1853–1908) as Professor of Philosophy at the Imperial University of Tokyo, and the arrival of his wealthy Boston friend William Bigelow, much more would have been lost. Together they purchased the huge collection of ancient Japanese Buddhist art which forms the core of the Asian collections in the Boston Museum of Fine Arts and the Freer Gallery of Art in Washington, D.C. More important for Japan, perhaps, was Fenollosa's advice to the Japanese government that indigenous artistic traditions should be preserved (even if adapted or modernized) – for at the time all branches of art studies, from oil painting to industrial design, were of Western origin.

The modified traditional Japanese painting style promoted by Fenollosa was called *Nihonga* (Japanese painting), to be distinguished from Western-style oil painting (*Yōga*). He maintained that the powerful, expressive Japanese Kanō line was essential but that it should be reinforced with more realistic Western *chiaroscuro* and a brighter range of colours. By 1891, when Fenollosa left Japan to become director of the Oriental art department of the Boston Museum of Fine Arts, the survival of *Nihonga* painting in Japan was assured. His brilliant disciple, the philosopher Okakura

153. *Fallen Leaves* by Hishida Shunsō. Right-hand screen of double six-fold pair; mineral pigments on paper, Japanese-style painting (*Nihonga*). 1910.

154. *Fruit* by Kobayashi Kokei. Hanging scroll; mineral pigments on paper. Early 20th century.

Tenshin (1862–1913) became director of the Tokyo College of Fine Arts. In contrast to Fenollosa's stress on the bold Kanō-school line, Okakura promoted a delicately expressive line derived from *Yamato-e*. (He wrote and lectured in English on Japanese aesthetics and was as instrumental in promoting Japanese art abroad as he was in retaining native traditions at home.)

Traditional Japanese influences and styles in *Nihonga* painting include pure ink landscapes, colour-wash styles and thick *impasto* screens with coloured designs on gold. (Although originally painted on screens or in hanging scroll format, *Nihonga* works today are usually set in Western-style frames since mineral pigments are easily damaged by repeated rolling and unrolling.) Themes include standard Eastern figures and landscape compositions, as well as Western motifs and near-abstract designs; the genre is unified by the materials (writing brush, and ink or mineral pigment, on silk or paper).

Among the major artists at the turn of the century was the short-lived Hishida Shunsō (1874–1910), a student of Okakura Tenshin. (He studied in Tokyo and later taught at Tenshin's Tokyo College of Fine Arts.) His style was a new departure for that time, using no overt line-work, and was condemned by critics as being muddled or incompetent. In *Fallen Leaves*, Shunsō combines Western realism with the poetry of space: trees seem to recede into an all-pervading mist, losing definition. (There is a reference to Tōhaku's magnificent *Pine Forest* but the statement is otherwise in the language of Western realism.)

153

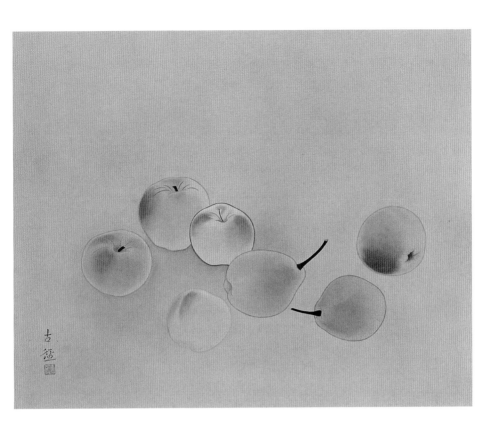

The giants of more typical, representative *Nihonga* are two old friends who toured Europe together in the twenties and visited China several times, Kobayashi Kokei (1883–1967) and Maeda Seison (1885–1977). Kokei encloses his forms with fine, taut lines which seem to have a life of their own. Often a subtle reverse shading from light to dark progresses from outline to centre of each form, as if the hues, startled by the line, had withdrawn in haste. Similarly, the delicate shading enveloping his motifs functions like the 'emotive cloud', 'blushing' or 'breathing' or both. A distinguished New York art critic confessed he found *Nihonga* lifeless and dull and wondered why the Japanese love it so. This is because he was waiting for the work to arouse him. Instead, he should have 'entered' the painting quietly and receptively. Then the dramatic tension of Kokei's *Fruit* which electrifies the still-life and charges the air, the subtle depiction of the fruit's colour, the quivering emotive space, would have transported him to the world of Japanese sensibilities which have quickened screens and scrolls for a thousand years.

154

Kokei's gentle perception of the world contrasts with the vigorous vision of Maeda Seison, his lifelong friend, and instructor to the Empress till his death in 1977. Most halls in the Gosho Imperial Palace in Tokyo display a single *Nihonga* work; Seison's magnificent *Lion Dancer Awaiting Cue* (1955) enlivens the enclosing space with typical tautness. The masked and robed actor is shown at the moment of highest psychological tension, just prior to breaking into dance. Seison's works are usually highly restrained, holding in reserve formidable energies. As in *onna-e* painting, he explores the world of inner emotional turbulence beneath surface calm. The difference is that Seison's subjects are not victims of affairs of the heart but often warriors before battle, medical students at the anatomy lesson (an autopsy), women at the bath, etc. In the manner of the *Frolicking Animals* scroll, Seison once painted a long ink monochrome hand-scroll of *Monkey's Journey to the West*. He explored all major traditions, bringing a new life to each. In 1930, he even rivalled the sumptuous Kōrin, challenging his *Iris* screen with a stupendous double six-fold screen of red and white *Poppies* on a gold ground: *impasto* flowers of the same height range across both screens in one daring,

155

155. *Lion Dancer Awaiting Cue* by Maeda Seison. *Nihonga* panel for the Imperial Palace, Tokyo. 1955.

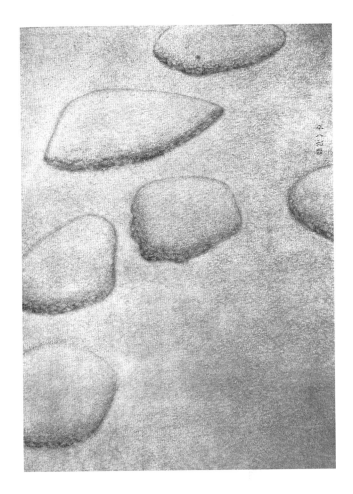

continuous horizontal band, on a flat, gold ground (white poppies in full bloom on the right screen, red poppies still in firm bud along the left). The relentless continuum is dramatically broken towards the end of the left screen where the field flowers have been trampled down, revealing a curved depression and – relieving the greens of the entire panel – one and a half full blooms in outrageous red. Seison is one of the very few Japanese artists ever to contrast primary red and green in this bold fashion and to convey a sense of continental grandeur and monumentality in his works.

In the *Nihonga* paintings of Fukuda Heichachirō (1892–1972) and Tokuoka Shinsen (1896–1972), done in traditional pigments on silk and paper, the forms are rendered in a near-abstract manner, like that common in non-Japanese abstract painting; but their expression is just as much suffused with Japanese aesthetic prefer-

ences as is the work of Kuroda Seiki. Fukuda's *Virgin Snow* of 1948 156
is an evocative portrait of white snow-softness in a garden setting
where six stepping stones are shaded in various hues. The description *yūgen*, 'mysterious and profound', has often been applied to
Tokuoka Shinsen whose *Stream* of 1954 can hardly be identified 157
without its title. In spite of their evocative mood or emotive clouds,
works such as this are entirely 'modern'; and without strained
mimicry of Western modernist techniques.

One of the greatest *Nihonga* artists whose works have influenced painters in Europe, China and Taiwan is Higashiyama Kaii 158
(born in 1908) whose intellectual approach brings a powerful min-
imalist dimension to this style of painting. Many of his works
exploit single motifs in single colours. The mineral pigment is
burned periodically to darken its hue as the work progresses.
When in 1977 his murals for the Tōshōdaiji in Nara were the subject of a major exhibition in Paris, the whole room was reproduced
to scale in order to show the size and function of his panels: they

157. *Stream* by Tokuoka
Shinsen. Colours on paper.
1954.

adorn the space in which the now secret image of Ganjin is kept. The exhibition demonstrated how the arts of the Japanese present relate intimately and harmoniously to those of the past. *Nihonga* in the Seventies, however, began to turn more towards the Viennese school of fantasy: today's works are often treated as if painted in oils in a congested manner and with high colour contrast. While losing its once unique potential in Japan, this mode is gaining momentum in Taiwan's academic painting in a rare reversal of cultural flow.

In recent years *Nihonga* has received much greater attention from the West where exhibitions and doctoral dissertations have established its importance as a major feature of Japanese art. And the modern print movement (in spite of the indifference of a government anxious to foster a Western image through conceptual art, steel and laser sculpture, etc.), has gone from strength to strength. In the Taishō era (1912–26) artists began to design, carve and pull their own prints in a 'creative print' movement (*sōsaku hanga*). Studies in black (such as black figures walking on rainy nights) reveal particular ingenuity. Kawase Hasui (1883–1957) produced landscapes where Japanese scenery is

reviewed in the light of new Western realism and dramatic colouration. By contrast, Yoshida Hiroshi (1876–1950) portrayed a world of pastel sentimentality echoing that of his Western counterpart J. Walter Phillips.

The most dynamic and original master who brought Japan's new print movement to international renown was Munakata Shikō (1905–77). His irrepressible energy and *joie de vivre* were translated into vigorous, unprecedented forms. To the end of his life he worked only with wood-block, even though most of his contemporaries had switched over to the more fashionable styles of mixed-media print. Like Enkū and Hakuin, Munakata was an anomaly in his own time, the creator of a torrent of frenzied works of alarming intensity and impulse: watching him work one formed the impression that the print possessed him rather than the other way round. His 'primitive' lack of inhibition earned him the derisive – or admiring – nickname 'Jōmon Man'.

Japanese artists today play a major part in world art, and a great many work in international circles. (Avant-garde imagery, despite vigorous promotion by the establishment and a very few brilliant exponents, lacks a genuine basis and remains an odd phenomenon within Japan. The other arts, however, rooted in

160

159. *Flight* sculpture by Nagare Masayuki, made of 400 tons of Swedish granite. For the Manhattan Trade Towers. *c.* 1970.

160. *The Visit* from *Uto no Hanga saku* by Munakata Shikō. Ink monochrome wood-block print. 1938.

long traditions, fairly burst with vitality.) The architect Tange Kenzō (b. 1913) whose revolutionary stadium and surrounding village for the 1964 Olympics animates all the space around, designs all manner of buildings in many countries. His influence is closely followed by that of Arata Isozaki who speaks through powerful masses. Japanese architecture, in both its traditional and its contemporary form, has made substantial contributions to modern concepts of modular construction and the inter-relation of outdoor and indoor space. Simple lines, diffused lighting and warm textures, standard attributes of Japanese buildings for centuries, are now commonplace. In the late twentieth century Japanese architects can be said to hold sway in major cities of the world. 161

Although Japanese sculpture lagged in the doldrums since the fourteenth century, the twentieth century has already offered the world two great masters. Isamu Noguchi (1904–1998) and more recently Nagare Masayuki (b. 1923). Both explore the contrast of rough stone finishes (*warehada*) and highly polished surfaces. Nagare, whose works have never been false to their Japanese roots, has been largely ignored by the establishment at home for fear of promoting antiquated standards, in spite of his growing prestige abroad. Like many Japanese artists of vision, he suffered from the post-war frenzy to create an international face for Japan (in commerce, shipbuilding and GNP, high fashion and 159

161. Olympic stadium in Tokyo by Tange Kenzō. Reinforced steel, concrete. 1964.

the arts) and the resulting imposition of a rather self-conscious Western standard on Japanese artists. Whether they have lived abroad or not, artists have been encouraged to emulate the latest innovation seen in foreign art journals (and immediately published in local monthlies). Contemporary art in Japan has become a political commodity and its managers are usually ignorant of Japan's own distinguished history and contributions. Professor

Ienaga Saburō, describing a similar situation in eighth-century Nara (where most art mirrored the Chinese), observed 'though it was possible to import material things . . . it was impossible to import the *social basis for their creation* (the italics are mine). Consequently continental influences extended only to such matters as exterior ornamentations . . . They failed to generate a profound change in the ways of thinking and living . . .' To a large

162. *Letter* by Yagi Kazuo. Black pottery. 1964.

extent, this has also been true for most of the twentieth century; whenever there have been self-doubts, Japan has held up its defensive mirror to the world and displayed art forms whose genesis lay outside Japan's own socio-cultural sphere. It is only in the last decade of the twentieth century that a Japanese couturier, Miyake Issei, has broken through the fashion frontiers to lead the world in a thorough rethinking of the human form, and the forms, social functions, and comfort of its coverings in works of high art.

The recent rise in nationalism has, however, produced signs of a changing attitude and a growing awareness that Japan's own traditions are vital and valid. The younger artists, many of whom have lived abroad, have developed a new perspective and make objective use of indigenous as well as foreign traditions. (For example, many Japanese printmakers from William Hayter's Atelier 17 in Paris have returned to Japan and contribute many of the finest works in prints.)

The oldest art industry of all, pottery, continues to provide exciting leadership with worldwide influence through the end of the twentieth century, overshadowing even the land that had given high-fired ceramics its Western name, China. Anonymous potters from regional folk kilns sell at Folk Art counters in department stores; potters like Yagi Kazuo (1919–1979) have introduced an urbane witticism to Japanese ceramics. His oeuvre is strikingly varied, ranging from glass and bronze to white and black pottery. The art of calligraphy, in a country which boasts one of the world's

162

163. *Uraurato tereru haru bi ni.* Calligraphy in *onnade* (now called *kana*) style by Kan Makiko. 1977.

164. *En* (Round) by Morita Shiryū. Avant-garde calligraphy; ink on paper. 1967.

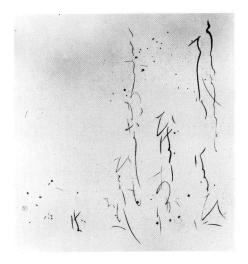

highest rates of literacy, has a large and active group of practitioners. Annual exhibitions include calligraphy in Chinese style, Japanese style, avant-garde style, and literary style (where instead of single or few words, entire poems or passages are executed in sensitive ink dances). Avant-garde calligraphers have broken the legibility barrier and produce pyrotechnics in ink or lacquer on silk, paper or board. Calligraphy enlivens book titles, magazine

164

covers, film titles, names on buildings, handbag clasps, textiles, bar signs and napkins. There is hardly an aspect of contemporary Japanese life untouched by the well-turned calligraph, be it in Chinese characters, the fluid *hiragana* or the angular *katakana* often used for foreign sounds. Interestingly, amid the frenzied push towards the frontiers of visual invention, the *omna-de* based *hiragana* calligraphy of Kan Makiko (b. 1933) continues to reign supreme in that domain. Intensely elegiac yet braced with an inner core of tensile steel, the brushwork bows to Heian courtiers but glorifies the power and resilience of her own times.

Although the average Japanese today is schooled to distinguish 'fine art' (placed on museum pedestals) from applied art (in clothing, houses, pottery, garden-design or trains), he is nevertheless as susceptible as ever to the beauty or sadness of things. For to him all things in nature are potentially beautiful – and, if they are made by man, ought to be. For the Japanese, as for peoples of few other nations, this quality of beauty which touches them, and its expression in art, is an inseparable part of life itself.

In the twenty-first century Japanese taste, like Zen and ceramics over the last half of the twentieth century, will influence most world arts, from architecture, auto-design, cinema, computer games, high fashion and interior design, to music, textile-design and video art. Subtly, perhaps not so subtly but surely, the follower of imperial days has become trend-setter of the space age.

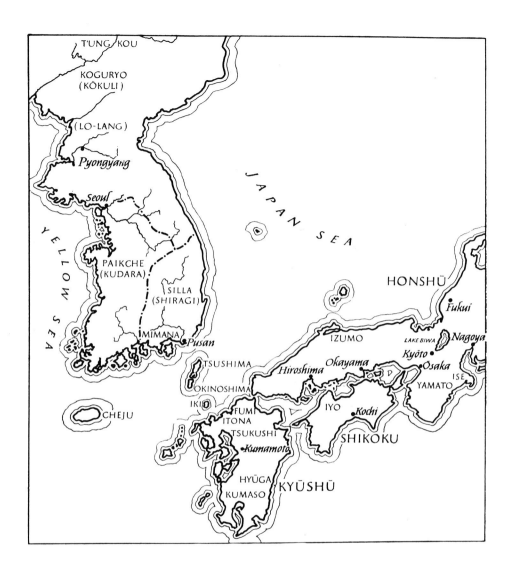

Korea and Japan in the
protohistoric period. (Modern
cities are marked in italics).

Japan, main districts and prefectures.

Select Bibliography

Thanks go to Sylvan Barnet and
William Burto, whose comprehensive
bibliography for The Asia Society New
York was last updated in 1998. See their
URL: http://www.asiasociety.org/arts/
japan-guide on the Internet.

General
Stephen Addiss, *How to Look at Japanese Art*, New York, 1996
Kendall H. Brown, *The Politics of Reclusion: Painting and Power in Momoyama Japan*, Honolulu, 1997
Martin Collcutt, *Court and Samurai in an Age of Transition*, New York, 1990
Michael Cunningham, *The Triumph of Style: 16th Century Art in Japan*, Cleveland, 1991
George Elison and Bardwell L. Smith (eds.), *Warlords, Artists and Commoners: Japan in the Sixteenth Century*, Honolulu, 1981
Danielle and Vadim Elisseeff, *Art of Japan*, (trans. I. Mark Paris), New York, 1985
Christine Guth, *Art of Edo Japan: The Artist and the City, 1615–1868*, New York, 1996
René Grousset, *Les Civilizations de l'Orient*, vol IV, *Le Japon*, Paris, 1930
The Grove Dictionary of Art, 34 vols, London, 1996
John Hall, et al., *Cambridge History of Japan*, 6 vols, Cambridge, 1988
John W. Hall and Toyoda Takeshi (eds.), *Japan in the Muromachi Age*, Berkeley, 1977
Rose Hempel, *The Golden Age of Japan, 194–1192*, (trans. Katherine Watson), New York, 1983
Money Hickman, et al., *Japan's Golden Age: Momoyama*, New Haven, 1996
The Dictionary of Japanese Art Terms, Tokyo, 1990
The Japan Foundation, *An Introductory Bibliography for Japanese Studies*
J. Edward Kidder, Jr., *Japanese Temples: Sculpture, Paintings, Gardens and Architecture*, London, 1964
J. Edward Kidder, Fr., *The Art of Japan*, New York, 1985
Kodansha Encyclopedia of Japan, 9 vols, Tokyo, 1983
Sherman E. Lee, *A History of Far Eastern Art*, New York and London, 1964
Sherman E. Lee, Michael R. Cunningham and James T. Ulak, *Reflections of Reality in Japanese Art*, Cleveland, 1983
Pamela Mason, *History of Japanese Art*, New York, 1993

Ivan Morris, *The World of the Shining Prince*, London, 1963
Miyeko Murase, *Japanese Art: Selections from the Mary and Jackson Burke Collection*, New York, 1975
Miyeko Murase, *Jewel Rivers: Japanese Art from the Mary and Jackson Burke Collection*, Richmond, 1993
Seiroku Noma, *The Arts of Japan*, 2 vols, trans. John Rosenfield and Glenn Webb, Tokyo, 1966–67
Kakuzō Okakura, *The Ideals of the East*, London, 1920
Kakuzō Okakura, *The Book of Tea*, 1906, Tokyo reprint, 1956.
Robert Treat Paine and Alexander C. Soper, *The Art and Architecture of Japan*, London 1955
Robert Treat Paine and Alexander C. Soper, *The Art and Architecture of Japan*, 3rd ed., Baltimore, 1981
David Pollack, *The Fracture of Meaning: Japan's Synthesis of China from the 8th through the 18th Centuries*, Princeton, 1986
Robert K. Reischauer, *Early Japanese History*, 2 vols, Princeton, 1937
Laurance P. Roberts, *A Connoisseur's Guide to Japanese Museums*, Tokyo, 1967
Laurance P. Roberts, *A Dictionary of Japanese Artists*, Tokyo, 1976
John M. Rosenfield, *Japanese Art of The Heian Period, 795–1185*, New York, 1967
John M. Rosenfield and Shūjirō Shimada, *Traditions of Japanese Art: Selections from the Kimiko and John Powers Collection*, Cambridge, Mass., 1970
John M. Rosenfield and Fumiko Cranston, *Extraordinary Persons*, Cambridge, Mass., 1998
George G. Sansom, *Japan, A Short Cultural History*, London, 1931, revised ed. London 1948
George G. Sansom, *A History of Japan*, 3 vols, Stanford, 1958–63
Timon Screech, *The Western Scientific Gaze and Popular Imagery in Later Edo Japan*, Cambridge, 1996
Yamasaki Shigehisa, *Chronological Table of Japanese Art*, Tokyo
Lawrence Smith, Victor Harris and Timothy Clark, *Japanese Masterpieces in the British Museum*, New York, 1990
Peter Swann, *A Concise History of Japanese Art*, Tokyo, 1979, revised ed. of *An Introduction to the Arts of Japan*, Oxford, 1958
Ryûsaku Tsunoda et al., *Sources of Japanese Tradition*, 2 vols, New York, 1958
H. Paul Varley and Isao Kumakura, (eds.), *Tea in Japan*, Honolulu, 1989
William Watson, (ed.), *The Great Japan

Exhibition: Art of the Edo Period, 1600–1868*, London, 1981
Carolyn Wheelwright, (ed.), *Word in Flower: The Visualization of Classical Literature in Seventeenth Century Japan*, New Haven, 1989
Yoko Woodson and Richard T. Mellott, *Exquisite Pursuits: Japanese Art in the Harry G.C. Packard Collection*, San Francisco, 1994
Yukio Yashiro (ed.), *Art Treasures of Japan*, 2 vols, Tokyo, 1960

Prehistory
C.M. Aikens and T. Higuchi, *Prehistory of Japan*, New York and London, 1982
Namio Egami, *The Beginnings of Japanese Art*, New York and Tokyo, 1973
J. Edward Kidder Jr., *Early Japanese Art: the Great Tombs and Treasures*, Princeton and London, 1964
J. Edward Kidder Jr., *The Birth of Japanese Art*, New York and Washington, 1965
J. Edward Kidder Jr., *Japan before Buddhism*, new ed., London, 1966
J. Edward Kidder Jr., *Prehistoric Japanese Arts: Jōmon Pottery*, Tokyo, 1968
Fumio Miki, *Haniwa*, New York and Tokyo, 1974
Douglas Moore Kenrick, *Jōmon of Japan: The World's Oldest Pottery*, London and New York, 1996
E.S. Morse, *Shell Mounds of Ōmori, Memoirs of the Science Department, University of Tokyo*, 1879, reprinted 1968
Richard J. Pearson, et al., *Windows on the Japanese Past*, Ann Arbor, 1986
Richard J. Pearson, et al., *Ancient Japan*, New York, 1992
Robert J. Smith and Richard K. Beardsley (eds.), *Japanese Culture: Its Development and Characteristics*, Chicago, 1962
Erica H. Weeder, (ed.), *The Rise of a Great Tradition: Japanese Archaeological Ceramics from the Jōmon through the Heian Periods, 10,500 BC–AD 1185*, New York, 1990

Architecture
Werner Blaser, *Japanese Temples and Tea Houses*, New York, 1956
Werner Blaser, *Structure and Form in Japan*, New York, 1963
William H. Coaldrake, *The Way of the Japanese Carpenter: Tools and Japanese Architecture*, New York, 1990
William H. Coaldrake, *Architecture and Authority in Japan*, London and New York, 1996
Y. Katsura Ishimoto, *Tradition and

Creation in Japanese Architecture (texts by Walter Gropius and Tange Kenzō), New Haven, 1960

Arata Isozaki: Four Decades of Architecture (with a preface by Richard Koshalek, essay by David Steward), London, 1998

Teiji Itō and Y. Futagawa, *The Essential Japanese House*, Tokyo, 1967

Teiji Itō and Y. Futagawa, *The Elegant Japanese House*, Tokyo, 1969

Japan Architect, English language ed. of *Shin-ken-chiku* (New Architecture), monthly journal published by Shin-kenchiku-sha, Tokyo

J. Edward Kidder Jr., *Japanese Temples*, Tokyo, 1966

Harumichi Kitao, *Shoin Architecture in Detailed Illustrations*, Tokyo, 1956

Bunji Kobayashi, *Japanese Architecture*, Tokyo, 1968, revised 1970

Kazuo Nishi and Kazuo Hozumi, *What is Japanese Architecture?* (trans. H. Mack Horton), New York, 1985

Hirotarō Ōta, *Japanese Architecture and Gardens*, Tokyo, 1966

Kakichi Suzuki, *Early Buddhist Architecture in Japan*, (trans. and adapted by Mary Neighbor Parent and Nancy Shatzman Steinhardt), New York, 1980

Kenzo Tange and Noboro Kawazoe, *Ise: Prototype of Japanese Architecture*, Cambridge, Mass., 1965

Buddhist Arts in Context

Toshio Fukuyama, *Heian Temples: Byodo-in and Chuson-ji*, (trans. Ronald K. Jones), New York, 1976

Roger Goepper, *Aizen-Myōō, the Esoteric King of Lust: An Iconographic Study*, Ascona, 1993

Elizabeth ten Grotenhuis, *Japanese Mandalas: Representations of Sacred Geography*, Honolulu, 1998

Hisatoyo Ishida, *Esoteric Buddhist Painting*, (trans. and adapted by E. Dale Saunders), New York, 1987

J. Edward Kidder, Jr., *Japanese Temples: Sculpture, Paintings, Gardens, and Architecture*, Tokyo, n.d.

Bunsaku Kurata, *Hōryūji-ji: Temple of the Exalted Law*, (trans. W. Chie Ishibashi), New York, 1981

Bunsaku Kurata and Yoshiro Tamura, (eds.), *Art of the Lotus Sutra*, Tokyo, 1987

Denise Patry Leidy and Robert A.F. Thurman, *Mandala: The Architecture of Enlightenment*, New York, 1997

Stephen Little, *Visions of the Dharma*, Honolulu, 1991

Donald F. McCallum, *Zonkoji and Its Icon: A Study in Medieval Japanese Religious Art*, Princeton, 1994

Yutaka Mino, et al., *The Great Eastern*

Temple: Treasures of Japanese Buddhist Art from Tōdaiji, Chicago, 1986

Anne Nishimura Morse and Samuel Crowell Morse, *Object as Insight: Japanese Buddhist Art and Ritual*, Katonah, N.Y., 1995

Jōji Okazaki, *Pure Land Buddhist Painting*, (trans. and adapted by Elizabeth ten Grotenhuis), New York, 1977

Pratapaditya Pal and Julia Meech-Pekarik, *Buddhists Book Ilumination*, New York, 1988

Takaaki Sawa, *Art in Esoteric Buddhism*, (trans. Richard L. Gage), New York, 1972

Willa J. Tanabe, *Paintings of the Lotus Sutra*, Tokyo, 1988

Ceramics

Rand Castile, *The Way of Tea*, New York and Tokyo, 1971

Louise Allison Cort, *Shigaraki, Potters' Valley*, Tokyo, 1979

Louise Allison Cort, *Seto and Mino Ceramics*, Washington, D.C., 1992

Patricia Graham, *Tea of the Sages: The Art of Sencha*, Honolulu, 1998

Williams Bowyer Honey, *The Ceramic Art of China and Other Countries of the Far East*, London 1948

Soame Jenyns, *Japanese Porcelain*, London, 1965

Soame Jenyns, *Japanese Pottery*, London, 1971

Fujio Koyama *The Heritage of Japanese Ceramics*, trans. and adapted by Sir John Figgess, New York and Tokyo, 1973

Bernard Leach, *A Potter in Japan*, London, 1971

Tsugio Mikami, *The Art of Japanese Ceramics*, New York and Tokyo, 1972

Roy Andrew Miller, *Japanese Ceramics*, Rutland and Tokyo, 1960

Hugo Munsterberg, *The Folk Arts of Japan*, Vermont and Tokyo, 1958

Daniel Rhodes, *Tamba Pottery*, Tokyo, 1970

Masahiko Satō, *Kyoto Ceramics*, New York and Tokyo, 1973

N. Saunders, *The World of Japanese Ceramics*, Tokyo, 1967

Joan Stanley-Baker, *Mingei: Folkcrafts of Japan*, Victoria, B.C., 1979

Richard L. Wilson, *Inside Japanese Ceramics: A Primer of Materials, Techniques, and Traditions*, New York, 1995

Donald Wood, Teruhisa Tanaka and Frank Chance, *Echizen: Eight Hundred Years of Japanese Stoneware*, Birmingham, Ala., 1994

Folk Art

Victor and Takako Hauge, *Folk*

Traditions in Japanese Art, New York, 1978

Victor and Takako Hauge, *Mingei: Masterpieces of Japanese Folkcraft*, New York, 1991

Hugo Munsterberg, *The Folk Arts of Japan*, Rutland, Vt., 1958

Kageo Muraoka and Kichiemon Okamura, *Folk Arts and Crafts of Japan*, (trans. Daphne D. Stegmaier), New York, 1973

Masataka Ogawa, et al., *The Enduring Crafts of Japan: 33 Living National Treasures*, New York, 1968

Matthew Welch, *Otsu-e: Japanese Folk Paintings from the Harriet and Edson Spencer Collection*, Minneapolis, 1994

Gardens

Masao Hayakawa, *The Garden Art of Japan*, New York and Tokyo, 1973

Masao Hayakawa, *The Garden Art of Japan*, trans. R.L.Cage, New York and Tokyo, 1974

Teiji Itoh, *Imperial Gardens of Japan*, New York, 1970

Teiji Itoh, *Space and Illusion in the Japanese Garden* (trans. adapted by Ralph Friedrich and Masahiro Shimamura), New York, 1973

Teiji Itoh, *The Gardens of Japan*, New York, 1984

Loraine E. Kuck, *The World of the Japanese Garden: From Chinese Origins to Modern Landscape Art*, New York and Tokyo, 1968

Osamu Mori, *Katsura Villa*, Tokyo, 1930, new ed. 1956

Osamu Mori, *Typical Japanese Gardens*, Tokyo, 1962

Osamu Mori, *Kobori Enshū*, Tokyo, 1974

P. and S. Rambach, *Sakuteiki ou le Livre Secret des Jardins Japonais*, Geneva, 1973

I. Schaarschmidt-Richter, *Japanische Garten*, Baden-Baden, 1977

I. Schaarschmidt-Richter and Osamu Mori, *Japanese Gardens*, New York, 1979

Kantō Shigemori, *The Japanese Courtyard Garden*, (trans. Pamela Pasti), New York, 1981

S. Shimoyama, *Sakutei-ki, The Book of Gardens*, Tokyo, 1976

David A. Slawson, *Secret Teachings in the Art of Japanese Gardens*, New York, 1987

Lacquers, Textiles and Armour

Raymond Bushell, *The Inrō Handbook*, New York and Tokyo, 1979

J. Earle, *An Introduction to Netsuke*, London, 1980

Helen Benton Minnich and Nomura Shōjirō, *Japanese Costume and the*

213

Makers of its Elegant Tradition, Vermont and Tokyo, 1963

Toshiko Ito, Tsujigahana, (trans. Monica Bethe), New York, 1985

Alan Kennedy, Japanese Costume, Paris, 1990

George Kuwayama, Shippō: The Art of Enamelling in Japan, Los Angeles, 1987

Kaneo Matsumoto, Jōdai Gire: 7th and 8th Century Textiles in Japan from the Shōsōn-in and Hōryū-ji, (trans. Shigeta Kaneko and Richard L. Mellott), Kyoto, 1984

Seiroku Noma, Japanese Costume and Textile Arts, New York and Tokyo, 1979

Beatrix von Ragué, A History of Japanese Lacquer-work, Toronto and Buffalo, 1976

William Rathbun, Beyond the Tanabata Bridge: Traditional Japanese Textiles, New York, 1993

W. Robinson, Arms and Armour of Old Japan, London, 1951

W. Robinson, The Arts of the Japanese Sword, London, 1961, 1970

Kanzan Satō, The Japanese Sword, (trans. Joe Earle), New York, 1983

Yoshiaki Shimizu, et al., Japan: The Shaping of Daimyo Culture, 1185–1868, Washington, D.C., 1988

The Tokugawa Collection: The Japan of the Shoguns, Montreal, 1989

James C. Watt and Barbara Brennan Ford, East Asian Lacquer: The Florence and Herbert Irving Collection, New York, 1991

Painting and Calligraphy

Court and Samurai in an Age of Transition, New York, 1990

Stephen Addiss, Tall Mountains and Flowing Waters: The Arts of Uragami Gyokudo, Honolulu, 1987

Terukazu Akiyama, Japanese Painting, Geneva, 1961, New York, 1977

Helmut Brinker, Zen in the Art of Painting, (trans. George Campbell), London, 1977

Helmut Brinker and Hiroshi Kanazawa, Zen, Masters of Meditation in Images and Writing, (trans. Andreas Leisinger), Zurich, 1995

James Cahill, Scholar Painters of Japan: the Nanga School, New York, 1972

Jan Fontein and Money L. Hickman, Zen Painting and Calligraphy, Boston, 1970

Calvin, L. French, Shiba Kokan: Artist, Innovator and Pioneer in the Westernization of Japan, New York and Tokyo, 1974

Calvin, L. French, Through Closed Doors: Western Influences on Japanese Art, 1639–1853, Rochester, Mich., 1977

Elise Grilli, The Art of the Japanese Screen, New York and Tokyo, 1970

Saburō Iengaga, Painting in the Yamato Style, (trans. John M. Shields), New York, 1973

Hiroshi Kanazawa, Japanese Ink Painting, Tokyo, 1979

Shigemi Komatsu, Kwan S. Wong and Fumiko Cranston, The Heinze Götze Collection, Munich, 1989

Taizo Kuroda, Melinda Takeuchi and Yuzo Yamane, Worlds Seen and Imagined: Japanese Screens from the Idemitsu Museum of Arts, New York, 1995

Richard Lane, Masters of the Japanese Print, London, 1962

Howard A. Link, Exquisite Visions: Rimpa Paintings from Japan, Honolulu, 1980

Takaaki Matsushita, Ink Painting, New York and Tokyo, 1974

Shin'ichi Miyajima and Yasuhiro Satō, Japanese Ink Painting, Los Angeles, 1985

Hiroshi Mizuo, Edo Painting: Sōtatsu and Kōrin, New York and Tokyo, 1972

Ivan Morris, The Tale of Genji Scroll, Tokyo, 1971

Miyeko Murase, Emaki: Narrative Scrolls from Japan, New York, 1983

Miyeko Murase, Tales of Japan, New York, 1986

Yūjirō Nakata, The Art of Japanese Calligraphy, New York and Tokyo, 1973

Yoshitomo Okamoto, The Namban Art of Japan, New York and Tokyo, 1972

Hideo Okudaira, Narrative Picture Scrolls, no. 5 in Arts of Japan series, New York and Tokyo, 1973

John M. Rosenfield and Fumiko and Edwin Cranston, The Courtly Tradition in Japanese Art and Literature, Tokyo, 1973

John M. Rosenfield and Shimada Shūjirō, Traditions of Japanese Art, Cambridge, Mass., 1970

J. Thomas Rimer, (ed.), Multiple Meanings, Washington, D.C., 1986

James H. Sandford, et al., (eds.), Glowing Traces, Princeton, 1992

Jōhei Sasaki, Ōkyo and the Maruyama-shijō School of Japanese Painting, St Louis, 1980

Dietrich Seckel and Akihisa Hase, Emakimono: the Art of the Japanese Painted Handscroll, London and New York, 1959

Yoshiaki Shimizu and Carolyn Wheelwright (eds.), Japanese Ink Paintings, Princeton, 1976

Yoshiaki Shimizu and John Rosenfield, Masters of Japanese Calligraphy: 8th–19th Century, New York, 1984

Joan Stanley-Baker, Nanga: Idealist Painting of Japan, Victoria, B.C., 1980

Joan Stanley-Baker, The Calligraphy of Kan Makiko, Victoria B.C., 1979

Joan Stanley-Baker, The Transmission of Chinese Idealist Painting to Japan: Notes on the Early Phase, Ann Arbor, 1992

Tsuneo Takeda, Kano Eitoku, (trans. and adapted by H. Mack Horton and Catherine Kaputa), New York, 1977

Ichimatsu Tanaka, Japanese Ink Painting: From Shūbun to Sesshū, vol. 12 in Survey of Japanese Art, New York and Tokyo, 1972

William Watson, Sōtatsu, London, 1959

William Watson, Buson, London, 1960

Prints

Laurence Binyon and J.I.O. Sexton, Japanese Colour Prints, New York 1923, 2nd ed. Basil and Grey (eds.), London, 1960

Catalogue of the Collection of Japanese Prints, 5 vols, Rijksmuseum, Amsterdam 1977–90

Timothy Clark, Ukyio-e Paintings in the British Museum, London, 1992

Timothy Clark, Donald Jenkins and Osamu Ueda, The Actor's Image: Printmakers of the Katsukawa School in the Art Institute of Chicago, Princeton, 1994

Arthur D. Ficke, Chats on Japanese Prints, London, 1928, reprint Vermont and Tokyo, 1958

Matthi Forrer, Hiroshige: Prints and Drawings, New York, 1997

Helen C. Gunsaulus and Margaret O. Gentles, The Clarence Buckingham Collection of Japanese Prints, 2 vols, Chicago, 1955 and 1965

Jack Hillier, Japanese Paintings and Prints in the Collection of Mr and Mrs Richard P. Gale, 2 vols, London, 1970

Jack Hillier, The Uninhibited Brush, London, 1974

Jack Hillier, The Japanese Print: a New Approach, Vermont and Tokyo, 1975

Jack Hillier, and L. Smith, Japanese Prints: 300 Years of Albums and Books, London, 1980

Richard Lane, Images from the Floating World: The Japanese Print, New York, 1978

Richard Lane, Hokusai, London, 1989

Kurt Meissner, Japanese Woodblock Prints in Miniature: the Genre of Surimono, Vermont and Tokyo, 1970

James A. Michener, Japanese Prints: From the Early Masters to the Modern, Vermont and Tokyo, 1959

Muneshige Narazaki, Ukiyo-e Masterpieces in European Collections, 12 vols, New York, 1988–90

Dean J. Schwaab, *Osaka Prints*, New York, 1989

Henry D. Smith II and Gian Carlo Calza, *Hokusai Paintings: Selected Essays*, Venice, 1994

Harold P. Stern, *Master Prints of Japan: Ukiyo-e Hanga*, New York, 1969

Seiichirō Takahashi, *Traditional Woodblock Prints of Japan*, New York and Tokyo, 1972

D.B. Waterhouse, *Harunobu and His Age: The Development of Colour Printing in Japan*, London, 1964

Sculpture

Christine Guth Kanda, *Shinzo*, Cambridge, Mass., 1985

Michiaki Kawakita, *Modern Currents in Japanese Art*, New York and Tokyo

J. Edward Kidder Jr., *Masterpieces of Japanese Sculpture*, Vermont and Tokyo, 1961

Nishikawa Kyotaro and Emily Sano, *The Great Age of Japanese Buddhist Sculpture AD 600–1300*, Fort Worth, 1982

Seiichi Mizuno, *Asuka Buddhist Art: Hōryū-ji*, New York and Tokyo, 1974

Hisashi Mori, *Sculpture of the Kamakura Period*, New York and Tokyo, 1974

Tanio Nakamura, *Contemporary Japanese-style Painting*, Tokyo, 1969

Minoru Ōoka, *Temples of Nara and Their Art*, New York and Tokyo, 1973

Takaaki Sawa, *Art in Japanese Esoteric Buddhism*, New York and Tokyo, 1972

Jiro Sugiyama, *Classic Buddhist Sculpture*, (Trans. and adapted by Samuel Crowell Morse), New York, 1982

William Watson, *Sculpture of Japan*, London, 1959

Women in Art

Sanna Saks Deutsch and Howard A. Link, *The Feminine Image*, Honolulu, 1985

Pat Fister, *Japanese Women Artists, 1600–1900*, Lawrence, Kans., 1988

Elizabeth Lillehoj, *Women in the Eyes of Men: Images of Women in Japanese Art*, Chicago, 1995

Andrew J. Pekarik (ed.), *The Thirty-Six Immortal Women Poets*, New York, 1991

Elizabeth Sabato Swinton, et al., *The Women of the Pleasure Quarter*, New York, 1996

Marsha Weidener, (ed.), *Flowering in the Shadows: Women in the History of Chinese and Japanese Painting*, Honolulu, 1990

List of Illustrations

42 Covered medicine jar. 811. Ash-glaze on shoulders. H. 18.5 (7.3) D. 23 (9.1). Shōsōin, Tōdaiji, Nara.

43 Landscape with figures: plectrum guard of *biwa* lute. Before 756. Shitan wood decorated with marquetry. H. 38.6 (15.2) L. 17.7 (6.7). Shōsōin, Tōdaiji, Nara.

44 Map of Tōdaiji, precincts (detail). 756. Ink and light colours on hemp. H. 297 (116.9) W. 221 (87). Shōsōin, Tōdaiji, Nara.

45 Womb Mandala (detail). Heian period, 859–880. Ink and colours on silk. H. 183.3 (72.2) W. 154 (60.6). Tōji, Kyoto.

46 Yakushi Nyorai (detail). Early 9th century. Painted cypress wood. H. 170.3 (67). Golden Hall, Jingōji, Kyoto.

47 Shaka Nyorai. Late 9th century. Wood. H. 238 (93.7). Golden Hall, Murōji, Nara.

48 *Blue Fudō and his dōji attendants* (detail). Mid-11th century. Colours on silk. H. 203.3 (80) W. 148.8 (58.6). Shōrenin, Kyoto.

49 *Amida on a cloud*: central panel of Amida triptych. Early 11th century. Colours on silk. H. 186.7 (73.5) W. 143.4 (56.5). Hokkeji, Nara.

50 View of the Phoenix Hall, *Byōdōin*, Uji, Kyoto, completed in 1053. Photo Orion Press, Tokyo.

51 *Buddha Amida* by Jōchō. 1053. Gold leaf and lacquer on wood. H. 295 (116). Phoenix Hall, Byōdōin, Uji, Kyoto. © Artephot, Paris (Ogawa).

52 Celestial bodhisattva on a cloud, by the school of Jōchō. 1053. Painted wood. H. c. 50 (c. 19.7). Phoenix Hall, Byōdōin, Uji, Kyoto.

53 *Raigō* Kannon Bosatsu. 1094. Lacquered and gilded wood. H. 96.7 (38.4). Sokujōji, Kyoto.

54 *Raigō* of *Amida and Celestial Host* (detail) from mural in Phoenix Hall. 1053. Colours on wood. H. 75 (29.5). W. 17.5 (8.9). Byōdōin, Uji, Kyoto.

55 *Suiten* (Water Deva), one of twelve. 1127. Colours and gold on silk. H. 144.2 (56.8) W. 126.6 (49.8). Tōji, Kyoto.

56 *Descent of Amida over the Mountains.* Early 13th century. Hanging scroll,

colours and gold on silk. H. 138 (49) W. 118 (32). Zenrinji, Kyoto.

57 *Haya Raigō* of Amida and bodhisattvas. 13th century. Hanging scroll, colours and gold on silk. H. 145.1 (57.1) W. 154.5 (60.8). Chionin, Kyoto.

58 *Early Spring Landscape*, door panel in Phoenix Hall. 1053. Painted wood. H. 374.5 (147.4) W. 138.6 (54.6). Byōdōin, Kyoto.

59 *Kashiwagi I*, detail from *The Tale of Genji*. Early 12th century. Handscroll, ink and colours on paper. H. 21.8 (8.6) W. 48.3 (19). Tokugawa Collection, Nagoya.

60 *Suzumushi II*, detail from *The Tale of Genji* handscrolls. Early 12th century. Ink and colour on paper. H. 21.8 (8.6) W. 48.3 (19). Gotō Museum, Tokyo.

61 Yakuō Bosatsu Honjibon. Frontispiece to the 23rd scroll of the *Heike Nōgyō. c.* 1164. Ink, colours and *kirigane* on paper. Itsukushima Shrine, Hiroshima.

62 *Ban Dainagon E-kotoba*, second of three scrolls. Late 12th century. Ink and colours on paper. Sakai Collection, Tokyo.

63 *The Flying Granary*, detail from the first *Shigisan Engi* handscroll. *c.* 1156–1180. Ink and colours on paper. H. 31.5 (12.4). Chōgosonshiji, Mt. Shigi, Nara.

64 *Simian Prelate worshipping frog Buddha* from the *Chōjū Giga* scroll I. First half of 12th century. Ink on paper. H. 31 (12.2). Kozanji Collection, Kyoto.

65 Enichi-bō Jōnin, *Zemmyō transformed into a Dragon*, detail from the *Kegon Engi* handscrolls. Early 13th century. Ink and colours on paper. H. 31.6 (12.4). Kōzanji, Kyoto.

66 *Hungry Ghosts wait to feast on Feces* from the *Gaki Zōshi* scroll (Kawamoto version). Late 12th century. Ink and colours on paper. H. 27.3 (10.7). National Museum, Tokyo.

67 Enichi-bō Jōnin, *Myōe Shōnin meditating.* Early 13th century. Hanging scroll, ink and colours on paper. H. 145 (57) W 48.8 (19.2). Kōzanji Collection, Kyoto.

68 *Burning of the Sanjō Palace.* Detail from the *Heiji monogatari* handscroll I.

Late 13th century. Ink and colours on paper. H. 41.3 (16.3) W. 699.7 (275.4). Courtesy, Museum of Fine Arts, Boston. Fenollosa-Weld Collection.

69 *Onnade* calligraphy of Kiyohara Fukayabu from one of the *Masu-shikishi* set of calligraphies ascribed to Fujiwara no Yukinari. Late 11th century. Album leaf mounted as *shikishi*. Ink on paper. H. 13.8 (5.4) W. 11.8 (4.7). Private collection, Japan.

70 Calligraphy fragment from the *Shigeyukishū* collection from the *Sanjūrokunin ka shū, c.* 1112. Ink on decorated paper. H. 20.1 (7.9) W. 31.8 (12.5). Nishi Honganji, Kyoto.

71 *So* (horizontal harp) with flowing stream and small birds. 12th century. Lacquered wood with *maki-e*. L. 151.9 (59.8). Kasuga-Taisha Shintō Shrine, Nara.

72 Armour with blue yarns from the Taira clan. 12th century. H. 39.5 (15.6). Itsukushima Shrine, Hiroshima.

73 *Furuna*, one of Ten Great Disciples. Nara period, *c.* 734. Painted dry lacquer. H. 149 (58.7). Kōfukuji, Nara.

74 Tankei (1173?–1256), *Basū-sen* (detail). Early 13th century. Polychrome painted wood. H. 154.7 (60.9). Myōhō-in, Kyoto.

75 Tankei (1173?–1256), *Mawara-nyō* (detail). Early 13th century. Polychrome painted wood. H. 153.7 (60.5). Myōhō-in, Kyoto.

76 Unkei (d. 1223), *Muchaku* (detail). 1208–12. Painted wood. H. 188 (74). Kōfukuji, Nara. © Artephot, Paris (Shogakukan).

77 *Lanqi Daolong* (1213–1278) (detail). 1271. Hanging scroll, ink and colours on silk. H. 104.8 (41.3) W. 46.4 (18.3). Kenchōji, Kamakura.

78 Goshin (active 1334–49), the Emperor *Hanazono*. 1338. Hanging scroll, ink and colours on paper. H. 31.2 (12.9) W. 97.3 (38.3). Chōfukuji, Kyoto.

79 Fujiwara Takanobu (1142–1205), *The Shōgun Minamoto no Yoritomo.* 12th century. Hanging scroll, ink and colours on silk. H. 139.4 (54) W. 111.8 (44). Jingōji, Kyoto.

80 Mokuan Reien (d. 1345), *Four Sleepers.* Inscription by Xiangfu Shaomi.

Hanging scroll, ink on paper. H. 73.4 (28.9) W. 32.4 (12.8). The Maeda Ikutokukai Collection, Tokyo.

81 Gyokuen Bompō (*c.* 1347–*c.* 1420), *Orchids and Rocks.* Hanging scroll, ink on paper. H. 106.5 (39.5) W. 34.5 (13.1). Metropolitan Museum of Art, Harry G. C. Packard Collection of Asian Art.

82 Gukei (active 1361–75), *White-robed Kannon* with flanking landscapes. Hanging scrolls, ink on silk. H. 98.6 (38.8) W. 40.3 (15.9) each. *White-robed Kannon* in Yamato Bunkakan Collection, Nara. Landscapes in Masuda Collection, Kyoto.

83 Ryōzen (active mid-14th century), *White Heron.* Hanging scroll, ink on paper. H. 35.1 (13.9) W. 32 (12.6). Nagatake Asano Collection.

84 Penglai, the immortals' isle. Arrangement of seven rocks in the pond garden of Tenryūji, Kyoto, completed by 1265.

85 Kinkaku (Golden Pavilion), Kyoto, 1398. Original destroyed by fire in 1950 and rebuilt in 1964. Photo Orion Press, Tokyo.

86 Josetsu (active early 15th century), *Catching Catfish with a Gourd.* 1408. Hanging scroll, ink and colours on paper with inscriptions by thirty monks. H. 111.5 (43.9) W. 76 (29.9). Taizōin, Kyoto.

87 Shūbun (active 1423–60), *Reading in the Bamboo Studio* (detail). See **88**.

88 *Reading in the Bamboo Studio* (complete). Mid-15th century. Hanging scroll, ink on paper. H. 134.8 (53) W. 33.3 (13). National Museum, Tokyo.

89 Shōkei Tenyū (active 1436–65), *Small Lake Landscape.* Hanging scroll, ink and colours on paper. H. 121.5 (47.8) W. 34.8 (13.7). Fujii Collection, Hyōgo.

90 Bunsei (active 1460s), *West Lake,* inscribed by Zuikei Shūhō and Ichijō Kanera. Before 1473. Hanging scroll, ink on paper. H. 80.8 (31.8) W. 33.4 (13.1). Masaki Art Museum, Osaka.

91 Sōami (d. 1525), *Eight Views of the Xiao and Xiang,* detail of one of the 23 sliding door panels. 1509. Ink on paper. H. 174.8 (68.8) W. 140.2 (55.2). Daisen-in, Daitokuji, Kyoto. Photo Richard Stanley-Baker.

92 Bokusai (d. 1492), *Ikkyū Sōjun.* Before 1481. Hanging scroll, ink and colours on paper. H. 46 (17) W. 26.5 (10). National Museum, Tokyo.

93 Sesshū Tōyō (1420–1506), *Landscape* (detail), inscribed by Ryōan Keigo in 1507. Hanging scroll, ink and light colours on paper. H. 119 (46.9) W. 35.3 (13.9). Ohara Kenichirō Collection, Osaka.

94 Sōen (active 1489–1500), *Haboku* landscape. Late 15th or early 16th century. Ink on paper. Andō Collection, Tokyo.

95 Tōshun (active first half of the 16th century), *Evening Snow* from *Eight Views of the Xiao and Xiang.* Hanging scroll, ink on paper. H. 22 (8.7) W. 31.7 (12.5). Masaki Art Museum, Osaka.

96 Sesson Shūkei (*c.* 1504–89), *Hawk on Pine.* Mid-16th century. One of a pair of hanging scrolls, ink on paper. H. 126.5 (49.9) W. 53.6 (21.1). National Museum, Tokyo.

97 *Dry landscape* garden in Ryōanji, Kyoto, constructed in the 1480s. Photo Orion Press, Tokyo.

98 Sesson Shūkei (*c.* 1504–89), *Landscape in Wind.* Hanging scroll, ink on paper. Late 16th century. H. 27.3 (10.8) W. 78.6 (18.8) (painting only). Sansō Collection, U.S.A.

99 Kanō Eitoku (1543–1590), *Pine and Crane,* 1566. Sliding door panels, ink on paper. H. 176 (69.3). Jukōin, Daitokuji, Kyoto.

100 Himeji castle, Hyōgo Prefecture, built late 16th century. Werner Forman Archive, London.

101 Kanō Sanraku (1559–1635), *White Peonies* (detail). Early 17th century. Sliding door panel, colours and *impasto* on gold foil. H. 184.5 (72.6) W. 99 (40). Daitokuji, Kyoto.

102 Kanō Tanyū (1602–74), *Night Fishing with Cormorants.* Mid-17th century. A six-fold screen in ink, colours and gold. Ōkura Bunkazaidan, Tokyo.

103 *Great Pine* murals in the Great Hall of Ninomaru Goten, attributed to Kanō Tanyū (1602–74). 1624–26. Detail. Ink and colours on gold-foiled paper panels. Nijō Castle, Kyoto. © Artephot, Paris (Zauho-Press).

104 Tosa school, *Landscape with Sun and Moon* (detail of the right-hand screen). Mid-16th century. Double six-fold screen, ink, colours and gold on paper. Each H. 147 (57.8) W. 316 (124.4). Kongōji, Osaka.

105 Kaihō Yūshō (1533–1615), *Pine and Plum by Moonlight.* Late 16th century. A pair of six-panel screens, ink and slight colour on paper. Each H. 169 (66.5) W. 353 (139). Atkins Museum of Fine Art, Kansas City, U.S.A.

106 Tawaraya Sōtatsu (active 1602–40?), *Matsushima (Pine Island).* Early 17th century. Double six-fold screen, ink, colours and gold on paper. H. 166 (59.8) W. 367.7 (141.3). Freer Gallery of Art, The Smithsonian Institution, Washington D.C.

107 Hasegawa Tōhaku (1539–1610), *Pine Forest.* Late 16th century. A pair of six-panel screens, ink on paper. Each H. 156 (61.4) W. 347 (136.6). National Museum, Tokyo.

108 (*exterior*), **109** (*interior*) Sen no Rikyū (1521–91), *Myōkian,* tea house. 1582. Myōkian, Kyoto.

110 Tanaka Chōjirō (1516–92), *Katsujishi, raku* ware tea bowl. 16th century. Black slip glaze. H. 8.8 (3.5) Diam. 10.9 (4.3). Mingei-kan Folk-craft Museum, Kyoto.

111 Yōmei-mon (Sunlight Gate), Tōshōgū. Early 17th century. Nikkō, Tochigi. Photo Orion Press, Tokyo.

112 *Katsura,* detached imperial villa and garden. 1642. Photo Orion Press, Tokyo.

113 *Portuguese Missionaries and Traders arriving in Japan. c.* 1600. *Namban* (Southern Barbarians) folding screen, ink, colours and gold on paper. H. 157.5 (62) W. 367 (144.5). V&A Picture Library, London.

114 *Kogan* (Ancient Shore) water-jar in Shino ware. Momoyama period, 16th–17th century. H. 17.5 (6.9) D. 19.2 (7.6). Hatakeyama Kinenkan Museum, Tokyo.

115 Small dish in *nezumi* Shino glaze with white slip painting of wagtail on rock. Momoyama period, 16th–17th century. H. 8.9 (3.5) D. 26.8 (10.6). Agency for Cultural Affairs, Tokyo.

116 *Yabure-Bukuro* (Torn Pouch) water-jar, Iga ware. Momoyama period, late 16th, early 17th century. Stoneware. H. 21.6 (8.5) D. of rim 15.8 (6.2). Gotō Museum, Tokyo.

117 Nabeshima ware plate with design of flowering buckwheat. Early 19th century. Overglaze enamels on porcelain. H. 9.1 (3.6) D. 30 (11.8).

118 Old Imari ware *sake* bottle depicting Europeans. Edo period, 17th century. Porcelain. H. 56 (22). © The Cleveland Museum of Art, 1999. Gift of Ralph King, 1919. 837.

119 Hon'ami Kōetsu (1558–1637), *Fujisan* (Mt. Fuji), *raku* ware tea bowl. Momoyama period, early 17th century. D. 11.6 (4.6). Sakai Tadamasa Collection, Tokyo.

120 Furuta Oribe (1543–1615), *Kuro Oribe Chawan*, tea bowl. Momoyama period, late 16th, early 17th century. H. 8.5 (3.4) D. 15 (5.9). Umezawa Memorial Museum, Tokyo.

121 Lacquered wooden chest with floral inlay of mother-of-pearl and metal, ivory handles. Early 17th century. H. 30.5 (12) W. 42.6 (16.8) D. 26.7 (10.5). V&A Picture Library, London.

122 Hon'ami Kōetsu (1558–1637), *Boat Bridge*, writing box. Early 17th century. Inkstone case, lead and mother-of-pearl on gold lacquer. H. 11.8 (4.6) W. 24.2 (9.5) D. 22.7 (8.9). National Museum, Tokyo.

123 *Waves and Wheel of Life* lacquer handbox. Heian period, 12th century. Gold and mother-of-pearl inlay. H. 13 (5.1) W. 22.5 (8.9) L. 30.5 (12). National Museum, Tokyo.

124 Tawaraya Sōtatsu (active 1602–40?), *Lotus and Swimming Birds*. Early 17th century. Hanging scroll, ink on paper. H. 116.5 (45) W. 50.3 (20). National Museum, Kyoto.

125 Hon'ami Kōetsu (1558–1637) (calligraphy) and Tawaraya Sōtatsu (1602–40?) (painting), *Flowers and Grasses of the Four Seasons* (detail). Momoyama period, early 17th century. Poem handscroll, ink, silver and gold on paper. H. 33.7 (13.3) W. 924.1 (363.8). Hatakeyama Kinenkan Museum, Tokyo.

126 Ogata Kenzan (1663–1743), five small plates. Edo period, early 18th century. White slip and rust glaze, decorated with grey and gold pigment. Each H. 2.4 (0.9) D. 11 (4.3). Nezu Institute of Fine Arts, Tokyo.

127 Ogata Kenzan (1663–1743), *Waterfall*, tea bowl. Early 18th century, White slip glaze and rust painting. H. 8 (3.2) D. 10.3 (4.1). Private collection.

128 Ogata Kōrin (1658–1716), *Irises*. Early 18th century. Double six-fold screen, colours on gold foil, over paper. Each H. 151.2 (59.5) W. 360.7 (142). Nezu Art Museum, Tokyo.

129 Ogata Kōrin, *Flowers and Grasses*, c. 1705. Framed handscroll, ink, colours and white pigment on paper. H. 36 (14.2) W. 131 (51.6). Private collection.

130 Inkstone box with *yatsu hashi* plank-bridge design by Ogata Kōrin (1658–1716). Edo period, 18th century. H. 14.2 (5.6) L. 27.4 (10.8) W. 19.7 (7.8). National Museum, Tokyo.

131 *Hawk and Dragon*, courtesan's *kosode*. Edo period, early 19th century. Gold and lamé on black velvet. National Museum, Tokyo.

132 Peacock *kosode* (short-sleeved robe) (detail) Edo period. Gold thread repoussé and embroidery.

133 *Rooster and Flowering Tree*. Meiji period, late 19th century. Cotton panel, probably a bedcover, resist-dyed on an indigo ground, mounted as a double screen. H. 146 (57.5) W. 125 (49.2). Collection of the Art Gallery of Greater Victoria, Canada.

134 Ikeno Taiga (1723–76). *Pine Tree and Waves*. c. 1765–70. One of double six-panel screen, light colours on paper. H. 58.5 (23) W. 118.9 (46.8).

135 Yosa Buson (1716–83), *Pine Tree at Karasaki* (detail), 1778. Handscroll now mounted on six-fold screen, ink and colours on paper. Hamaguchi Gihei Collection, Chiba.

136 Yosa Buson (1716–83), *Sumō Wrestling*, inscribed with *haiku* verses by Buson. Mid-18th century. Hanging scroll, ink and light colours on paper. H. 261 (102.8) W. 22.8 (9). Private collection, Japan.

137 Uragami Gyokudō (1745–1820), *High Winds and Banking Geese*. 1817. Album leaf from *Kokin Yojijō*. Ink and light colours on paper. H. 31 (12.2) W. 25 (9.8). Takemoto Collection, Aichi.

138 Aoki Mokubei (1767–1833), *Birthday Felicitations*. 1830. Hanging scroll, ink and light colours on satin. H. 17 (6.7) W. 23.5 (9.3). Setsu Collection, Kanagawa.

139 Maruyama Ōkyo (1733–95), *Sketches of Cicadas* (detail) from *Sketchbook of Insects*. Mid-18th century. Ink and light colours on paper. Size of sketchbook H. 26.7 (10.5) W. 19.4 (7.6). National Museum, Tokyo.

140 Nagasawa Rosetsu (1754–99), *The Itsukushima Shrine*, fifth view of *Eight Views of Miyajima* (Hiroshima). 1794. Album leaf, ink and colours on silk. H. 34.5 (13.6) W. 46.5 (18.3). Yasuda Chūzō Collection, Hiroshima.

141 Itō Jakuchū (1716–1800), *Phoenix and White Elephant*. Mid-18th century. One of pair of six-fold screens, ink and colour *impasto* on paper. H. 176 (69.3) W. 376 (148). National Museum, Tokyo.

142 Gibon Sengai (1750–1837), *Frog and Snail*. Early 19th century. Hanging scroll, ink on paper. H. 35.1 (13.8) W. 52.7 (20.7). Sansō Collection, California.

143 Enkū (1628–95), *Shō Kannon Bosatsu*. Late 17th century. Unpainted wood. H. 157.1 (61.9). Seihōji, Gifu.

144 Hakuin Ekaku (1685–1768), *Daruma* (Bodhidharma). 1751. Hanging scroll, ink on paper. H. 222.8 (87.7) W. 36.5 (14.3). Shōjūji, Aichi.

145 Kanō Naganobu (1577–1654), *Dancing under the Cherry Trees* (detail). Early 17th century. One of pair of six-fold screens, colours on paper. H. 149 (58.7) W. 348 (137). National Museum, Tokyo.

146 *Shijō-Kawara*. Early 17th century. One of pair of bi-fold screens, colours on gold paper. H. 152.2 (59.9) W. 157.2 (61.9). Seikadō Collection, Tokyo.

147 Suzuki Harunobu (1724–70), *Viewing Maple Leaves by the Waterfall*. Late 1760s. 'Brocade print' (*chūban nishiki-e*). H. 27.6 (10.9) W. 20.4 (8).

148 Kitagawa Utamaro (1754–1806), *The Coquettish Type* from the series *Ten Physiognomic Types of Women*. Late 18th Century. Polychrome wood block print. H. 37.9 (14.9) W. 24.4 (9.6).

149 Sharaku (active 1794–95), *Sakata Hangorō III as the Villain Mizuyemon*, from *Hana-ayame Bunroku Soga*. 1794. Polychrome wood-block print, with a mica-dusted background. Art Institute of Chicago.

150 Katsushika Hokusai (1760–1849), *View on a Fine Breezy Day*, from *Thirty-Six Views of Mount Fuji*, 1822–32. Polychrome wood-block print. H. 25.5 (10) L. 38 (15). Sekai-Kyūsei-kyō Collection, Atami Museum, Shizuoka.

151 Andō Hiroshige (1797–1858), *Snow at Kambara* from *Fifty-Three Stations of the Tokaido*. 1833. Polychrome wood-block print. H. 24.2 (9.5) W. 36.7 (14.5).

152 Kuroda Seiki (1866–1924), *Lake Shore*, 1897. Oil on canvas. H. 68 (26.8) L. 83.3 (32.8). National Institute of Art Research, Tokyo.

153 Hishida Shunsō (1874–1910), *Fallen Leaves*. Right-hand screen of double six-fold pair, 1910. Mineral pigments on paper. Each H. 156.2 (61.5) W. 365

(143.8). Courtesy of the Eiseibunko Museum, Tokyo.

154 Kobayashi Kokei (1883–1957), *Fruit*. Early 20th century. Hanging scroll, mineral pigments on paper. Yamatane Museum of Art, Tokyo.

155 Maeda Seison (1885–1977), *Lion Dancer Awaiting Cue*. 1955. Painting set in wall, mineral pigments on gold foiled paper. H. 159.5 (62.8) W. 201.5 (79.3). Hall of the Lion Dance, Imperial Palace Collection, Tokyo.

156 Fukuda Heihachirō (1892–1972), *Virgin Snow*. 1948. Colours on silk. H. 113 (44.5) W. 81.9 (32.3). Private collection.

157 Tokuoka Shinsen (1896–1972), *Stream*. 1954. Colours on paper. H. 133.4 (52.5) W. 177.3 (69.8). Private collection.

158 Higashiyama Kaii (b. 1908), *Rhythm of Snow Country*. 1963. Colour on paper. H. 156.2 (61.5) L. 213 (84). National Theatre, Tokyo.

159 Nagare Masayuki (b. 1923), *Flight*. c. 1970. 400 tons of black Swedish granite. World Trade Centre, New York. Photo courtesy of Bank of America.

160 Munakata Shikō (1908–75), *The Visit* from *Uto no Hanga saku*. 1938. Ink monochrome wood-block print. H. 25.4 (10) W. 28.7 (11.3).

161 Olympic stadium in Tokyo, designed by Tange Kenzō (b. 1913). 1964. Reinforced steel, concrete. Photo Orion Press, Tokyo.

162 Yagi Kazuō (1919–1979), *Letter*. 1964. Black burnished clay. H. 28.5 (11.2) L. 41 (16) W. 10.5 (4.1).

163 Kan Makiko (b. 1933), *Uraurato tereru haru bi ni*. 1977. Hanging scroll, ink on coloured and speckled *ryōshi* paper. H. 37 (14.6) W. 33 (13). Collection the author.

164 Morita Shiryū (b. 1912), *En* (Round). 1967. Ink on paper H. 69 (27.2) W. 91 (35.8). Private Collection, Japan.

Index